Content Area Literacy Instruction for the Elementary Grades

Donna E. Alvermann
University of Georgia

Jeanne Swafford
Mississippi State University

M. Kristiina Montero
University of Georgia

PEARSON

Boston   New York   San Francisco
Mexico City   Montreal   Toronto   London   Madrid   Munich   Paris
Hong Kong   Singapore   Tokyo   Cape Town   Sydney

For Jack.
D.E.A.

To my husband Vance, whose love, patience and encouragement
made it possible for me to write for hours, days, and weeks on end.
To my son Isaac, who is always willing to read with me
and teach me more about how readers grow.
J.S.

To my parents, Elsa and Juan Montero, who taught me
their languages, cultures, and histories through the texts
of Finland and Spain.
M.K.M.

Series Editor: Aurora Martínez Ramos
Editorial Assistant: Katie Freddoso
Senior Marketing Manager: Elizabeth Fogarty
Production Editor: Marissa Falco
Electronic Composition: Publishers' Design and Production Services, Inc.
Composition and Prepress Buyer: Linda Cox
Manufacturing Buyer: Andrew Turso
Cover Administrator: Linda Knowles
Editorial-Production Service: Matrix Productions, Inc.

For related titles and support materials, visit our online catalog at www.ablongman.com

Library of Congress Cataloging-in-Publication Data

Alvermann, Donna E.
    Content area literacy instruction for the elementary grades / Donna Alvermann, Jeanne Swafford, M. Kristiina Montero.
        p. cm.
    Includes bibliographical references (p.) and indexes.
    ISBN 0-205-36619-8
    1. Language arts (Elementary)—United States. 2. Content area reading— United States. I. Swafford, Jeanne. II. Montero, M. Kristiina. III. Title.
    LB1576.A6158 2004
    372.6—dc21

                                                                        2003048224

Printed in the United States of America
10 9 8 7 6 5 4 3 2 1   HAM   08 07 06 05 04 03

Credits appear on p. 302, which should be considered an extension of the copyright page.

CONTENTS

PREFACE

Why did we write this book? As teachers we know the excitement generated by good instruction, especially when that instruction involves teaching young children to read, write, and communicate using a variety of texts (print, visual, symbolic, and digital). One of the delights of teaching content is watching youngsters' eyes light up as they discover the marvels of science, the significance of their historical past, or the repeating patterns in mathematics, music, and art. Another is the satisfaction of knowing that you have taught a child not only to read, but also how to read to learn, for we believe the two processes co-occur and reinforce one another. It would be the rare child (or person of any age, for that matter) who did not read for *something*—to find out about world events, to share an enjoyable story with a friend, to figure out how to do something by reading the instructions, or to simply find answers to one of life's many questions.

We believe that youngsters, growing up in a digital world and surrounded by media on all sides, are unusually adept at negotiating meaning regardless of the form a text may take. But it takes good instruction to focus their negotiations and to help them apply what they learn. That's what this book is about. It is the first one, to our knowledge, to focus specifically on teaching content literacy in pre-kindergarten through grade 6. Toward that end, this book is complete with age-appropriate examples and illustrations of children's work. It is also filled with methods and strategies for teaching and learning content through reading, writing, and other communicative and visual arts. It is more than a compendium of such methods and strategies, however, for we have focused on introducing them as part of actual classroom practices across the curriculum.

Recently, a number of issues have come to our attention that reinforce our belief that the time is right to introduce a methods text devoted fully to teaching and learning content in the elementary grades. One of these issues is the proverbial "fourth-grade slump"—the grade in which many children begin to struggle with reading and learning with texts. This is often a trying time because the stories (narrative texts) children have become accustomed to reading in school are no longer the mainstay of the curriculum. Instead, they are expected to make meaning with, to learn with, and to make use of expository texts, which are quite different from stories.

A second reason for focusing on content area literacy instruction at the elementary school level is tied to the standards-based reform movement presently afoot. Whether or not we agree with the direction such reform is taking (including high-stakes testing), the fact remains that youngsters in the elementary grades are expected to read more academically challenging texts, write in more expository-based genres, and communicate with greater efficiency using some of the world's most advanced technologies. Content area literacy instruction is needed if these expectations are to materialize beyond the rhetoric presently fueling them.

Finally, a third impetus for writing a book that focuses solely on content area literacy instruction in the elementary grades stems from the fact that increasingly more pre-K through grade 6 preservice and inservice teachers are enrolling in content area literacy courses, many of which focus on middle school or high school students. It has become increasingly clear that these courses (and their accompanying texts) no longer meet elementary school teachers' needs. Furthermore, state, regional, and local school officials are encouraging many teachers to enroll in professional development programs that prepare them to become peer leaders in content area literacy instruction, and in some states, certification requirements for reading specialists call for a course in content area literacy instruction.

For these reasons, we have designed the text specifically for pre-K through grade 6 classroom teachers. We hope it will provide alternatives for teaching content literacy that reach beyond the traditional assignment of reading and answering the questions at the end of the chapter. Our overarching goal has been to write a book that supports teachers in their mission to help children become independent readers and lifelong learners.

Important Features of This Text

Remembering, Reflection, Reconsidering

Innovative in its 3R's framework—Remembering—Reflection—Reconsidering—this book will help students make connections and improve comprehension.

Remembering

What do you remember about how you learned content area material? What was considered important in your content area class—the content or communication about the content? Do you remember the use of textbooks and worksheets? How were you presented information in the content areas? How was your content area knowledge assessed? What made learning the content enjoyable for you? What made learning the content not so enjoyable for you?

Kristiina began her "teacher" years in Ontario, Canada, where she was trained to teach students French as a second language (differentiated from French as a foreign language because in Canada French and English are the two official languages). She not only had to teach the language, but also certain aspects of the cultures and histories of the Francophone world. The textbooks she was given to use in the classroom were categorically divided up into neat lessons. There was one lesson on each of the

This section helps readers link their personal experiences to the content of each chapter, thus activating the readers' schema and piquing curiosity. The authors also link their own experiences with the chapter content in the Reflection section, providing a concrete example with which readers may connect.

Reflection

What is your opinion about the role of state or provincial achievement testing in the classroom? What do you think about the fear of "teaching to the test?" Do you think standardized tests can impact student learning? How can you use standardized tests to your advantage?

Assessing Texts and Learners

Three crucial questions a teacher must ask herself or himself when thinking about evaluating texts and learners in relation to instruction are "why am I doing what I am

Readers are asked to reflect in strategic places in each chapter, giving opportunities for readers to stop and reflect about the content they just read, and linking it to classroom practice, and to their own experiences.

Reconsidering

Now that you've read this chapter, what do you think about curriculum as inquiry? What advantages do you see? What disadvantages? Perhaps you agree philosophically with the notion that students' inquiries should guide the curriculum. If so, how can you begin to organize student knowledge and interests, your knowledge and interests, and curriculum standards to make learning in your classroom more inquiry based? What questions do you have? To support your future inquiries, we recommend you read Short, Harste, and Burke's (1996) book *Creating Classrooms for Authors and Inquirers*. There's so much more to explore, ponder, and reflect upon. Your journey has just begun.

At the end of each chapter, readers are encouraged to recondsider the content of a chapter and the ideas presented, in view of classroom practice. This section will allow readers to critique their own experiences or classroom practices in light of the ideas presented in the chapter.

Every chapter is embedded with boxed material highlighting key information on **struggling readers, ELL learners, activities aligned to standards,** and **technology links** to show students how to adapt their instruction. In addition, there are entire chapters devoted to these topics.

ELL: Quality Spanish-Language Informational Trade Books

While Spanish is not the sole primary language of English language learners, it certainly dominates many classrooms. If you have Spanish-speaking children in your classroom and would like to provide them access to books written in their home language, you may want to browse the recommended books by http://cuatrogatos.org/mejores.html. They dedicate a section to informational books. Haga clic en ¡Los mejores del 2001! (Click on "The best of 2001!") to find the recommended books for children and adolescents written in Spanish.

A Web Link for Promoting Media Literacy Instruction

Log on to the Alliance for a Media Literate America's website at http://www.amedialitamerica.org and find out what you can do as a teacher to promote media literacy that focuses on critical inquiry, learning, and skill building rather than on media bashing and blame. Click on the link "Email Newsletter" and select something of interest to the class that you can report on or use in your own teaching.

Struggling Readers and the Web

If you are wondering where to start teaching struggling readers to judge the trustworthiness of what they see on the Web, we suggest that you observe firsthand what and how they are currently reading online. For example, you might sit beside a child while he or she is reading online. Attend especially to how this child is responding to competing visual and auditory images that may contradict what the so-called story line of a website is supposedly trying to communicate. Discuss with the child possible reasons for these contradictions and help him or her develop criteria for assessing the credibility of the site. (See Chapter 6 for ideas on how to help students assess the credibility of particular websites.)

Linking ELA Standards with Inquiry

An inquiry curriculum is consistent with ELA Standards 1, 3, 4, 5, 7, 8, and 12, which state that students engage in personal inquiries, comprehend, interpret, evaluate, and synthesize data from a variety of sources, including technological and other informational resources, and communicate their discoveries in writing and other ways, depending on their purposes and audience.

Inquiry also supports Standards 2 and 9, which relate to understanding different aspects of human experiences and understanding and appreciating differences in the classroom community. (www.ncte.org/standards/standards.shtml)

Marginal Icons

 "Evidence-based Research" icons in every chapter signal the reader that the information presented in the text has been drawn from evidence-based research articles.

to use text structure as they read (Pearson & Fielding, 1991). To review from Chapter 2, explanations of the how's, when's, where's, and why's of using text structure, along with teacher modeling and thinking aloud, are essential elements of instruction. Likewise, guided practice in large and small group contexts and independent practice are important to give students opportunities to apply their knowledge of text structure, yet have access to teacher support. As necessary, the teacher may extend or pull back the amounts and kinds of support she or he provides, depending on students' develop-

 The **"Teaching and Learning Toolbox,"** (Part IV), also denoted by icons in chapter margins, prepares students for National accountability standards by explaining the purpose and implementation of instruction strategies supported by the National Reading Panel.

ideas. She read the book aloud and then went back and modeled her thinking about its structure. She and her students discussed similarities described in the book and, using shared writing, constructed a Venn diagram.

The next day, Julie chose to use information from their "ocean" K-W-L chart (Bryan, 1998) to continue their study of the comparison/contrast structure. Because there was lots of information in the "K" column about whales and sharks that could be compared and contrasted, she chose to guide students in constructing a Venn

---

Technology Try It! Turn on the Tube

What? You want us to watch TV?! Yes! Go to your local TV listings and find the Magic School Bus cartoon. (If you don't have cable, some episodes are available at local video rental stores.) Get your pencil and paper out, sit back, and watch cartoons! As you watch, jot down information you learn from the cartoon. You'll probably need to watch the episode more than once to learn everything; it's amazing how much information can be packed into a thirty-minute cartoon!

"Try-It" exercises in every chapter illustrate main points and engage readers in participating in their own learning.

Additional Resources

- Annotated bibliography of children's literature represents some of the authors' favorite books to use for content instruction. Books are alphabetized by author and organized by content area.
- **Appendix A** includes lists of **leveled information books (preK–2)** organized by content area and reading level (A–J) providing easy access to titles for emergent and beginning reading and content instruction, a valuable tool for in-service teachers.

- Features **"English Language Arts Standards"** textboxes in each chapter, and **"English Language Arts Standards and Reading Professionals Standards Matrices"** in Appendix C to help students understand how standards are addressed in the text. **At-a-glance chart** is also included at the beginning of the book for easy reference.

  In addition, students can access the book's **Companion Website** which offers a wealth of enriching activities that capture a students attention including **"You Be the Historian,"** an interactive online activity giving students choices on how to meet ELA Standard #7, a glossary of terms, case studies, discussion questions, study/test questions, and correlated readings.

Acknowledgments

This book is truly the result of a collaborative effort—one in which each of us brought our particular strengths and interests to the table, shared our knowledge, and worked hard to represent that knowledge in a way that will hopefully engage our readers. It also reflects the vision and practices of the many preservice and inservice teachers with whom we have worked in our education courses. We are thankful to them because they were willing to share their inquiries with us, and as a result we learned from and with them.

Jeanne would particularly like to thank the teachers and students in the public schools of Lubbock, Texas, who worked with her for over a decade, bringing content literacy to life in primary grade classrooms. Special thanks go to Judy Rogers, who shared her classroom with Jeanne, putting up with tape recorders, cordless microphones, video cameras, and the like for over a year. Also, to the students in Judy's classroom for sharing their wonderings and feelings, a special thank you.

With warmth and admiration, Kristiina would like to thank Jorge Gonzalez Outeiriño for his expertise and support when technological difficulties were at their worst, Jonathan Eakle who enriched the book by sharing his knowledge about museum literacies and art, Carla Michelle Manning for sharing ideas about the teaching profession, and Maria Rossi, Henrietta Coole, Elsa Glover, and Jorge García Lara who, through numerous dialogues across geographical boundaries and time, helped connect many ideas to the world found on the other side of the classroom walls.

In addition, we especially thank the following reviewers who took the time to respond thoughtfully and in great detail to an earlier draft of this book: Paul Blohm, Indiana University Northwest; Lee A. Dubert, Boise State University; Lois E. Huffman, North Carolina State University; Patricia Joann Williams Pollifrone, Gannon University; and Nina L. Rynberg, Lake Superior State University. We trust they will see many of their ideas represented here. For the patience, skill, good cheer, and support that went into the preparation of the manuscript, we thank Terri Coley, Chris Fedorczak, and Barry Robinson. We also wish to thank Marissa Falco for assistance in the day-to-day production process. Finally, we wish to acknowledge and especially thank Aurora Martínez Ramos for her enthusiasm, keen sense of the literacy field, and attention to detail. Without her guidance and support, this book would not have materialized.

PART ONE

Introduction

CHAPTER

1

Content Area Literacy for Pre-K through Grade 6

In this introductory chapter, you will go on a Literacy Dig to learn about the multiple literacies around you. Learning about multiple literacies and their relation to children's everyday worlds will help you think about content area literacy instruction and students' motivation for learning from and with a wide range of texts—print, visual, digital, and so on. It will also help you to see the connection between the standards movement and your own instruction. Information on the reading process as viewed from a social constructionist perspective will become part of your professional knowledge base as you engage in activities designed to make abstract concepts more concrete.

Try It!

This chapter begins with a Literacy Dig. Like archaeologists, you are about to participate in an activity that may lead to some surprises or unknowns. Your task is straightforward: "Dig" for evidence that literacy is going on all about you—wherever you are—in the classroom, at home, on campus, in the mall, and so on. Keep a notebook in which you record what you find. Be creative—use words, photographs, drawings, symbols, audio or video recordings—and then share what you find in class.

Remembering

When Donna Bell, a pre-kindergarten teacher at Kilbourne Elementary School in Columbia, South Carolina, and Donna Jarvis, a kindergarten teacher in the same school, went on a Literacy Dig in their homes and community, they discovered they had to redefine what they thought literacy involved. In their words:

> Prior to this experience, we defined literacy as knowing how to read in "school-styled" ways—reading words, sentences, and paragraphs in books, newspapers, magazines—but when the members of our reading initiative group shared the results of our "digs," we were amazed. Literacy was everywhere—on shampoo bottles, the microwave, the washing machine, videotapes, soup cans, coins, photographs, scribbled grocery lists, receipts. And literacy wasn't just about reading words. It was about reading all kinds of symbols that help us get along in our world—road signs, logos, traffic lights. Our definition of literacy broadened to encompass all of the bits and pieces of communication that make up our lives. (Bell & Jarvis, 2002, p. 10)

Now it's your turn. What do you remember thinking literacy involved before you went on your Literacy Dig? How did your thinking compare or contrast with the definition of literacy that Donna Bell and Donna Jarvis held prior to their dig? What's your definition now? If your definition didn't change as a result of going on a Literacy Dig, speculate as to why it didn't. If it did change, consider whether your new definition encompasses the view that kids of the net generation are increasingly making use of their multiple literacies to communicate on a broad range of topics with an ever-widening audience (*Newsweek/Score*, 2000).

Engaging in a thoughtful response to these questions will prepare you to read the rest of this chapter, which is about a special kind of literacy—one that involves teaching and learning in the content areas, such as social studies, language arts, math, science, foreign languages, health, art, music, and physical education. A good working definition of *content area literacy* is the ability to use reading, writing, speaking, listening, representing, viewing, and other sign systems to construct meaning with print and nonprint texts (Swafford & Kallus, 2002).

We begin with an example of how Felix, a third-grade boy in Athens, Georgia, used his multiple literacies—that is, his knowledge of print-based, visual, and digital texts—to work collaboratively with peers in making an electronic get-well card for an absent classmate. Following that we focus on how you, as a classroom teacher, can use a social constructionist perspective on the reading process to tap into your students' multiple literacies as you simultaneously teach them how to learn in the content areas. We also highlight how the standards movement and the influence of media and new communication technologies can affect what you do in teaching content area literacy. Finally, we provide a brief overview of why you will want to key in on the importance of motivation for engaging your students in content area literacy and learning—a theme that is threaded through (and elaborated further) in the chapters that follow.

Multiple Literacies at Work: Felix and the Electronic Get-Well Card

Felix (not his real name) attends an elementary school where many of the students are children of newly arrived immigrant parents. Located only a few blocks from the University of Georgia, the school is proud of its literacy-rich curriculum designed especially for students whose first language is other than English. These English language learners (ELLs) work side by side with their English-only peers in learning to read and write in social studies, science, math, and other content areas. The day that one of us (Donna) visited Felix's class, he was engaged with a small group of peers in creating an electronic get-well card for a classmate who was ill. Here's what Donna wrote in her journal as she observed the multiple literacies at work in this small group:

Donna's Journal Entry

First, the teacher invites the class to brainstorm words appropriate for a get-well message. Felix volunteers several words in Spanish, and some of his classmates nod approvingly as the teacher writes them on the board. After the brainstorming session, Felix works in a small group to craft a message for the absent classmate. At one point, just as the group is on the verge of finishing, Felix dashes to the computer that has Web access and hits the "favorites" button. Up pops a list of the class's favorite websites. He clicks on http://free.bluemountain.com and scrolls down until he finds the category labeled "Get Well." Clicking on it, he copies the words from one of his favorite animated get-well cards and dashes back to his group. Paper in hand, Felix reads the commercially prepared message that he's selected. Except for one girl in the group, his peers seem ready to toss aside their group-constructed message and substitute the one from Blue Mountain. When Emily asks if he'd consider using "half and half" (meaning a blend of the group's original message and the message from the Blue Mountain site), Felix seems agreeable and sets to work combining the two. He adds a hastily sketched cartoon-like illustration "to make Richard [the absent classmate] laugh." Amidst peels of laughter, Felix and the others finish the greeting card and sign up for a turn at emailing it to Richard.

Reflection

What were some of the literacies that Felix and his peers used in making the electronic get-well card? Do you think these literacies were all "taught" in school? How do you know? As a teacher (or prospective teacher), how would you capitalize on the literacies that Felix has at his command to interest him in social studies, science, health, art, or some other content-related subject area?

The Reading Process

Learning to read and reading to learn are not separate processes. Indeed, separating the act of reading from one of its functions—reading to learn *something*—makes no sense. Developmentally speaking, emergent and beginning readers are different from skilled readers, but the difference lies more with the content or subject matter materials the two read than with their *purposes* for reading. Thus, when we hear the oft-repeated slogan that children must first learn to read before they can read to learn from their content area texts (broadly defined), we shake our heads in disbelief. How long will this myth live on, we ask ourselves.

Part of our rationale for deciding to write this book was to dispel the notion that there is a "natural" break in the reading process between learning to read and reading to learn. Another part was to provide alternatives to the way content area literacy is typically taught in elementary classrooms. It has been our observation (as well as others, perhaps including you) that teaching content through fill-in-the-blank worksheets and unit tests is not very appealing to young minds accustomed to exploring the "real" world outside of school through the ever-widening lenses made possible by the interactive media technologies that surround them on all sides (Alvermann, 2002; Dyson, 1997, 2002). How to make use of these lenses and the multiple literacies that children like Felix bring to their content area learning—while still addressing standards-based instruction—is the overarching goal of this book.

But first, let's consider how you experience reading this excerpt from a text that Donna uses to teach preservice and in-service teachers at the University of Georgia about the reading process.

Try It!

Imagine that you are reading right along in your health textbook on people's phobias and you come upon the word *triskaidekaphobia*. The sentence in which this word appears is the following: Claudia's tendency to suffer from triskaidekaphobia prevented her from ever staying on the thirteenth floor of a hotel. Describe to a classmate the process you used to unlock the meaning of triskaidekaphobia.

In the foregoing activity, simply being able to decode (e.g., sound out or break the word into smaller parts) was probably not as helpful to comprehending the sentence as was your ability to associate a fear of the number thirteen with staying on a particular hotel floor. Getting the gist of the sentence, even if you were unable to pronounce the word triskaidekaphobia, is what is important. (Of course, if you were reading the sentence aloud to a group of people you wanted to impress, it's likely that being able to pronounce the word correctly would also be important!)

What this activity also demonstrates is how you can simultaneously be a "code breaker" and a "meaning maker"—two elements of Luke and Freebody's (1999) four resources model. The other two elements—"text user" and "text critic"—involve such things as acting on your fear of the number thirteen, and like Claudia, refuse to stay on the thirteenth floor of a hotel. Such an action would entail being a "text user"—that is, making functional use of a piece of information to inform your actions. If instead you decide to tackle head-on the superstition that the number thirteen is necessarily an unlucky number, then you might become what Freebody and Luke describe as a "text critic." That is, you would look for the assumptions underlying the fear of the number thirteen and then decide for yourself whether your actions will be guided by such assumptions. All four of the processes just described (code breaker, meaning maker, text user, and text critic) are part and parcel of a social constructionist perspective on the reading process.

Social Constructionism: The View That "Truth" Is Made, Not Found

From your experiences as a reader of various content area texts, you probably recognize that the kinds of texts you encountered (and the people with whom you interacted while reading those texts) had a considerable influence on what you eventually came to understand about the subject matter. The same holds for the children you teach. In fact, several labels exist in the research literature for describing this view of the reading process. Sometimes it is broadly referred to as a sociocultural perspective on reading; at other times, it is described as coming from the theoretical and research literature on social constructivism (Vygotsky, 1978) and social constructionism (Bruner, 1986, Gergen, 1999).

Social constructivism and social constructionism should not be confused or used synonymously. Although both terms are derived from the theoretical notion that learners use their lived experiences to make meanings of different concepts (e.g., content area concepts such as *democracy, addition, wildlife,* and *transportation*), social constructionist learning theory looks to language as a prime mediator (or intervening factor) in terms of what children will understand about a particular concept. Thus, how children hear language used, and how they use language themselves, will influence what they learn in any given content area. It will also influence how they come to see and address each other in classroom discussions, as the following exercise illustrates.

Try It!

In the excerpt that follows, put yourself in the role of the teacher and tell a colleague or classmate what you would say following Anthony's and Ray's responses to Maya's observation.

E. [A FEMALE INSTRUCTOR]:   What makes this a girl's book? (holding up a book in the *Babysitters Club* series)

CHILDREN (ALL AT ONE TIME):   There are girls on the cover! There are girls on it.

MAYA: And it's pink.

ANTHONY: Boys don't really babysit much.

MAYA: I haven't ever seen a boy babysit.

ANTHONY: I have.

RAY: I did. (Dutro, 2001, p. 382)

Reflection

Did you note that it was a female adult leading the discussion who introduced the notion of the *Babysitters* book being "a girl's book?" Did you also note how quickly the sexist labeling was taken up and defended by another female, Maya? Why do you think the only two students to challenge the sexist label were the two boys?

The excerpt of the *Babysitters* book discussion, which is from a longer discussion a group of fifth graders had on the topic of what makes a girl's book different from other books, is an example of how knowledge is socially constructed. It makes use of certain conventions of language (e.g., sexist talk) that go unchallenged over time and eventually become accepted "as the truth" or "the norm." Working from a social constructionist perspective on how content area learning occurs, we believe it is possible to show youngsters that "truth" about content information (e.g., Christopher Columbus discovering an America that was already inhabited by Native Americans) is largely made (or constructed) through language as opposed to being some kind of unalterable "truth." How is this possible? According to Gavelek and Raphael (1996):

> [The social constructionist] perspective has the potential to shift our focus on talk about text away from seeking "facts" or "truths" [in textbooks and other kinds of texts] toward constructing "interpretations" and offering "warranted justifications" for interpretations. From this perspective, the teacher's role would shift from asking questions to ensure that students arrive at the "right" meaning to creating prompts that encourage students' exploratory talk. . . . Teachers would encourage talk that elicits a range of possible interpretations among individuals reading and responding at any given time. Teachers would also encourage talking about previously read texts because individuals construct different readings at different periods in life or within different contexts. . . . Textual meaning is not "out there" to be acquired: It is something that is constructed by individuals through their interactions with each other and the world. (p. 183)

Although it is the case that the same reader can construct different meanings for the same text, over time and in different contexts, it is also worth noting that the way readers have responded in the past does in fact channel or help frame their future responses. We all have cultural histories and identities that make us somewhat predictable. Acknowledging this, however, does not give us license to fall headlong into an essentializing trap of sorts—one in which we assume that students of the same race, ethnicity, gender, language group, religious affiliation, and the like will necessarily think alike. It should come as no surprise that children who share common cultural and linguistic backgrounds will have had unique life experiences and different ways of using language to interpret those experiences (Gee, 1996; Heath, 1983).

Using a Social Constructionist Perspective to Plan Content Literacy Instruction

Theory aside, you might wonder what a teacher who subscribes to a social constructionist view of the reading process thinks about as he or she plans a social studies unit or sets up learning centers for a hands-on science experiment. Although there are different ways of helping teachers accomplish this kind of planning, we particularly like Unsworth and O'Toole's (1993) literacy development cycle (LDC). The LDC calls for instruction that integrates content and process and enlists active student participation. It is grounded in the research literature on literacy teaching and learning that makes use of a variety of print and nonprint texts (Wade & Moje, 2000), such as newspapers, magazines, children's literature, textbooks, trade books, biographies, CD-ROMs, videos, photographs, rhymes, jokes, songs, personal writings (e.g., diaries), and popular culture texts (e.g., rap, instant messaging).

The literacy development cycle is built on the following premises:

- The texts children encounter should be composed for genuine communicative purposes and not those constructed principally to include repetitions of sound/ symbol relations, vocabulary items or grammatical structures [such as controlled vocabulary texts].
- Children's engagement with texts should be enjoyable and functional in meeting their own social purposes.
- Literary texts for young children [arouse] children's active, interpretive orientations to the construction of meaning in texts.
- As well as literary narratives, many other texts such as rhymes, jokes, songs, traditional tales, informational texts associated with curriculum area learning, environmental texts, personal texts, and texts of popular culture have an important role in early development.
- Young children's literacy learning is like an apprenticeship, involving both guidance and explicit teaching from a master practitioner.
- Early literacy development is enhanced by the provision of recurrent, enjoyable and supportive contexts where the same texts are revisited over time.
- The development of children's control of the conventions of written text in their reading and writing is characterized by gradual approximation to the accepted practices of the community. (Unsworth, 2001, p. 184)

Although this list of premises, which we tend to see as guiding principles, is by no means exhaustive, we think the ideas presented in it fit well with our overarching goal of helping teachers connect children's out-of-school literacies to literacy learning in the content areas. The LDC is also compatible with the social constructionist view of learning and takes into account the influences of language, multiple literacies, and motivation on children's learning across the curriculum.

Reflecting on the Reading Process

Take a few minutes to think back on how you were taught to read content area texts when you were in elementary school. Do you recall discussing what you read with peers, or was content area reading mostly an individual effort? How does a social constructionist perspective on the reading process support group learning? How does it support teaching in the content areas?

The Standards and You

If you have ever wondered why the reading process and the policies and standards regulating how reading is taught generate so much media coverage, you're not alone. We, too, have marveled at how hardly a week goes by without some news about standards-based instruction and its connection to high-stakes testing (see Chapter 10, this volume). Perhaps one of the most momentous (although not unexpected) stories to break on the topic of reading in the United States occurred on January 8, 2002. On that day a bill was signed into law by Congress that vows to leave no child behind—meaning that *all* children must be reading on grade level by the time they exit third grade (U.S. Department of Education, 2002). Under the new law—*No Child Left Behind*—schools must use "evidence-based" research to make decisions about classroom literacy practices including, of course, the way in which students are taught to read their content area texts.

No Child Left Behind has drawn mixed responses from teachers and other professionals in early literacy education. Some applaud it; others worry about its implications for teaching children whose first language is not English, and still others vehemently oppose the law on the basis that it oversimplifies the reading process and the ability of all children to read at grade level. In other words, the critics wonder, "Is the new law realistic?" And how does it play out for teachers of children who speak a language other than English at home?

English Language Learners and No Child Left Behind Legislation

It is unclear how teachers whose classrooms are filled with youngsters from homes where English is not the first language, and who themselves are monolingual, are supposed to teach students content from materials written largely in English. Nor do researchers agree on the level of proficiency that is needed in English to support an English language learner's ability to comprehend content area materials written in English. To learn more about this controversy, you may want to refer to *Educating Language-Minority Children* issued by the National Research Council (1998).

Add to this mix the accountability required of teachers by the standards movement (to say nothing of high stakes testing) and you will soon understand why your choice of professions has to be one of the most challenging ones around. We say this not to frighten you (or, worse yet, to discourage you from entering the teaching profession), but rather to impress upon you the need to pay particular attention to what students need to know and the competencies required of you if you are to be accountable. Basically, the information on standards for teaching and learning content area literacy can be grouped into three categories: the *Standards for the English Language Arts* (International Reading Association and the National Council of Teachers of English, 1996); the *Standards for Reading Professionals* (International Reading Association, 1998); and other content area specialty groups' standards, such as the *National Science Education Standards* (National Research Council, 1996), the *National Council for the Social Studies Standards* (NCSS, 1994), the *National Council of Teachers of Mathematics Standards* (NCTM, 1991), and *Teachers of English to Speakers of Other Languages* (TESOL, 2001).

You will find the student standards (grades K–12)—that is, the *Standards for the English Language Arts* (ELAs)—listed on the inside of this textbook's front cover under the title *ELA Standards at a Glance*. They are also highlighted in the body of the text and called out as "boxed material" for your convenience in seeing how the chapter information ties to the student standards.

The *Standards for Reading Professionals*—that is, the standards which the International Reading Association deems colleges of education should require of preservice and in-service teachers—are listed on the inside of this textbook's back cover under the title *Reading Professional Standards at a Glance*. So that you can see the relation between the K–12 student standards and the standards required of professionals such as yourselves, we have included a matrix in Appendix C. This matrix also lists the chapters in which each of the student standards and the reading professional standards is addressed.

The standards of the content area specialties are embedded in the body of the text where appropriate and when mention is made of a particular content practice that is part of the content area specialty's organization. Further information can be obtained on the various content standards by logging onto the appropriate professional organization website sponsoring those standards (see reference list for URLs).

So that you have a sense of how all this works, consider the *Babysitters Club* book discussion described earlier in the chapter. The fourth standard in the *Standards for the English Language Arts* (1996) states the following:

ELA Standard #4

Students adjust their use of spoken, written, and visual language (e.g., conventions, style, vocabulary) to communicate effectively with a variety of audiences and for different purposes. (http://www.reading.org./advocacy/elastandards/standards.html)

Because we see a connection between ELA Standard #4 and the example provided in the *Babysitters Club* excerpt, we would typically have placed the boxed-in standard in the vicinity of the text where the *Babysitters Club* book discussion appeared. We placed it here, in this section of the chapter titled "The Standards and You," for strictly illustrative purposes.

Media and New Communication Technologies

We have read an article by two Australian educators, Allan Luke and Vicki Carrington at the University of Queensland, in which they discussed the speed and flexibility of learning accessible to some, but not all, children in this age of global networking and digital literacies. Commenting on the changes in youngsters' everyday experiences and uses of space and time, they wrote: "Whether in Bangkok or Brisbane, a particular new species and social class of 'world kids' play and learn in shopping malls and basketball courts, on the internet and in schools" (Luke & Carrington, 2003, p. 3).

The changes engulfing the youngest of our world citizens in Asia and the Pacific Rim are no less recognizable closer to home. For instance, Felix (with his ability to traverse multiple literacies in completing a school project) is part of that new species of "world kids" whom Luke and Carrington describe. Like their contemporaries around the globe, these kids, in many instances, are more at ease than their teachers in exploring the capabilities of new technologies. And, like their teachers, they may find it difficult at times to comprehend what is often contradictory information streaming endlessly across the Web. Which sites to trust, which to question, and which to avoid are part and parcel of living at a time in history when information is imploding upon itself and criteria for judging the credibility of that information are in short supply. Nowhere is the need for these criteria more evident than when teaching students who struggle to read content that is Web based.

Struggling Readers and the Web

If you are wondering where to start teaching struggling readers to judge the trustworthiness of what they see on the Web, we suggest that you observe firsthand what and how they are currently reading online. For example, you might sit beside a child while he or she is reading online. Attend especially to how this child is responding to competing visual and auditory images that may contradict what the so-called story line of a website is supposedly trying to communicate. Discuss with the child possible reasons for these contradictions and help him or her develop criteria for assessing the credibility of the site. (See Chapter 6 for ideas on how to help students assess the credibility of particular websites.)

Developing a Critical Awareness through Media Literacy

Using media and interactive communication technologies to enhance young children's background knowledge of the content you expect them to learn in social studies and science, for example, involves helping them develop a critical awareness of what they see, hear, and read. All literacies are *situated*; that is, they are located in particular times and places, and they are linked to broad social issues, such as inequities around race, ethnicity, social class, and gender (Barton, Hamilton, & Ivanic, 2000). As you might imagine, media literacy is no exception. Depending on your perspective, the term media literacy may be characterized uncritically as yet another form of reading and viewing or, alternatively, as the ability to choose selectively among texts, taking into account issues of race, social class, gender, and other identity markers.

Planning your instruction so that you give appropriate attention to developing children's ability to read critically is crucial to their growth as learners (Freebody & Luke, 1990). At the center of much of the discussion around the need for critical literacy to permeate content area classrooms is the perceived need to develop children's critical awareness of how all texts (print, visual, oral, and internet mediated) position them as readers and viewers within different social, cultural, and historical contexts. This need, however, should not be translated into a call for critical literacy instruction that would have students searching for the villains or heroes in texts, for the oppressors or emancipators among us, or for opportunities to label people holding different views as occupying opposing and discrete categories—the proverbial "us" and "them." Rather, according to Morgan (1997), it is a summons to set aside these overly simplistic categories that serve to divide us so that we become open to, in her words, "a different view of how people may act, provisionally, at a particular time and within particular conditions" (p. 26).

A Web Link for Promoting Media Literacy Instruction

Log on to the Alliance for a Media Literate America's website at http://www.amedialitamerica .org and find out what you can do as a teacher to promote media literacy that focuses on critical inquiry, learning, and skill building rather than on media bashing and blame. Click on the link "Email Newsletter" and select something of interest to the class that you can report on or use in your own teaching.

The Role of Popular Culture in Content Learning

Although much of the research on popular culture's influence on content area learning has involved older students in the middle grades and higher, we believe that younger children in the primary and intermediate grades also demonstrate competencies in the use of popular culture texts and should not be excluded from the conversation (Alvermann, Moon, & Hagood, 1999; Dyson, 1997; 2002). We also know of two studies in which teachers (preservice, in-service, and a teaching assistant) successfully integrated primary-grade children's popular culture into their regular curriculum (Xu, 2001; 2003).

When Jeanne's son Isaac was in second grade, he used a cellular phone and checked his email regularly. Like many youngsters his age, Isaac is fond of playing computer games, and though he learns content mostly through reading traditional print materials (e.g., textbooks, nonfiction trade books, newspapers, magazines), he also uses the internet to search for information that interests him. New media and communication technologies are only a part of Isaac's repertoire of everyday literacy practices, however. He also uses face-to-face oral communication strategies (e.g., he asks the media specialist in his school to help him locate materials he's interested in, and he shares what he learns through writing, drawing, music, and drama) (Swafford & Kallus, 2002). In short, Isaac is one of the "world kids" that Luke and Carrington (2003) write about.

Reflecting on Media and New Communication Technologies

Are you favorably inclined toward content literacy instruction that takes advantage of media and the new interactive communication technologies? If you use pencils, highlighters, overhead transparencies, and printed materials to teach content, you have already developed a degree of expertise in using what some people refer to as "older" technologies. What might your students teach you about the newer technologies? How might you reciprocate by teaching them to develop a critical eye toward what they read, see, and hear on-line and off-line?

Importance of Motivation in Content Area Literacy Teaching and Learning

When you provide literacy instruction that connects a child's everyday experiences with learning from content area texts, you are almost guaranteeing that such instruction will be motivating and conducive to maintaining high interest and engaged learning. Children will find almost any content engaging and worth learning if it is presented in a way that motivates them to connect it with what they know outside of school. Skimping on content in an attempt to concentrate on basic literacy skill and drill activities is a mistake. This is especially the case when working with children deemed at risk of school failure. As Luke (2001) argues,

> Basic skills are necessary but not sufficient. No matter what we do with [at-risk kids] in terms of basic reading and writing skills, numeracy and literacy skills, unless the activities are somehow connected to the world and unless there is a critical intellectual engagement with knowledge—unless there is an educative act going on—we might as well pack up and go home. (p. 25)

To support this claim, Luke shares two contrasting vignettes that have their bases in classroom observations drawn from a data bank of 1000 lessons. The first vignette (see Table 1.1) captures a lesson featuring a shared book experience on *Flipper*. The lesson itself was well orchestrated in every respect, save one: it was content free.

TABLE 1.1 Vignette 1

The Year 3 and 4 kids watched a video on *Flipper*, and they did some enlarged print materials with *Flipper*. All of these things in a wonderfully socially supportive environment. If I were a principal or teacher supervisor who walked past the lesson I would have said, "Five out of five! A beautifully run lesson, no behaviour management problems, great teacher." At the end of the lesson, at the end of forty minutes, what had the kids gained? Flipper. They knew Paul Hogan had starred in *Flipper*. They knew that Flipper was a dolphin that could talk and that it had been a movie, but that was about it. . . . Content-free teaching, or teaching that is about having a good time but in which [there is] no substantive engagement with a . . . discipline [area] is occurring . . . [with the result being] no depth of engagement. (Luke, 2001, p. 24)

The second vignette (see Table 1.2), which was also exemplary in terms of execution, engaged children with the content of the lesson while simultaneously sharpening their question-asking skills.

Content-free teaching is a problem in more ways than one. In addition to having missed opportunities for exploring related content in the foregoing example—the type of marine life that supports dolphins, the characteristics of a dolphin that causes it to be classified as different from a whale, and so on—the teacher in vignette 1 may have underestimated her students' ability to engage in sustained inquiry about subject-matter material. Perhaps she was operating under the assumption that young children prefer learning from what sometimes is called "soft text" to distinguish it from more factual-oriented "hard text." This assumption may be more widespread than one might imagine. For example, Donna recalls a conversation she had several years ago with a second-grade teacher who told her that she was surprised to discover young children preferred to read books *about* worms rather than *how to eat fried worms*, which is also the title of a well-known children's book (Rockwell, 1973).

This teacher's discovery would come as no surprise to Guthrie and colleagues (Guthrie, McGough, Bennett, & Rice, 1996; Guthrie & Wigfield, 1997), however. Their research on Concept-Oriented Reading Instruction (CORI) documents the effectiveness

TABLE 1.2 Vignette 2

By contrast, I went into one of our outstanding primary schools in Queensland (in a lower socio-economic area), and I observed a shared book lesson with *Paperbag Princess* in which the kids and the teacher did a shared book experience and then the teacher said, "Well kids, what questions would we ask of the text?" And I thought, "Good critical literacy lesson." The kids were generating the questions and not answering the questions. She listed them. Then she said, "Which of these questions go together in the same family?" Then I thought, ". . . What's going on here?" And then she said, "Who can write a question that actually can cover the other three questions in the same family?" She was teaching taxonomy and meta-language and doing it with a fair degree of precision. (Luke, 2001, p. 24) of integrating science content with language arts instruction in the elementary grades. It also supports the notion that young children can indeed sustain an interest in so-called hard texts when teachers introduce strategies for promoting the acquisition of content knowledge, conceptual understanding, social interaction, and motivation for literacy. Children as young as kindergarteners, in fact, are known to benefit from developmentally appropriate instruction that integrates informational texts and other media with language arts learning (Richgels, 2002).

In a review of the research literature on motivation, reading engagement, and academic performance, Guthrie and Wigfield (2000) concluded that various instructional practices, while important, do not directly impact student outcomes such as time spent reading independently, achievement on standardized tests, performance assessments, and beliefs about reading. Instead, the level of student engagement, including its sustainability over time, is what mediates classroom instruction and thereby indirectly influences student outcomes. Guthrie and Wigfield's conception of the engagement model of content area reading calls for instruction that fosters student motivation, strategy use, learning from a variety of texts, and social interaction—all of which are dealt with at length in the chapters that follow.

Reconsidering

Now that you've had an opportunity to consider a broad sweep of what counts as content literacy instruction in the elementary grades and the role that the standards play in such instruction, we invite you to rethink what you learned in your personal Literacy Dig. Try to relate what you found as evidence of literacy practices in your world to the multiple literacies that today's children have at their disposal. As a classroom teacher charged with the responsibility of teaching students to read and learn with content area texts (broadly defined), are you ready to invite them to bring their everyday literacies into the classroom? Why or why not? What are some of the advantages and disadvantages to introducing out-of-school literacies into content area lessons?

PART TWO

Knowledge Base

CHAPTER

2 Teaching Comprehension

In this chapter, we focus on teaching comprehension. To understand how to teach comprehension, first it's important to recognize what research has shown about the comprehension process. Then we look at strategies used by proficient readers when they read. We illustrate each strategy with examples of how they are used. We also include excerpts from reading experiences of an eight-year-old boy. Finally, we describe the gradual release of responsibility teaching model—an effective model for teaching comprehension.

Open your social studies book to Chapter 5. Read pages 35–42 and answer the questions at the end of the section. Be sure to write the questions and answers on your paper. If you have time, do the "challenge questions" too.

After giving this assignment, Ms. Bell watched her fourth-grade students working diligently. They flipped through the pages of the chapter, found answers, and wrote them down. It did not appear that students were actually reading. Were they simply reading the questions and scanning for answers?

When the teacher began checking their assignment, she noticed a pattern. The answers were very similar—in fact, most were copied verbatim from the textbook. The same questions were left blank or the answers were totally off base. Curious, Ms. Bell wondered what it was about these questions that caused students' problems. After careful analysis, she discovered that those questions required students to make inferences, connections to their lives outside of school, and to synthesize information.

Remembering

Does this assignment sound familiar? If so, do you remember having difficulty locating answers to questions? Did you actually read the textbook chapters or scan the text for answers? If you are a teacher, do you make similar assignments? Have you noticed that students seem to experience difficulties with the same questions? If you do, you're not alone.

Ms. Bell's assignment reflects Jeanne's memories of reading and writing assignments when she was an elementary school student. The intent of such assignments was probably to help students comprehend and learn the most important information in the chapter. In reality, however, the assignment merely tested students' skillfulness in scanning and locating answers to questions.

Why do students have difficulty answering what are sometimes referred to as "higher level" questions? One reason may be that, for years, the common assumption was that comprehension was "caught, not taught." The problem was: this assumption was incorrect! So, what's a teacher to do?

In this chapter, we hope to shed some light on this question. We begin by briefly considering research that has helped us better understand the comprehension process. Then we examine strategies "good readers" use and how to teach those strategies to all students. Finally, we describe a model for teaching reading comprehension.

Comprehension Research

During the first half of the twentieth century, research in reading was concerned with teaching students how to read and on best methods for doing this. (Hmmm, sounds like today!) It was not until the mid-1970s that researchers turned their attention to reading comprehension. At this time, the National Institute of Education (NIE) put out a call to establish The Center for the Study of Reading (CSR)—subsequently awarded to the University of Illinois—to study reading comprehension. This was quite a shift; up until this time, decoding had received most of the funding.

One study based at the CSR was Dolores Durkin's research (1978–1979) to determine how much time was spent teaching reading comprehension and what comprehension instruction looked like. What she found across grades three through six in nine schools was that reading comprehension instruction did not occur during reading or social studies. Rather, time was devoted to assessing (testing) comprehension.

Worksheets were prevalent in all classrooms. Although some teachers spent time help-ing students with assignments, much time was spent doing non-instructional tasks, such as taking care of discipline problems or grading the plethora of worksheets that was generated.

Continuing in the 1980s at the CSR, research grounded in schema theory helped shed more light on the reading comprehension process. From this theory grew the notion that comprehension is a complex, interactive process in which readers construct meaning by (1) connecting what they know (schema) to what is written in a text and (2) engaging in discussions with other readers in a variety of contexts and for a variety of purposes. All of these things—the reader's own knowledge, others' knowledge, the context in which reading takes place, and the purpose for reading—influence a reader's comprehension of a text.

"Think-aloud" research also contributed much to what we know about the read-ing comprehension process. "Expert" readers were asked to "think aloud" as they read a text, thus making their comprehension strategies visible. Other research differenti-ated between strategies "expert" and "novice" readers used during reading. The result of this work was the identification of strategies expert readers use flexibly and as needed before, during, and after they read. These strategies include the following:

- making connections with their background knowledge,
- creating images,
- drawing inferences,
- asking questions,
- distinguishing between important and less important information,
- summarizing information, and
- monitoring comprehension (Pressley, 2002).

Reflecting

Do you remember being taught to use the strategies listed above? Have you ever thought about what reading strategies you use to process text? Do you use some strate-gies more proficiently than others?

More research in the mid-1980s and 1990s demonstrated that, contrary to the thinking in the 1950s, 60s, and 70s, comprehension strategies can be taught (Duke & Pearson, 2002). In addition, determining how to teach students to orchestrate their use of the strategies was of interest to researchers. Different instructional frameworks, such as reciprocal teaching (Palincsar & Brown, 1984), explained in the *Teaching Tool-box* and transactional strategies instruction (Pressley, El-Dinary, Gaskins, Schuder, Bergman, Almasi, et al., 1992; Brown, Pressley, Van Meter, & Schuder, 1996), have been effective for teaching students to use a variety of strategies flexibly.

So, what does comprehension instruction look like today? We wish we could say that things have changed across the country. However, in a 1999 study published by the Center for Improvement of Early Reading Achievement (CIERA), researchers found similar teaching practices as those observed by Durkin twenty years ago (Tay-lor, Pearson, Clark, & Walpole, 1999). Of the seventy first-, second-, and third-grade teachers observed—all identified as exemplary by their school principals—the "primary modes of working on comprehension included asking questions (many of which were literal) about the story as children were reading . . . and having children write in response to stories they had read" (p. 42). The writing children did was typically to answer questions or to write in a journal. Only eleven out of seventy teachers were observed "asking higher level questions about children's feelings or about their lives in relation to a story. . . . Only 5 teachers were frequently observed providing instruction (not including worksheet completion) about a comprehension skill or strategy" (p. 42). On top of that, little or no discussion occurred.

Is this an indictment on teachers? We think not. We believe that this finding is an artifact of many things, including the inordinate amount of attention on decoding by funding agencies and thus by publishing companies, almost to the exclusion of reading comprehension. The underlying assumption (although an inaccurate one) is that if children can decode, then they can comprehend (understand) what they read. Teachers are well aware that this is not always the case. You have undoubtedly worked with students who could decode beautifully but could tell you nothing about what they read. Things are looking up in the political arena, however. In 2002, the RAND Corporation Reading Study Group (under contract by the U.S. Department of Education) published a report entitled *Reading for Understanding: Toward an R&D* [research and development] *Program in Reading Comprehension*, which recommended that research is needed to determine effective reading comprehension curriculum, instructional practices, and assessment.

Keeping Current

We recommend that you bookmark the following websites: www.reading.org and www.ncte.org. Check out the link, "Reading Headlines," on the www.reading.org website for current news reports related to literacy. Position statements for IRA and NCTE are also available on these websites. Another website with current news is www.edweek.org. You can check out past articles by clicking on the "Archives and Special Reports" icon.

Reflecting

Consider how politics drives curriculum and instructional decisions in schools today. What has directly impacted you or teachers you know? Why is it important for you to be knowledgeable about the research agendas set by the federal government?

Research-Based Comprehension Strategies

This section of the chapter describes comprehension strategies that have been shown to facilitate comprehension. We provide examples from lessons with children and activities for you to participate in as you read. The purpose of these activities is to help you become more consciously aware of your own comprehension strategies. Record your strategies on sticky notes and place them in the text at points where you use different strategies.

Making Connections

Have you ever thought about all the connections you make when you're reading? Does a book or magazine article remind you of an experience you've had? Perhaps one book reminds you of another. Do you ever think about someone else's experience when you're reading? If you do, you may be a strategic reader.

Strategic readers make connections and integrate their existing knowledge (schemata) with new information. Schemata are developed from various sources, such as one's personal experiences, experiences of others, books, television, movies, music, newspapers, magazines, artwork, and websites. Making connections helps readers:

- deepen their understanding of a text
- make predictions
- know what to expect in terms of text structure, genre, format, author, cue words, writing style, and literary features, thus improving comprehension
- understand a character's feelings, motivations, actions
- stay engaged with a text (i.e., sustain interest in reading a particular text)
- learn new information
- evaluate the meaning of a text (i.e., is it logical?)
- remember what they read
- enjoy reading a text!
- want to learn more! (The more you know, the more you want to learn!)

To help readers think broadly about the connections they make, Keene and Zimmerman (1997) suggested that readers make basically three kinds of connections: text-to-self (T-S), text-to-world (T-W), and text-to-text (T-T). Connections readers make between their own personal experiences and a book are referred to as text-to-self connections. Young children typically make text-to-self connections quite naturally. If you are a pre-K, kindergarten, first-, or second-grade teacher, you have probably experienced the read aloud that seems to never end. Your students just *have* to share all their text-to-self connections with the class! They may not understand how these connections help make them better readers, however. Teaching students how to use connecting strategically requires explicit instruction, including teacher modeling and guidance about what kinds of connections enhance comprehension and what kinds do not.

Another kind of connection that strategic readers make is a "text-to-text" (intertextual) connection. We define "text" broadly to include print text (books, magazines, newspapers, and computer-generated print) and nonprint text (television shows, videos, movies, and computer games). If when you're reading a book, it reminds you of another book, you are making a text-to-text connection. Classroom teachers often use text sets, organized by a common theme, issue, genre, author, or illustrator, to foster text-to-text connections.

Strategic readers also make text-to-world connections as they read. These connections relate to knowledge readers acquire, based on someone else's experiences—vicarious experiences. For example, you may not have attended segregated schools, but your grandmother has told you stories about her experiences growing up. When your class reads *Through My Eyes* by Ruby Bridges (1999), you make a text-to-world connection; you have not experienced segregated schools personally but you make a connection with your grandmother's stories.

To illustrate how a second grader made T-S, T-T, and T-W connections, we provide a description of interactions between Jeanne and her son Isaac when he was eight years old. She read aloud to Isaac the first four pages of *The Most Beautiful Roof in the World* by Kathryn Lasky (1997). In this photographic essay, the reader is introduced to Meg Lowman, a rainforest scientist, and learns about some of her explorations. Early in the book, we learn that Meg's interest in science began when she was a young child. We enter the dialogue between Jeanne and Isaac there.

> **JEANNE READING:** "As a child she [Meg] had "a bird's nest collection, a rock collection, a shell collection, . . . (unpaged).
>
> **ISAAC:** I made a text-to-me [text-to-self] connection. I used to have a rock collection when we lived in Lubbock.
>
> **JEANNE:** How does that connection help you understand this part of the book?
>
> **ISAAC:** I know what it's like to have a rock collection and what kinds of rocks she might have collected.
>
> **JEANNE READING:** "When Meg was ten years old, she was intrigued by two women: Rachel Carson, one of the first environmentalists, who studied and wrote about the delicate relationships in the web of life . . ." (unpaged).
>
> **JEANNE:** Do you know what it means by the "web of life?"
>
> **ISAAC:** It's like the "circle of life" in the *Lion King*. (He explained how everything is linked to everything else and talked about the cycle of birth to death.)
>
> **JEANNE:** You made a text-to-video [text-to-text] connection! How do you think making that connection helped you understand the book?
>
> **ISAAC:** I might have thought the "web of life" had to do with a spider if I didn't make that connection.
>
> **JEANNE REREAD THE PREVIOUS SENTENCE AND THEN CONTINUED:** "She [Meg] was intrigued by two women: Rachel Carson . . . and Harriet Tubman, the most famous 'conductor' of the Underground Railroad . . . Harriet Tubman guided countless African Americans out of slavery." (The book continues, telling how Tubman used what she knew about the environment to "guide her people on their perilous journey. Harriet Tubman, says Meg, was a pioneer field naturalist, one of the first women field naturalists in this country.")
>
> **ISAAC:** I made a text-to-history [text-to-world] connection here. I know about a girl who was a slave and she escaped and helped other slaves escape from slavery.

Isaac's personal experiences (rock collection), knowledge of other texts and their meanings (*Lion King* and the circle of life), and his knowledge of the world (history and Harriet Tubman) all contributed to enhancing his understanding of the text.

Although connections may help students understand a text, others may interfere with their comprehension. When students' connections do not facilitate comprehension, the teacher must guide them to make appropriate connections and, when appropriate, provide experiences that will build relevant knowledge. To illustrate, we continue examining Isaac's connections.

> **JEANNE READING:** "To gather species of plants and insects, Meg has climbed ropes to pluck leaves, sailed aloft in hot-air balloons . . . even hung over the side of an inflatable raft resting on the canopy" (unpaged).
>
> **ISAAC:** I made a text-to-TV [text-to-text] connection with the *Wild Thornberrys*. One day on the Thornberry's, they used an inflatable raft in a river to go fishing. They were leaning over the side of the raft and almost fell in.

This connection did not help Isaac understand the text. In fact, it could have led to misunderstandings. To help expand Isaac's schema for inflatable rafts, Jeanne located a photograph in the book that illustrated a rain forest canopy raft. (If you want to know about the *Wild Thornberrys* and rainforest canopy rafts, check out the web activity.)

Web Activity: Wild Thornberrys and Rainforest Canopy Raft

Wild Thornberrys: If you're not familiar with the adventures of the *Wild Thornberrys*, check out these websites: www.cooltoons.com and www.nwf.org/wildthornberrys. Knowing what cartoons your students watch will help you understand the connections they make.

Rainforest Canopy Raft: Go to www.google.com. Search for rainforest canopy raft. Try to locate a site that includes photographs. Sometimes they're designated as "main photo page." After viewing the photographs, do you more clearly understand how scientists like Meg Lowman explore the rainforest canopy?

To summarize, the sample dialogue illustrates several things.

1. Even young readers can make connections when books, with difficult concepts, are read aloud to them. Capitalizing on their previous experiences and building new ones will help students better comprehend texts.
2. Students may make up their own labels to identify their connections. What's important to remember is the purpose for making connections. Agreeing on the labels for instructional purposes, however, is important so everyone understands the vocabulary.
3. A reader's background knowledge is critical for understanding both print and nonprint (illustrations) text. However, irrelevant connections or lack of background knowledge may hinder comprehension.

   A word of caution: When students make connections that do not help them comprehend a text, they need your help to make relevant connections. One way to do this is by modeling your own connections. Think aloud as you read a text, describe your connections, and explain how they help (or hinder) your comprehension. Tell students what you do when you realize a connection doesn't help you—how you "fix" your comprehension. In doing this, you are also demonstrating comprehension monitoring (metacognitive) strategies you use while reading.

4. Even young readers use their experiences with multiple literacies to help them construct meaning with text. (See Chapter 6 for more about media and visual literacies.)

Readers Who Lack Background Knowledge about a Topic

One reason some children may struggle with comprehension is that they do not have background knowledge about topics they read about. To build students' background knowledge about the rainforest, for example, provide students with experiences in which they explore artifacts, examine photographs, and view videos. Then explicitly model the connections you make with these experiences as you read aloud *and* explain how these connections help you understand what you read. Invite students to share their connections too.

Reflecting

Think about the connecting strategy. Did you find yourself making any text-to-self connections as you read? For example, did you make a text-to-self connection with the social studies assignment at the beginning of the chapter? Or maybe you, like Meg, were fascinated by Rachel Carson's biography, a T-T connection. Perhaps you made a text-to-world connection and linked Lasky's book with your knowledge of the rapid deforestation of rainforests.

As you continue reading this chapter, continue using sticky notes to jot down your connections. But this strategy is only one of many that strategic readers use. Now we turn to sensory images. Do you use an author's words and your background knowledge to create sensory images when you read? If you do, you may be a strategic reader.

Creating Sensory Images

Do you ever "see" pictures or "mind movies" in your head when you read? Perhaps you've imagined what the setting or your favorite character looks like. When you read a complicated text, do you ever visualize (or perhaps draw) a diagram to help you understand how parts are related? Visualizing personalizes a text, keeps the reader engaged with a text, and aids remembering and understanding.

Have you ever thought about using your other senses to help you understand a text? Strategic readers often use their other senses and experience emotional reactions when reading. Read the following text and try to experience it as you read. Think about what you see, hear, feel, and smell. Also, notice your emotions as you read this biographical text.

> The diver stood like a statue on the springboard, visualizing her dive. Suddenly, she launched herself off the board into the air, turned a seemingly effortless forward somersault, and entered the water straight as an arrow. Only a small splash marked the spot where she had, seconds earlier, entered the water. Loud shouts of victory and waves of applause filled the chlorine-scented air as the diver swam to the side of the pool, lifted herself out, and headed for the soothing water of the whirlpool.

What did you imagine? Did you *see* a swimmer at the local pool doing a flip off the board or did you *see* a diver at the Olympics? Did you *hear* the springboard bounce on its supports as the diver jumped into the air? Did you *hear* the roar of the crowd applauding as the dive was perfectly executed? Did you *hear* the water splash ever so slightly? Did you *smell* the chlorine in the air? Did you anticipate the dive and then *hold your breath* until the dive was complete? Perhaps you pictured yourself as the diver rather than a member of the crowd. In that case, you saw, heard, smelled, and felt different things. You probably *visualized* the perfect dive as you stood on the end of the board. After the dive, did you feel *jubilant* and *relieved* because you executed the dive perfectly?

It is important to note that creating images is closely linked to a reader's schema. The more a reader knows about a topic, the more information a reader has available from which to create vivid sensory images. Think about it. If you've never seen a glacier, for example, nor seen an image on television or in a photograph, you must depend solely on an author's words to help you generate an image. If you have some kind of experience with a glacier, then you have more information available from which to create an image.

Reflecting

Do you understand how using many of your senses can help you comprehend, even experience, a text more fully? If you don't use your senses, consider why you may not. As you continue reading this chapter, consider how you use (or do not use) your senses. Continue jotting down your connections too.

Making Inferences

Think back to Ms. Bell's students and their difficulties answering some of the questions. Why do you think this was the case? One reason may be that the answers for those questions were inferred, rather than stated explicitly, in the textbook. To make inferences, a reader must figure out what an author meant but did not say! Teaching students how to infer what the author meant is important.

To make inferences, readers may be likened to detectives. When they read the words, readers look for clues in the print, consider what the clues mean and how they are linked, and then determine the meaning of the text or, in the case of a detective, solve the crime. (Sherlock Holmes was a genius at making inferences.)

We make inferences every day outside the context of reading; children do too. Remember when a particular teacher turned your way and raised an eyebrow or when your mom called you by your full name? You inferred that you were in trouble! You knew this because you had experienced the consequences of the raised eyebrow or the sound of your full name. No one had to tell you that "you were in for it now!" You knew. You put together the raised eyebrow—like the words that are stated in a text—with past experiences and what you were doing at the time (made text-to-self connections) and then made an inference.

Inferring is a "way of life" for teachers and students of mathematics and science. To solve mathematical word problems, inferences are crucial. The words don't tell the reader explicitly how to solve the problem. Rather, readers consider the pieces, sift through them, determine what's important (more about determining importance later), decide how the pieces fit together, determine appropriate operations, and then solve the problem. In science, students make hypotheses, based on the information they have (what they know). In effect, they are making an inference about what will happen.

Try It! Making Inferences in Mathematics and Science

Here's the math problem:

You have 75 children's picture storybooks. Each one averages about $14.95. Three-fourths of them you bought at a half-price sale. How much money do you have invested in your library?

What information is stated explicitly? _____

What is inferred? _____

How do you know what to do to solve the problem? _____

Does your answer make sense? _____

Here's the science problem:

Your hair dryer won't turn on. What's wrong?

What's your hypothesis—what do you think (infer) is wrong? _____

What questions do you have? _____

What procedures will you use to answer your questions? _____

How can you find out if you're right—what data can you collect? _____

Did you accept or reject your hypothesis? _____

When readers use context clues to determine the meaning of a word, they are also making inferences. They infer what a word means based on words that occur before and after the unknown word (i.e., the context). Context clues are to a reader like clues are to a detective. (See Chapter 4 for more about context clues.)

Asking Questions

Let's examine questioning in general first. Think about the last time you asked a question. Perhaps you asked directions to a friend's house or maybe you asked a friend about her children or a recent vacation. Generally speaking, people ask questions because they are curious, intrigued, confused, or need information. There are times, however, when individuals ask questions to find out what someone else knows, to challenge an idea, to intrigue, or to test one's own or someone else's knowledge.

Think about questions that are asked in elementary school classrooms. Who typically asks questions? If you're a teacher, you may think about little Anthony who *always* has a question! If you're a preservice teacher, you may think about all the questions your professors ask. But have you ever thought about the questions you ask yourself before, during, and after you read? When readers ask themselves questions during reading, they are monitoring—keeping track of—their comprehension. When readers monitor their comprehension, they are said to be metacognitively aware—you are aware of what you are thinking as you read. Do you ask yourself questions as you read? If you do, you may be a strategic reader.

Teachers in one of Jeanne's graduate courses were curious about their own use of questioning because many of them did not think they asked questions as they read. To examine their use of questioning, they read wordless picture books such as David Weisner's *Sector 7* (1999) and Tom Feelings' *The Middle Passage* (1995). They "read" the illustrations in pairs, thinking aloud and discussing as they "read." Then they recorded their questions on sticky notes.

What did the teachers learn from this experience? First, they learned that they approached the texts with a questioning attitude, although sometimes they didn't actually ask questions. Comments on sticky notes reflected their predictions, wonderings, uncertainties, and questions. Second, teachers concluded that asking questions (approaching the text with a questioning attitude) helped them stay actively engaged with the books, facilitated thinking as they read, and encouraged them to focus on information that might answer their questions. Third, several teachers reflected that they needed to teach their students to ask questions during reading. Until this time, they did not fully understand the importance of reader-generated questioning as a comprehension-enhancing and comprehension-monitoring strategy.

Try It! Ask Sticky Questions

Get some sticky notes; small ones will work. As you read, jot down your questions. Place the sticky note where you had the question. If you find the answer as you continue reading, write "A" for answer and move the note to the page where your question was answered. Kids of all ages love to use this strategy! As a teacher, you can use students' sticky questions to assess how you might assist them with their comprehension. Perhaps they need more background knowledge or more instruction about how to make inferences or images as they read.

Raphael (1986) described a strategy for helping students become more aware of the relationship among questions, information in a text, and students' background knowledge. This strategy, Question-Answer Relationships (QAR), is especially useful for students who, even when they ask their own questions, can not find the answers unless they are explicitly stated. Particular vocabulary enables students to more easily talk about the relationships among questions and answers. "Right There" denotes questions explicitly answered in a text. "Think and Search" signals that answers are inferred in a text. "On My Own" or "Author and Me" implies that a reader must use his or her own knowledge from a variety of sources to answer questions. Instruction with QARs helps "reduce the mystery of how questions are created and how responses to questions may be formed" (Raphael & Hiebert, 1996, p. 212).

Reflecting

As you read this book, have you noticed yourself asking questions? Perhaps you wrote a question mark in the margin beside a paragraph you didn't understand. If so, you're monitoring your comprehension through questioning. Maybe you asked yourself how many more pages are in this chapter! Have you noticed the questions we ask you? Have you guessed the purposes of those questions?

Determining Important Ideas

How do you make decisions about what's important in your daily life? You set priorities—consciously or unconsciously—that help you decide. If you are a strategic reader, you make decisions about what information receives most of your attention and what information receives less. In other words, you determine the priority the information has for you. This section focuses on determining important *ideas* in a text, not a single "main idea." Strategic readers need to be able to differentiate between important and less important information in their daily reading, not just on forced-choice (multiple choice) tests.

Typically children learn early in their school careers how to determine important ideas in stories. They know that the setting, characters, problem, and resolution are the most important elements of a story. Determining important ideas in informational texts requires different understandings. Textbooks and other informational texts include organizational features, such as a table of contents, index, glossary, introduction, summary, and headings, to help readers differentiate between important information and less important details. (See Chapter 5 for more information.) In addition, most paragraphs are structured with the most important ideas in the first or last sentence.

All of these features help readers determine what the author considers most important, which is what teachers are most concerned with when teaching content. But have you considered that a *reader's* purpose ultimately determines what he or she thinks is important? For example, your purpose for reading a particular journal article may be to find book titles you can share with your fifth graders. The authors' purpose, as stated in the article, may have been to describe what students learned from reading these books. *Your* purpose determined what information was most important to you.

Reflecting

Do you use a highlighter when you read? (Maybe you're using a highlighter right now!) How do you determine what ideas to highlight and which ones to leave in black and white? Perhaps you have struggled with distinguishing important ideas and less important ones when reading your college textbooks. This is more likely the case when you're reading a book for which you have little background knowledge because everything looks important. What features of text do you use to help you determine what an author considers to be important?

Summarizing

When you read this section heading, "summarizing," what was your first thought? Perhaps it was "augh!" Elementary school students may think of the dreaded book report. Perhaps you thought about the "journal abstract" assignments you've undoubtedly encountered during your university work. These "connections" may contribute to the bad reputation of summarizing. But that need not be the case. We use summarizing throughout each day. For example, when you tell a friend about a movie you saw last Friday night, you summarize the film in a way that hits the highlights but doesn't give away the whole story. You've probably learned to summarize very succinctly for email communication too. In these circumstances, it probably seems natural to summarize your experiences without retelling every detail.

Why, then, does summarizing of text seem so difficult? One reason may be because we were not taught *how* to summarize. But don't despair, research shows that summarizing can be taught (Pearson & Fielding, 1991). General rules for summarizing developed by Kintsch and van Dijk (1978) are useful for teaching students how to summarize. They include the following:

1. delete irrelevant information,
2. delete redundant information,
3. use a general idea (category) to describe a list of ideas,
4. look for topic sentences that may be used in the summary, and
5. create your own topic sentences when authors don't provide them.

The aforementioned rules reflect the intricate relationship between summarizing and determining importance. The first two steps focus on sorting through ideas to identify the most important (relevant) ideas and to remove repetitive (redundant) ideas. Then those ideas must be pulled together—synthesized—into a new "whole," which provides an accurate representation of the original text (Dole, Duffy, Roehler, & Pearson, 1991).

To illustrate summarizing, we turn again to interactions between Jeanne and her son Isaac during the summer after his second-grade year. Together, they read the book *My Man Blue* by Grimes (1999). The book is written as a series of poems describing the relationship between a young African American boy, Damon, and Blue, an old friend of Damon's mother. After Jeanne and Isaac read each poem, they recorded characteristics about Blue on a sticky note—one note per poem—in preparation for writing a biopoem about Blue (see Figure 2.1 for sample notes). When they finished reading the book, they read over their notes and identified information that best represented Blue, deleting unnecessary and redundant information (similar to the summarizing rules given earlier). The biopoem stems (see Toolbox for examples) provided category labels—much like topic sentences—to help Isaac organize his ideas. See Figure 2.2 for his completed biopoem about Blue.

After Isaac finished writing the biopoem, Jeanne was curious to see how he would summarize the book. He said: "This book is about a guy named Blue and a boy named Damon. They get to know each other and fill up each other's missing feelings of having a son and a father." Isaac's summary says it all—it captures the essence of the relationship between Damon and Blue beautifully.

The Interrelationship of Strategy Use

Summarizing required that Isaac use comprehension strategies flexibly. In one poem, "Grounded," he made a *text-to-self connection* to predict why it was titled "Grounded." He predicted that the boy was grounded because he had done something he shouldn't have. He revised his prediction after reading a few lines and *inferred* that Damon was "grounded" because his asthma was acting up and prevented him from playing "stick ball." Isaac made a *text-to-world connection* with asthma; one of his friends had asthma and was hospitalized. In "Grounded," Blue gives Damon a hot dog to cheer him up. Isaac wrote on a sticky note that Blue was a good cook. Jeanne asked why he thought that and he described a detailed scenario that demonstrated he had created images, inferred, and made text-to-self connections to *infer* that Blue had cooked the hot dog he gave to Damon. Isaac *asked* Jeanne what "stick ball" was. To answer his question, she made a *text-to-self connection* for him by explaining that "stick ball" was like baseball. When Isaac identified characteristics of Blue on sticky notes, he selected what he considered to be *important information* and ignored other information. When he wrote the biopoem and *summarized* the book in two sentences, he *synthesized* the information.

When Isaac and Jeanne read this book, he was not accustomed to reading poetry in a book format. Although it's not apparent in the description given earlier, Jeanne

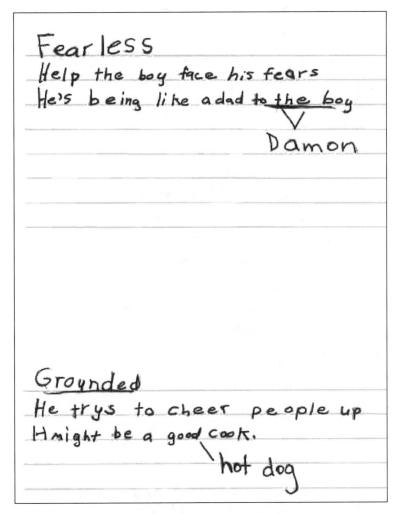

FIGURE 2.1 Notes from *My Man Blue*

provided support and instruction for Isaac throughout the book when he seemed confused or when he asked questions. She also modeled how to compose a biopoem and how and why to use sticky notes. When Isaac was composing his biopoem about Blue, they discussed their notes and how to decide which information to include. He composed the summary independently. We wonder what his summary would have been like if he had been told to read the book and summarize it without instruction or support. We strongly suspect that his engagement with the text, his understanding of the "whole," and his writing would have been very different.

Blue
Gives people good advice,
a guardian angel,
tries to cheer people up,
brightens people's lives.
Friend of Damon.
Father of Zeke.
Loves Zeke and Damon.
Feels scared, happy and sad.
        Fears Damon getting hurt.
Would like to see Zeke,
people being kind to each other,
and other people being a good influence on
others.
Lives in a big city close to the water.
Angel

FIGURE 2.2   Isaac's Biopoem

Reflecting

If you were to summarize this chapter thus far, what procedures would you follow? Try using the rules suggested earlier. Did they help you?

Earlier in this chapter, we asked you to record your strategy use on sticky notes. Look back at your notes. Did you use a variety of strategies flexibly? If you did, you are a strategic reader!

Try It! Read a Mathematical Word Problem Strategically

Go back to the mathematical word problem in the *Try It!* box. How did you decide what information was important to use when solving the problem? What questions did you ask yourself as you tried to solve the problem? Did you try to picture the information in the problem? Did you make connections as you solved the problem? Now try it with another word problem. Go to www.google.com and type in "math word problems." You can solve math problems strategically to your heart's content.

FIGURE 2.3   Text Selection Hints*

Strategy	Hints
Making connections	Organize text sets around a theme, topic, issue, genre, author, illustrator Use texts about which students have had experiences Use nonprint texts such as video, photographs, etc. to build students' background knowledge
Creating sensory images	Select texts with rich description: Poetry Provide sensory experiences and read related books: *The Popcorn Book* (Tomie de Paola) Author ideas: Joanne Ryder, Seymour Simon, Karen Hesse Suggested titles: *Listen to the Rain* (Bill Martin Jr. and John Archambault), *Out of the Dust* and *Come on Rain!* (Karen Hesse), *My Man Blue* (Nicki Grimes)
Inferring	Select texts that require inferring: Mysteries, wordless picture books, poetry, e.g., *Hoops* (Robert Burleigh) Conduct science experiments and make inferences (predictions) Think aloud when reading and solving mathematical word problems
Asking questions	Select texts that arouse curiosity: Books by Chris Van Allsburg (e.g., *Mysteries of Harris Burdick*), wordless picture books, Dorling Kindersley science books
Determining importance	Select well-structured text: expository texts (e.g., textbooks and informational trade books) with various organizational features Examine and write riddles, time lines
Summarizing	Select short texts such as newspaper and magazine articles when beginning instruction. Later move on to texts with headings and subheadings, and then to summarizing across multiple texts. (See Chapter 3 for periodicals information.)

*See Appendix B for more examples of texts for teaching strategies.

Teachers have frequently asked us what kinds of texts are good for teaching the different strategies. Figure 2.3 provides a few suggestions for choosing books. In addition, Appendix B has an extended list of trade books that can be used for content and literacy instruction.

Comprehension Monitoring

When we discussed making connections, we mentioned comprehension monitoring and metacognitive awareness. Perhaps you placed a question mark there. If you did, you were monitoring your reading comprehension. Perhaps you've never really thought about this or realized that it's an important strategy to use when reading.

Consider this situation: You're reading a textbook chapter (not this one of course!) and realize after reading a few pages that you don't remember anything you've read. Realizing that you haven't paid attention means you are metacognitively aware of your mental processes during reading. When you decide to "fix" your comprehension, you have several alternatives to choose from. Your decision about which strategy to use depends on which one you believe will be most effective. So, how does this example relate to metacognition? To explain precisely, we refer to the definition from *The Literacy Dictionary* (Harris & Hodges, 1995); metacognition is the "awareness and knowledge of one's mental processes such that one can monitor, regulate, and direct them" (p. 153).

Reflecting: Are You a Strategic Reader?

Strategic readers monitor (keep track of) their comprehension process. They have access to a variety of strategies, which they use flexibly and deliberately to construct meaning with texts. The coordinated use of the strategies is characteristic of strategic readers. They are also knowledgeable about strategies that may be used to repair comprehension when it breaks down. If a strategy does not work effectively, they select another strategy from their repertoire. Strategic readers adapt to different kinds of texts, tasks, and contexts. So, there you have it; now what do you think? Are you a strategic reader?

Readers Who Struggle

Struggling readers, especially, have difficulty asking questions before, during, and after they read. They may read passively and engage little with the text because of lack of interest or understanding of comprehension strategies for engaging with the text. They often concentrate so much on decoding that they don't think about the meaning of a text. Furthermore, they make few connections, create few images, and make few inferences. Explicit teaching, including teacher modeling, is essential for struggling or reluctant readers to ensure that they understand what strategies to use, how to use them, and when to use them.

Fluency

Much has been written about the importance of fluency in terms of word recognition. Only recently has it been suggested that fluency should be examined in relation to the coordinated use of comprehension processes (Samuels, 2002). Pressley (2001) wrote:

> . . . [M]uch needs to be learned about how to increase fluency of higher order reading processes, including the automatic use of comprehension and monitoring strategies.

According to this perspective, comprehension will only be maximized when readers are fluent in all the processes of skilled reading, from letter recognition and sounding out of words to articulation of the diverse comprehension strategies used by good readers. . . . That use of comprehension processes must be automatic is one of the reasons that successful teaching of higher order comprehension processes occurs over years. Automatic, fluid articulation of comprehension strategies develops slowly, when it develops at all. . . . Although much is known about how to teach comprehension strategies when students are first learning them, very little is known about how teaching should occur as students are internalizing and automatizing strategies.

Perhaps this is the challenge. How can comprehension strategies be taught so that readers use them automatically, flexibly, and strategically? Perhaps with the new research agenda proposed by the RAND Corporation Reading Study Group, we will learn more.

Gradual Release of Responsibility Teaching Model

A model for teaching reading comprehension that is supported by evidence-based research (Duke & Pearson, 2002) is sometimes referred to as the gradual release of responsibility (GRR) model (Pearson & Gallagher, 1983). We list the components and include sample dialogue to demonstrate what each component "sounds like."

1. The teacher describes explicitly a strategy, including when and how to use it.

   "Using mental imagery is like making a movie in your mind. You imagine what things look like, smell like, sound like, feel like, and taste like. It's also about how the author makes you feel—your heart feelings. When you read a book without illustrations, it's especially important to create mind movies from the author's words. Let's begin by reading one page and then stop and describe our mind movies."

2. The teacher models a strategy in action.

   "I'm going to read *Christmas in the Big House, Christmas in the Quarters* and share my mind movies with you. I'll read a section, put the book in my lap, and then describe my movie. Let's start right here where the children are hanging up their stockings. [Read the text.] In the Quarters I hear the slave children, three girls, laughing and giggling as they hang up their stockings, which are probably old socks. I think they're probably young and have to stand on their tiptoes and reach with their arms outstretched to hang up their stockings. The fireplace is a big square hole in the wall, a fire is burning, and over it is a great big cast iron pot with something cooking in it. I can feel the heat and smell something wonderful—maybe it's chicken. I can feel the children's excitement in my heart; I remember how excited I always felt on Christmas Eve. Imagining what the girls were doing, what the fireplace looked like, and how the room smelled, helps me understand how different their home was from mine. Thinking about their excitement on Christmas Eve helps me think about how similar my feeling are to theirs."

3. The teacher and students use the strategy collaboratively.

"Now that I've described for you what my movie was like, I'm going to give you a chance. I'll read a section from the book. As I read, I want you to make your own movie about what the author is describing. When I stop reading, we'll share what we imagined and why. Ready?"

4. The teacher guides students' practice, gradually releasing responsibility to them.

"Now that we've practiced making mind movies together, I'd like you to meet with your reading buddies. Read two pages of your book silently, then stop, and describe your mind movie to each other. Remember to share how imaging helped you with your reading. I'll be coming around to listen in and see what you come up with."

5. Students practice using strategies independently.

"Today during silent reading, I'd like you to think about making mind movies as you read. We'll read for about fifteen minutes and then when you get to a stopping place, I want you to draw your favorite image. Then we'll talk about how your mind movies helped you understand and enjoy your book."

We want to expand a little on the guided practice component of the model. This is not a time for students to work independently on worksheets, simply practicing a skill. Rather, Miller (2002) recommends that a teacher should explain explicitly what she wants students to do in their groups, how they should do it, and why it's important. As students work in their small groups, the teacher observes to assess students' progress with strategy use, to encourage them, and to provide additional instruction and guidance, which propels students to more proficient and independent strategy use. The social interactions between the teacher and small groups are essential during guided practice, as is social interaction during large group when students share their strategy use with one another.

In *Mosaic of Thought* (Keene & Zimmerman, 1997) and *Strategies that Work* (Harvey & Goudvis, 2000), the authors recommend that each strategy should be taught until students use them independently and flexibly. This process does not happen overnight. In fact, Miller writes extensively about her six- to eight-week strategy teaching plans in her book, *Reading with Meaning* (2002). Strategies are not taught in a vacuum. When a new strategy is introduced, instructional engagements focus on the "new" strategy. In addition, the teacher continues to encourage students to use other familiar strategies, especially during independent reading. Inevitably, students begin to share how they use familiar strategies *and* the "new" strategy while reading. These incidents provide a teacher with opportunities to talk about and demonstrate how expert readers coordinate the use of multiple strategies. After all, the ultimate goal of reading instruction is that readers can flexibly orchestrate strategy use independently.

Routman (2003) cautions teachers about how they teach comprehension. If too much emphasis is placed on isolated strategy instruction, it could make reading more difficult. Strategies are "tool[s] for facilitating and extending comprehension," (p. 119) not an end in themselves. For students to benefit from strategy instruction, they must also have plenty of independent reading time in which they can practice using these strategies. Just like anything else, remembering the ultimate purpose for comprehension strategy instruction is important for students to "become proficient and independent readers" (p. 119).

Learning to use comprehension strategies is not an all-or-nothing proposition. Strategic readers continue to develop their use of strategies more efficiently and effectively throughout their lives. With new technologies evolving every day, even proficient readers will develop new strategies for processing and negotiating text.

Reconsidering

Early in the chapter we asked you to record the strategies you used while reading this chapter. What strategies did you use? Did you find that you use some strategies more than others? Were there some strategies you used rarely? If you are a teacher, what comprehension strategies do you teach explicitly? Consider how your growing metacognitive awareness of your own comprehension process can help you become a better teacher of reading.

3 Using Textbooks and Trade Books for Content Area Instruction

This chapter examines the strengths and limitations of textbooks and trade books, commonly used to teach content in elementary school classrooms. Then we briefly describe evidence-based research that supports the use of trade books for content area teaching and learning. Finally, we consider the impact of a reader's purpose (or stance) on understanding and experiencing content area texts.

Picture this: a third-grade classroom. Each desk contains a reading textbook, reading workbook, a social studies textbook, a science textbook, paper, pencils, crayons, a handwriting book, a library book, and a three-ring binder. Are these images from classrooms today, a decade ago, or forty to fifty years ago?

Remembering

Does the description of the third-grade classroom sound familiar to you? What was in your desk in first grade, third grade, or sixth grade? What do you think fills students' desks today?

Would you be surprised to learn that the third-grade classroom "picture" was from our memories that go back fifty years, forty years, and twenty years?! From our recent classroom observations, the tools of the school trade—textbooks, workbooks, library books, paper, pencils, and crayons—have changed little, except that worksheets are prevalent and magic markers are a "must." Yet two prominent additions have been made in many classrooms: a classroom library with trade books of varying genres and reading levels and computer workstations.

Strengths and Limitations of Textbooks

You are undoubtedly very familiar with textbooks, like the one you're reading now! You've probably used them throughout your school career. Textbooks have been a mainstay in public school classrooms in the United States for decades. Elementary school students probably expect to have a textbook for most subjects. Even in graduate school, students typically expect to have access to a textbook. Why do you think this is the case?

In the best cases, textbooks offer several strengths for content area teaching and learning (see Figure 3.1).

First, they provide an overview or introduction to a particular body of knowledge. Second, each publishing company designs their textbooks so that content is presented in a systematic, sequential way across the grade levels. That is, textbooks provide a scope and sequence teachers may follow exactly or simply as a guide. Third, knowledgeable individuals in a field serve as consultants for textbook development, which should ensure accurate and current information. Fourth, textbook content and suggested teaching practices are ideally consistent with national standards such as *Principles and Standards for School Mathematics* (2000), *National Science Education Standards* (1996), *Expectations for Excellence: Curriculum Standards for Social Studies* (1994), and *Standards for English Language Arts* (1997). Fifth, the best textbook series provide teachers with research-based instructional strategies and up-to-date resources that can be used to intrigue, motivate, and teach students. Sixth, organizational features are chosen to support readers as they construct meaning with the text. Seventh, textbooks are revised regularly.

Knowing these *potential* strengths, you might wonder why textbooks have such a bad reputation. As you might expect, there are two sides to the story. Textbooks also have their limitations (see Figure 3.1). First, textbooks provide only an overview of many topics, a strength, if your objective is to get a "glimpse" into a topic. If, however, your objective is to encourage in-depth inquiry or concept development, an overview is insufficient.

Second, textbooks used in elementary schools are typically difficult to read. There are several reasons for this:

FIGURE 3.1   Strengths and Limitations of Textbooks

Strengths	Limitations
1. Provide overview or introduction to body of knowledge.	1. No in-depth coverage of concepts
2. Content is presented systematically and sequentially across grade levels	2. Difficult for many students to read
3. Authors/consultants are knowledgeable, contributing to accuracy	3. Physically unappealing
4. Practices advocated are consistent with standards of learned societies	4. Outdated quickly. Inaccuracies occur if attempt to publish too quickly
5. Research-based strategies and up-to-date resources are advocated	5. Textbook adoption may be politically motivated
6. Organizational features support readers	6. Expensive
7. Revised regularly	

- the readability levels are often higher than the grade level in which they are intended (e.g., a third-grade social studies book may be written on a fourth- or fifth-grade reading level), although more publishers strive to write textbooks "on grade level" than in the past;
- a single textbook cannot meet the needs of students who have a wide range of reading levels;
- technical vocabulary, often specific to a particular content area, is unfamiliar to students;
- concept load in textbooks is often dense; a lot of information is packed into a small space;
- content is unfamiliar to students; they lack background knowledge (schema) so reading is more difficult;
- authors often over rely on a descriptive text structure, which does not support the understanding and retention of information as well as expository text structures such as compare contrast, sequence, and cause effect; and
- transition words, which explicitly signal the relationships among ideas, are often lacking.

Third, textbooks are typically physically unappealing. Sometimes the sheer size and weight of textbooks are intimidating. Moreover, textbooks typically do not include physical features such as intriguing illustrations and photographs that often serve to invite students to *step into* and *move through* (Langer, 1995, pp. 16–17) a text, although recent textbooks are much more interesting in terms of their use of photographs and visuals than in the past.

Fourth, textbooks become outdated quickly; this is due in part to the virtual explosion of information in the late twentieth and early twenty-first centuries. Also contributing are state textbook adoption policies; typically textbook adoptions occur every five to eight years. Relatedly, when textbooks are published too quickly in an attempt to provide students with up-to-date information, more errors in content information tend to occur.

Fifth, the politics of textbook adoption is a complicated factor. Who makes decisions about textbook adoptions—classroom teachers or administrators? Why do they make the selections they do? Do marketing strategies influence decisions more strongly than the quality of materials, the match with students' needs, and research-based features? Do relationships with salespeople make the difference? And then there are the supplemental materials offered. Do the materials actually support student learning?

Sixth, textbooks are very expensive. The inclusion of features that may make a textbook more appealing to readers also increases the cost. Is the money well spent? Are textbooks good enough and used enough to warrant the expense?

Reflecting

Think about the textbook you're reading right now. How does it measure up in terms of strengths and limitations just noted? What could we do in our next edition that would increase the strengths of this book?

If you are a teacher, think about the textbooks available for teaching social studies, science, and mathematics. Do they embody the strengths noted earlier? What are the limitations?

As you can probably guess, we do not advocate the exclusive use of textbooks for content area teaching and learning. In fact, few educators do. We believe that a variety of print and nonprint resources should be used to supplement textbooks and to help compensate for their limitations. Trade books are one kind of print resource advocated by researchers and teachers alike.

Strengths and Limitations of Trade Books

We start with a definition of trade books. Trade books are books available to the general public (Harris & Hodges, 1995) and are found in libraries and bookstores. Textbooks and reference books are not considered trade books. The terms *trade books* and *children's literature* are used interchangeably by many educators. Children's trade books include a variety of genres: realistic fiction, informational books (nonfiction books), biographies and autobiographies, historical fiction, fantasy, science fiction, picture books, traditional literature, and poetry.

The publication of children's literature is a major industry. According to the *Bowker Annual Library and Book Trade Almanac* (Ink & Grabois, 2001), over 9000 children's books were published in 1998 and 1999. Preliminary estimates for the year 2000 were over 6000, although it's likely the actual figures were higher.

The quality of children's trade books has improved over the last decade with advancing technologies. To recognize outstanding children's literature, numerous awards, such as the Caldecott Award for picture books, the Hans Christian Andersen Award for an author and illustrator who have made important contributions to children's literature internationally, the *Orbis Pictus* Award for nonfiction, and the Boston Globe-Horn Book Award for Nonfiction are presented regularly. The Washington Post-Children's Book Guild honors annually an author of children's books who has contributed significantly to informational books for children. Authors such as Jim Murphy, Diane Stanley, Laurence Pringle, Seymour Simon, Russell Freedman, Joanna Cole, Gail Gibbons, and Kathryn Lasky have received this award. Content specific book awards are also presented each year. For example, the National Science Teachers Association and the Children's Book Council publish lists of outstanding science trade books in the March issue of *Science and Children*. Books are organized in categories such as biography, life science, environment and ecology, earth and space science, and science-related careers. The National Council for the Social Studies also publishes their annual list of Notable Social Studies Trade Books for Young People in the May/June issue of *Social Education*. These books are organized in broad categories, are correlated with the national standards, and include annotations with general reading levels—primary, intermediate, and advanced.

Web Activity: Noteworthy Children's Literature

What do you know about award-winning informational children's books? Check out the following websites to familiarize yourself with some of the most noteworthy. The Washington Post-Children's Book Guild website is www.childrensbookguild.org. Do you recognize the nonfiction authors who have been honored? For outstanding social studies books, see www.socialstudies.org/resources/notable. Notable science books can be accessed at www.nsta.org. Click on "Teacher Resources" and then scroll down to "Outstanding Science Trade Books for Children." The winners of the *Orbis Pictus* Award for Outstanding Nonfiction for Children can be found at www.ncte.org/elem/orbispictus.

ELL: Quality Spanish-Language Informational Trade Books

While Spanish is not the sole primary language of English language learners, it certainly dominates many classrooms. If you have Spanish-speaking children in your classroom and would like to provide them access to books written in their home language, you may want to browse the recommended books by http://cuatrogatos.org/mejores.html. They dedicate a section to informational books. Haga clic en ¡Los mejores del 2001! (Click on "The best of 2001!") to find the recommended books for children and adolescents written in Spanish.

FIGURE 3.2   Strengths and Limitations of Trade Books

Strengths	Limitations
1. Many up-to-date books are available	**1.** Accessibility of reasonably current trade books
2. Expert authors	**2.** Teachers' lack of knowledge about available books
3. Wide range of reading levels for children across grade levels	
4. Provide struggling readers with access to content	
5. Written from varying perspectives about a plethora of topics	
6. Facilitate favorable attitudes toward reading and content area learning	
7. Help build students' background knowledge for topics and language of a discipline.	
8. Varied expository text structures	
9. Appealing formats	
10. Provide opportunities to develop critical reading skills	

Much has been written about the strengths of trade books for content area instruction (see Figure 3.2).

First, because the publication of informational trade books for children and young adults has grown tremendously over the last few years, many up-to-date informational trade books are available from a variety of sources such as local bookstores, on-line, and from book clubs such as Scholastic and Trumpet.

Second, informational trade books are written by experts. Authors' credentials are much more credible than in years past. Information about the resources authors use to write a book is often included in a preface or afterward. Sometimes information is also included about how long an author studied a topic before writing the book. Authors also often acknowledge experts who have helped them with the development of a book.

Third, informational books are available at all reading levels. Since about the mid-1990s, publication of informational books for the primary grades, in particular, has exploded. Until then, few informational books were appropriate for young readers to read independently. Publishers such as Rigby, Sunshine, and Newbridge have whole catalogs listing and describing informational books for emergent, early, and transitional readers.

These changes came about, in part, as a result of research sparked by Christine Pappas's ground-breaking study (1991, 1993). In her study of kindergarten students' understanding of expository and narrative structures, she found that kindergartners understood expository texts as easily as narrative texts. These results called into question the assumption that narrative texts should dominate primary grade reading instruction. Pappas (1991) proposed that children are denied "full access to literacy" (p. 461) when the kinds of texts used in the early grades are limited.

Moss (1997) drew similar conclusions in a study of first-grade students. She found that young children understood informational trade books that were read to them. Moreover, she found that they could summarize, identify ideas they deemed important, make text-to-self connections, and draw inferences.

Other researchers examined the impact of using informational texts with narrative texts for beginning reading instruction. Kamil and Lane (1997) conducted a two-year observational, intervention study of two first-grade classrooms. Informational texts accounted for 50 percent of materials used in the classrooms, and instruction for negotiating informational texts was an integral component of the curriculum. Results revealed that students in these classrooms not only learned to read, they learned to read and write a variety of genres. This study was important to provide more evidence that young readers *can* learn to read with texts other than stories.

A fourth strength of trade books is their potential for providing struggling readers access to literacy. Less proficient readers typically spend less time reading than more proficient readers. Carefully selected trade books can provide opportunities for struggling readers to successfully negotiate materials that are better matched to their reading levels than textbooks. Likewise, because trade books are written about a plethora of topics, it's likely that books of interest can be found. For many struggling readers, using informational trade books for integrated reading and content instruction can open doors to literacy when traditional remedial methods—isolated phonics drill and practice and use of narrative text or controlled text—have not worked. In addition, Abrahamson and Carter (as cited in Moss & Hendershot, 2002) suggest that informational books can motivate reluctant readers to become lifelong readers.

A small number of studies have demonstrated that informational texts can promote reading development. Caswell and Duke (1998) found this to be the case for two students who attended the Harvard Literacy Laboratory for assistance with reading. Both students had a history of reading difficulties, although their reading profiles were quite different. Peter had a history of reading difficulties but demonstrated strengths in the areas of social studies and science. He repeated kindergarten and first grades and began individual tutoring at the end of his initial first-grade year. Isaac, a fourth grader,

moved to the United States from Cape Verde, off the coast of West Africa, when he was five years. His native language, Capeverdean Creole, was the primary language spoken at home and he also spoke English, learned primarily from watching television. When Isaac entered kindergarten he had no knowledge of the alphabet or concepts of print and had few experiences with books. At the beginning of third grade, he could neither read nor write and at the beginning of fourth grade, when he began work at the literacy laboratory, he was reading on a first-grade level. Isaac demonstrated a phenomenal memory for facts and a well-developed schema for topics in which he was interested. As it turned out, both boys progressed most successfully when the teachers planned tutorials based on informational texts in which the boys were interested and had well-developed schemata. The students demonstrated increased motivation for reading, more active engagement with texts, more perseverance when tackling difficult texts, and more confidence in their reading abilities.

In interviews with twelve highly successful adult dyslexics who had difficulty learning to read, Fink (1995–1996) found that *passionate interest* was a key factor for these individuals. Although the majority did not really learn to read until they were between ten and twelve years old, that did not stop them from reading; most said they read voraciously, even before they read fluently. Typically they chose to read in-depth about a topic in which they were passionately interested. Extensive reading enhanced their background knowledge, vocabulary, and knowledge of text structures used in writing about this topic. Although many of these adults continue to experience difficulties with decoding, this does not block their reading. Rather, they rely on their highly developed schemata (background knowledge) about particular topics to access meaning from context.

In the book *Learning Denied* (1991), Taylor writes of her experience with a family whose young son was basically denied access to learning by a school district. He was labeled as having all kinds of learning problems in kindergarten and was unsuccessful learning to read with isolated phonics instruction. His parents' observations of their son's abilities were inconsistent with those described by various school officials. Taylor began working with Patrick at home. During their time together, Patrick demonstrated quite sophisticated literacy skills. We use Patrick as an example because informational texts provided him access to literacy when narratives in basal reading programs did not. In the box that follows, we list ways to support struggling readers by using informational texts.

Struggling Readers and English Language Learners

1. Determine students' interests and/or strengths. What students do when they're not in school can give you clues about interests and strengths.
2. Design instruction so that it builds on their interests and strengths. Don't discredit students' interest in popular culture; starting where students are is important.
3. Provide students with access to materials that capitalize on their strengths and interests. Web-based materials, which incorporate various methods of communication, have potential. Also, don't forget about popular magazines and newspapers. Struggling readers may read magazines when they won't touch other print materials.
4. Provide students with time to examine and read materials. The more reading they do, the more experienced they become.
5. Don't focus on teaching decoding to the exclusion of reading meaningful, interesting text. Try a different approach. For example, students may self-select words they wish to learn within the context of reading material they find interesting and for which they have a well-developed schema. Don't rule out the possibility of popular magazines, such as *Sports Illustrated for Kids* and other content-related periodicals written especially for children and young adolescents. *Magazines for Kids and Teens* (Stoll, 1997) is a good resource for learning more about periodicals for kids. It includes magazine annotations, lists by subject area, and by grade level. If you are searching for magazines that publish student work, check the "Audiences for Student Writing" list Kristiina compiled in *Improving Writing* by Johns and Lenski (2000).

Web Resources for Enhancing Fluency with Content-Related Text

Books on tape have been advocated by many to increase fluency. Scholastic.com has a web feature called "Listen and Read" that accompanies their *Scholastic News* website. Students can listen to a feature article each week on-line. The slow, yet fluent, voice reads a paragraph at a time, controlled by the student, who clicks on the text he or she wishes to hear. Accompanying each paragraph is an illustration. A feature called "Sound It Out" helps readers negotiate difficult, unfamiliar words. All a student has to do is click on the word and listen! This is a great feature for struggling readers and English language learners.

Try It!

Check out the "Read and Listen" feature for *Scholastic News*. First, go to the Scholastic website www.scholastic.com. Click on the site map, click on product information, then classroom magazines, and last *Scholastic News*. Choose grade level one or two and then go to the "Listen and Read" icon. Listen, read, view, and learn!!!

A fifth strength of informational trade books is that they are written from a variety of perspectives and about almost every topic imaginable. Therefore, in-depth information is available related to students' interests, backgrounds, questions, problems, and concerns, not to mention information about the natural, historical, multicultural, and international world and related social issues. Other genres can contribute to helping students view content from a variety of perspectives. For example, historical fiction often provides insights into the people of history, a perspective often omitted in textbooks. To get an international perspective on issues, be sure to choose books originally published in another country and/or another language. (Information about international children's literature can be found on The Children's Literature Web Guide http://www.acs.ucalgary.ca/~dkbrown/awards.html and http://www.ibby.org—the International Board on Books for Young People.) In addition, Tomlinson (1998) notes that international children's literature (both fictional and informational) may introduce topics or themes that U.S. authors are reluctant to talk about, such as "alienation, living with disabilities, human sexuality, interracial marriage, and poverty" (p. 5).

Sixth, trade books encourage favorable attitudes toward reading and content area learning. When students determine their own purposes for reading and choose books they wish to read, they enjoy reading—yes, even content-related books! Teachers may need to help students make connections between the trade books they enjoy reading and content area studies. A case in point: When Jeanne was in fourth grade, she read all the biographies in the school library about famous American women but did not relate her reading to social studies content. In her mind, social studies was related to the textbook and occasionally reports copied from the encyclopedia. Imagine how much more interested she would have been and how much more she could have learned if she had made the connection between social studies and biographies.

Seventh, trade books can be used to develop background knowledge for a variety of topics, including the language of a discipline. The more well developed a student's schema for a subject (and, as mentioned earlier, the more interested a student is), the more likely he or she will understand and remember what is read. Realistic fiction, poetry, picture books, and historical fiction can also be used to help build students' background knowledge about content, as can magazines and newspapers written especially for children. (See Figure 3.3 for a list of periodicals for elementary school students.) See Appendix B for titles of our favorite informational trade books for teaching content.

Web Activity: Check out Websites for Children's Periodicals

Browse through some of the websites for magazines written especially for children pre-K–6 listed in Figure 3.3. The link for teachers is usually a good place to start. Information abounds related to standards, contents of back issues, lesson plans, reproducibles, and much, much more! You can even find some articles on-line!

Eighth, the appealing format, including beautifully and creatively designed illustrations, color photographs, and other graphics entice students to *step into* informational trade books. Moss and Hendershot (2002) found that 48 percent of sixth graders in their classroom study reported selecting informational books because of the cover art, photographs, and illustrations inside the books. Once students step into a book, the illustrations, the way print information is presented, and various access features encourage and support students as they *move through* books of their own volition. Also, the physical size of trade books makes them portable and less intimidating than textbooks. See Figure 3.4 for a sample of especially visually appealing books.

Ninth, trade books provide students with opportunities to become acquainted with various expository text structures (e.g., cause–effect, compare contrast, problem solution, description, and sequence), which are rarely present in basal reading materials. (See Chapter 5 for more details about text structure.) Some concepts can be understood more easily when information is framed using a particular structure. Also, these texts provide students with good models for nonfiction writing. Reading expository text extensively is good practice for taking standardized reading comprehension tests because they rely heavily on expository passages. Although this reason is the least compelling strength to us, the reality in today's schools is that much hinges on test scores. Perhaps this rationale will support the purchase of more high-quality, current informational books across the grade levels.

Finally, informational trade books provide opportunities for students to develop critical reading skills such as evaluating the credibility of authors and authenticity of

FIGURE 3.3 Periodicals for Elementary School Students

Content Area	Title	Publisher	Grade Level
Science	*Wild Animal Baby*	National Wildlife Federation www.nwf.org	Preschool
All areas	*Let's Find Out*	Scholastic www.scholastic.com	Pre-K–K
Science	*Your Big Backyard*	National Wildlife Federation www.nwf.org	Pre-K–1
All areas	*Click*	Cobblestone Publication www.cobblestone.pub.com	1–2
All areas	*Weekly Reader* (weekly news)	Weekly Reader www.weeklyreaders.com	Pre-K–6
All areas	*Scholastic News* (weekly news)	Scholastic www.scholastic.com	1–6
		Go to site map, product information, classroom magazines, then select publication	1–3 also in Spanish
Science and Social Studies	*Kids Discover*	Kids Discover www.kidsdiscover.com	1–6
All areas	*Spider*	Cobblestone Publication www.cobblestone.pub.com	2–3
History	*Appleseeds*	Cobblestone Publication www.cobblestone.pub.com	2–4
Science	*Ranger Rick*	National Wildlife Federation www.nwf.org	2–6
Science and Social Studies	*National Geographic for Kids*	National Geographic www.nationalgeographic.com/education	3–6
African American History	*Footsteps*	Cobblestone Publication www.cobblestone.pub.com	4 and up
World Culture and Geography	*Faces*	Cobblestone Publication www.cobblestone.pub.com	4 and up
American History	*Cobblestone*	Cobblestone Publication www.cobblestone.pub.com	4 and up
World History	*Calliope*	Cobblestone Publication www.cobblestone.pub.com	4 and up

FIGURE 3.4 Visually Appealing Books

Bridges, R. (1999). *Through my eyes*. NY: Scholastic Press. (black and white photographs, Coretta Scott King award)

Jordan, M., & Jordan, T. (1996). *Amazon alphabet*. NY: Kingfisher. (vivid paintings)

Martin, J. B. (1998). *Snowflake Bentley*. Boston: Houghton Mifflin. (wood block print, marginal notes, 1999 Caldecott Winner)

Simon, S. (2001). *Animals nobody loves*. NY: SeaStar Books. ("up-close and personal" color photos of scary-looking animals)

St. George, J. (2000). *So you want to be president?* NY: Philomel Books. (hysterical caricatures, 2001 Caldecott winner)

Taylor, B. (1992). *Rain forest*. NY: Dorling Kindersley. (Look Closer series) (up-close color photos with captions on each two-page spread)

Jeunesse, G., & de Bourgoing, P. (1995). *Under the ground*. NY: Scholastic. (First Discovery Series) (overlays, cross sections, color illustrations)

National Geographic Society. (1996). *Whales*. Washington, DC: National Geographic Society. (National Geographic Action Book) (moveable parts—pop-ups, tabs, fold-outs—and sound effects)

Sandved, K. B. (1999). *Butterfly alphabet*. NY: Scholastic. (vivid, close-up photographs of designs on butterfly wings, each resembling a letter of the alphabet)

materials. These skills are more relevant than ever with the widespread use of the Internet for resources. So often, in the past, individuals falsely assumed that if information was in print, then it must be true. Although this was always a fallacy, students need to become more critical consumers of information for today and tomorrow.

Trade books also have their limitations. The most obvious is how to get access to enough reasonably current trade books. As mentioned earlier, more informational books are being published each year than ever before, so they're out there, but where? The school and public libraries are, of course, a place to start. We have found that librarians are very willing to help teachers locate books that may be appropriate for teaching science and social studies. Interlibrary loan is also an option to consider if you need a particular book. Some librarians will even purchase titles they know children and teachers will use. Book clubs, such as Scholastic, have increased their monthly nonfiction offerings. Scholastic even offers periodic flyers that focus solely on math, science, or social studies. Sometimes parent organizations ask teachers for "wish lists" of books that parents can purchase for classrooms. And then there are garage sales, library book sales, and, of course, bookstore chains, many of which give teachers 10 to 15 percent discounts. And don't forget discount book tables. Jeanne has also found that some airports have good selections of literature about a particular part of the country, as do some hotel gift shops. Then there are magazines, newspapers, and the Internet. (See Figure 3.3 for magazines for elementary age students.)

Website: Book Prices for the Frugal

Check out www.scholastic.com or www.troll.com to peruse the latest books available from book clubs. While you're there, check out the teacher resources and other links. A site to consider that has recycled books and other inexpensive books is www.literacyempowerment.org. Also, check www.ebay.com for inexpensive books. You never know what you'll find!

Another limitation related to trade books is that there are so many! Why is this a limitation? It's important to choose informational trade books carefully; all informational books are not created equal. Figure 3.5 lists general criteria for selecting informational books.

Another reason the sheer number of books may appear like a limitation is that some teachers believe they have to read every single book in their classroom libraries. If you believe that the teacher must be "all knowing" about the content, then "all those books" would be enough to make you want to use a single textbook. If, however, you approach learning from a social constructionist perspective, then you know that you can learn from and with your students. They will share books with you and their classmates about specific content.

Knowing about the advantages of using informational trade books and their widespread availability, you might expect that informational trade books are used more than ever before for reading and content area instruction. While this may be true, Duke's (2000) study of twenty first-grade classrooms and the kinds of texts available to students revealed alarming results. She found that informational texts were used only an average of 3.6 minutes a day! In low socioeconomic status classrooms, informational

---

FIGURE 3.5   Criteria for Choosing Informational Books

1. *Accuracy.* Is the book current? What are the author's credentials? Did the author explain his or her research process? Is the author biased?

2. *Organizational structure.* Does the structure support readers' construction of meaning? Is the text organized logically? Is the text cohesive and clear? Are examples well chosen? How accessible is the content? How effective are the access features for guiding readers?

3. *Author's style.* Does the author's style entice the reader to step into and then move through the book? Does the author's style capture and hold readers' attention? Does the style support understanding, learning, and appreciation of a topic? Is the author obviously passionate about the topic?

4. *Focus.* Is the focus manageable? Is it too broad or too narrow?

5. *Age appropriateness.*

6. *Visual appeal.* Do the visuals shout "you have to see this!"? Do the visuals establish the content of the book? Does the aesthetic information scaffold understanding?

texts were used an average of only 1.9 minutes a day, and in some classrooms no informational texts were used at all. These results are troublesome, especially when we consider that the American Library Association determined that students must be able to read and use informational texts throughout their lives if they are to be considered literate in the twenty-first century.

Research: Textbook and Trade Book Use

The limitations of textbooks, the strengths of trade books, and easier access to informational trade books resulted in an increased use of trade books for content area instruction. Research to determine the effectiveness of trade books for teaching content began to appear in the early 1990s.

Romance and Vitale (1992) investigated the effectiveness of integrating science and reading instruction in fourth-grade classrooms. Students who received instruction using trade books, basals, hands-on activities, and science process skills scored higher on standardized science and reading tests than students who received traditional textbook instruction. Smith (1993) found similar results in social studies. Fourth-grade students who studied social studies with trade books scored as well or better on measures of reading and social studies content knowledge than students who used textbooks. Similarly, Guzzetti and colleagues found that sixth-grade students who received reading and social studies instruction with trade books scored higher on a multiple choice test used to evaluate concept acquisition in social studies and reading.

A number of studies have investigated students' attitudes toward mathematics (Murphy, 2000). It seems that many students have negative attitudes toward mathematics because they do not understand its relevance. To remedy this, educators recommend the use of trade books. Whitin and Whitin (2000) suggest that reading aloud books with mathematical themes helps set a nonthreatening atmosphere for mathematics lessons. Schiro (1997) suggests that presenting concepts within the contexts of stories relevant to students' lives makes mathematics more interesting and meaningful. Furthermore, he writes that trade books can help children learn to use mathematical language and to think like a mathematician.

Toward the end of the 1990s, research comparing the effectiveness of textbooks and trade books all but disappeared. Juxtaposing textbooks and trade books against each other seemed counterproductive. Capitalizing on the strengths of both textbooks and trade books seemed a worthwhile compromise.

Using Textbooks with Trade Books

How teachers use textbooks and trade books for content area instruction varies. At one end of the continuum, some teachers rely exclusively on textbooks, despite their limitations. An overreliance on textbooks and related activities (e.g., lectures and worksheets) stifles student interest and their use of higher level cognitive skills (Dunn, 2000). At the other end of the continuum, some teachers do not use textbooks at all.

Other teachers use textbooks as they would any other resource, as one source of information. Most teachers use trade books with content area textbooks.

To illustrate how a teacher can capitalize on the strengths of both textbooks and trade books, we use an example from Laura Pardo's third-grade class (Pardo & Raphael, 1991). In a social studies unit focusing on communication, she used textbooks to provide students with an overview of the topic and for modeling strategies for determining important information, taking notes, and organizing information, among other things. In this classroom, which demonstrates a social constructionist perspective, students and teacher work together as they develop their understandings of new content.

To begin their study of communication, students wrote what they knew about communication in their journals. Ms. Pardo asked one student to read the textbook aloud to the class. To prepare, he practiced reading the text until he could read it aloud fluently. As he read to the class, the other students listened. He paused after reading each section in the chapter. Then the teacher modeled how she determined what ideas she considered most important. She also elicited ideas students thought were important. Throughout the discussion, Ms. Pardo modeled how to take notes from the textbook. After reading the textbook, students shared the ideas they had written earlier in their journals. Ms. Pardo added this information to the notes taken from the textbook. After identifying topics for small group investigation, students used trade books to research various means of communication. They also collected information from other sources: interviews and field trips. Ms. Pardo capitalized on the strengths of textbooks and trade books to organize social studies instruction. (See Figure 3.6 for informational books about communication.)

Textbooks are also effective materials for teaching students how to use access features typically found in other informational texts, such as trade books, magazines, and newspapers. As students become familiar with the purposes of these features and how to use them, they will be better able to read other informational texts more independently. (See Chapter 5 for more about organizational structures and access features of expository texts.)

Primary Sources: The Neglected Resource

Don't forget about primary sources when selecting materials to plan your content area lessons. What is a primary source? It is "a document or object that was created by an individual or group as part of their daily lives. Primary sources include birth certificates, photographs, diaries, letters, embroidered samplers, clothing, household implements, and newspapers. A document that is a primary source may contain both first person testimony and second hand testimony" (Smithsonian Institution, ¶2, http://www.si.edu/archives/documents/exercise.htm). A first-person testimony is "the account of a person who actually participated in an event;" a second-hand or hearsay testimony is "an account repeated by someone who did not actually participate in the event." Check out the Smithsonian Institute's website for access to primary source documents and classroom activities using these documents.

FIGURE 3.6 Communication-Related Informational Books

Aliki. (1993). *Communication*. NY: Scholastic.

Aliki. (1986). *How a book is made*. NY: Scholastic

Davidson, M. (1989). *The story of Alexander Graham Bell, inventor of the telephone*. NY: Dell.

Fain, K. (1995). *Handsigns: A sign language alphabet*. NY: Scholastic.

Gibbon, G. (1993). *Puff. . . Flash . . . Bang! A book about signals*. NY: Morrow Junior.

King, M. L. (1999). *I have a dream*. NY: Scholastic.

Lincoln, A. (1995). *The Gettysburg Address*. NY: Scholastic.

Peterson, J. W. (1977). *I have a sister my sister is deaf*. NY: Harper & Row.

Reflecting

When you were in elementary school, did your teachers use textbooks? Did they encourage you to read content-related trade books? Do you remember checking out informational books from the library or purchasing them from a book club or bookstore?

If you are a teacher, are informational trade books available for you and your students to use? If someone asked you what percentage of informational books you use for reading and content area instruction, what would be your estimate? Why do you think informational trade books aren't used more regularly in elementary school classrooms?

Reader's Purpose and Stance

The transactional view of reading advocated by Rosenblatt in her books *Literature as Exploration* (fifth edition, 1995) and *The Reader, the Text, and the Poem* (1994) influenced how researchers and teachers viewed reading and the use of literature. This view emphasizes the critical role of readers and their experiences for constructing meaning with text rather than simply focusing on the text, as other theories have done. She contends that readers approach texts differently, depending on their purposes for reading. If their intent is to acquire information, they selectively attend to the *public* aspect of meaning, or an efferent stance. This stance is what we typically associate with textbooks and informational books. If, however, a reader's purposes are "experiencing, thinking, and feeling *during* the reading" (Rosenblatt, 1991, p. 444)—the more "private" aspects of reading—then an aesthetic stance is fitting. Rosenblatt contends that these stances are not opposites, rather they "form a continuum of possible transactions with a text" (Rosenblatt, 1995, p. xvii). Furthermore, she suggests that most reading events fall some place near the middle of the continuum and represent a *mix* of attention to the public and private aspects of reading (Karolides, 1999); a reader's attention shifts back and forth during reading. That is, a reader may attend to facts in a text

FIGURE 3.7   Shifting Stances: 9-11

Do you remember reading newspaper articles about the September 11, 2001, tragedy right after it happened? Perhaps you read for information first, thus taking an efferent stance; you wanted to know the details: *who, what, when, where,* and *why.* Undoubtedly, however, your attention shifted abruptly, because your reading stirred up a plethora of emotions—horror, anger, loss—aesthetic responses. Your attention to the private aspects of your reading may have interfered, at least momentarily, perhaps longer, with your original intent.

Perhaps as we reminded you about the tragedy, your stance toward reading this textbook changed. For a few moments, all your feelings about 9-11 came flooding back. Do you see how your efferent approach to this chapter shifted to an aesthetic one? Perhaps you are considering how our lives have changed since that fateful day.

because he or she is intent on knowing particular information. His or her attention may shift, however, when the transaction evokes an emotional reaction. Figure 3.7 illustrates how your experiences can affect your reading stance.

Traditional *in-school* reading has been dominated by an efferent approach, especially in the content areas; the emphasis has been on determining what the author thinks is important. The transactional view of reading takes some of the emphasis away from the text (and author) and accentuates the "to-and-fro, spiraling, nonlinear, continuously reciprocal influence of reader and text in the making of meaning" (Rosenblatt, 1995, p. xvi). As noted in Chapter 2, reader-determined importance is also appropriate at times. What a reader deems important depends a great deal on what he or she brings to the text. It also depends on a reader's purpose. It is the teacher's responsibility to make it clear to students if they should read a particular text from a predominantly efferent or aesthetic stance. This guidance is important for students across the elementary grades.

Judy Rogers, a second-grade teacher in Lubbock, Texas, guides her second-grade students to approach multiple texts from different stances, depending on their purposes for reading. When the class began a study of the Amazon rainforest, Judy instructed small groups of students to choose from the classroom library a few trade books that looked interesting. Then they were to browse through the books. This browsing time provided students with a chance to *step into* and *move through* (Langer, 1995) the books at their own pace, directed by their own curiosities. They thumbed through pages, stopped and examined illustrations, read the captions in some instances, and oooo'ed and ahhhh'd over intriguing illustrations. The browsing time was done for a predominantly private (aesthetic) purpose. In Figure 3.8, Josh and Alan are browsing through the book *Rain Forest* (Taylor, 1992) from the *Look Closer* series. Their dialogue illustrates their combined aesthetic and efferent stances toward this informational book. This activity also demonstrates how its social constructionist nature supports content learning and interest.

As the browsing time came to an end, Judy directed students to shift their attention to a predominantly efferent stance. She asked them to record in their journals an interesting fact they had learned or a question they would like to answer. Judy had dis-

FIGURE 3.8   Boys' Efferent and Aesthetic Responses to Informational Text

ALAN READING THE CAPTION AND POINTING TO THE PHOTOGRAPH: The curly haired tarantula!

JOSH: Neato dude!

JOSH AND ALAN READING THE CAPTION TOGETHER: The cur I us [Cuvier's]

JOSH: toucan

ALAN: toucan!

JOSH: Oh look at this! [referring to a photo of a passion flower]

ALAN: What is it? [Reading]: The passion

JOSH AND ALAN READING TOGETHER: flowers

JOSH: Cool!

[A few seconds later they turned to the page titled "Murder by Poison."]

JOSH AND ALAN: AHHHH! Goodness!

JOSH: Cool dude! Centipedes. Neat!

ALAN READING: "Each segment of the body has 1 breathing hole called a spiracle."

JOSH: Oh, you can see it!

[The boys continued browsing through the engaging photographs, reading the captions, assisting one another as needed, making connections, and exclaiming excitedly for at least fifteen minutes. They were browsing to learn and enjoyed doing it!]

covered in previous years that if she directed students to use an efferent approach before they had a chance to browse, then they got bogged down in the fact-gathering and question-generating tasks.

Later in their study, students examined illustrations in trade books, such as *At Home in the Rain Forest* by Diane Willow, *Birds* by Diane James and Sara Lynn, *Jungle Life at Your Fingertips* by Judy Nayer, and *A Walk in the Rainforest* by Kristin Joy Pratt, so that they could accurately depict a particular plant or animal for their rain forest mural. They also engaged in research using multiple texts to gather facts regarding the appearance, habitat, and diet of an animal of their choice. Each child used his or her facts to write a book. Their reading at this point was for predominantly efferent purposes.

The use of trade books can entice students to read and learn with texts. When readers read more and varied texts from varying stances, they become better readers, experience texts more personally, and, as a result, learn more deeply.

Reflecting

Consider the consequences if students read history from a predominantly efferent stance—to learn the facts. Would they have an in-depth understanding of World War

II, for example? Why or why not? Under what circumstances do you enjoy reading to learn? In what ways could you help students enjoy reading to learn?

Reconsidering

Think back to the beginning of the chapter. If you were asked to describe what the optimal "tools of the trade" for content area reading and learning should be in the twenty-first century, what would you say? What would be the role of trade books and textbooks and other informational texts, such as newspapers and magazines? How would you balance the use of informational books with other genres? What recommendations would you make to textbook adoption committees? What would your classroom instruction look like if you and your students used multiple texts to explore content information? How would you broach the subject of reading information for both efferent and aesthetic perspectives?

CHAPTER

4 Developing Vocabulary for Content Area Learning

In Chapter 4, you will learn about the size and nature of students' vocabularies. You will also find evidence-based research that backs up the strategies we suggest you use in teaching students new meanings for known words, new words for "old" concepts, and new words for new concepts. In addition to vocabulary strategies, you will find ideas for adapting your instruction so that it meets the needs of English language learners and readers who struggle in the content areas. Adapting in this way is part and parcel of being a teacher who views children's learning from a social constructionist perspective.

In A *Word* About *Vocabulary* Instruction (Figure 4.1), the poet Steven Layne (2001) humorously illustrates what it means to "know" a word. Although the individual

*T*eacher says we gots to work on improving our

Volac~~a~~berry

Voba~~ca~~larry

Vucb~~aca~~berry...

Words.

FIGURE 4.1   A *Word* About *Vocabulary* Instruction

Source: Figure 10-1 from Steven L. Layne. *Life's literacy lessons: Poems for teachers.*
Newark, DE: International Reading Association, 2001. Reprinted with permission
of Steven L. Layne and the International Reading Association.

attempting to spell *vocabulary* was having a difficult time, there was no mistaking the
fact that this same individual knew what it meant. Substituting *words* for *vocabulary*
solved the problem. It also demonstrated what content area teachers have known for a
long time, and that is: "The easiest words to teach [though perhaps not to spell, as
Layne's poem would suggest] are those for which students already have the concepts"
(Blachowicz & Fisher, 2002, p. 106).

Remembering

When you were in elementary school, do you remember looking up the meanings of
long lists of content-related words in social studies and science (sometimes twenty or
more per week) and then copying the dictionary meanings verbatim in a spiral-bound
vocabulary notebook? Perhaps you remember your teacher telling you to look up the
new words in a dictionary and use them in sentences that you made up. What happened when you didn't understand a dictionary meaning? Did the sentences you wrote
sometimes make little sense? Or perhaps you remember something a particular teacher
did that made learning vocabulary interesting or fun. What was it? Why do you think
it worked so well in that particular teacher's classroom?

Although we attended different schools (Donna, a small town elementary school
in upstate New York; Jeanne, a large city school in Tennessee; and Kristiina, a small
city elementary school in Ontario, Canada), the way we learned vocabulary didn't vary
much. Jeanne and Donna looked up the meanings of new words in a dictionary, wrote
them in their vocabulary notebooks, and then promptly stored the notebooks in their
desks. There the notebooks lay, undisturbed, until it was time to study for a test, at
which point all the words and their associated meanings were committed to memory
in anticipation of "the Friday test." Kristiina remembers a similar routine. She learned
French vocabulary through lists, once again, only this time the English word was on

the left-hand side of the page and the French word on the right. Her word knowledge was tested through the famous "Dictée" (Dictation), in which the teacher read a sentence and Kristiina wrote it. Comprehension didn't matter—the important thing was that she could hear the word, identify it, and spell it correctly. As for learning Spanish and Finnish vocabulary—well, that was primarily through reading storybooks and through conversation with her parents, who are from Spain and Finland.

Not surprisingly perhaps, we began our teaching careers with the expectation that our students would learn content area vocabulary in the same way we had learned it. Eventually, of course, we discovered through graduate courses and professional texts more effective ways to engage young learners in word study. But that's another story—one that we hope will become patently visible in this chapter on developing children's vocabulary for content area learning.

As you think back to your elementary years, try to relate what you remember to the information presented in this chapter. Here, you'll find sections on the following topics: the size and nature of students' vocabularies; what the research on vocabulary instruction can and cannot tell us; strategies for teaching new meanings for known words, new words for "old" concepts, and new words for new concepts; and some instructional adaptations that can help you assist learners with special needs.

The Size and Nature of Students' Vocabularies

Why should you be interested in the size and nature of your students' vocabularies? For nearly six decades, professionals in the reading field have held that vocabulary knowledge is a powerful predictor of comprehension (e.g., Davis, 1944; National Reading Panel, 2000). Although a causal link between vocabulary size and comprehension ability has not been demonstrated empirically, researchers generally agree that "vocabulary is strongly related to comprehension" (National Reading Panel, 2000, pp. 4–15).

Estimates vary concerning the number of words elementary school children know. The range can be large (e.g., between 2562 and 26,000 words for first graders) and can also vary according to a family's socioeconomic status (SES), with middle-class learners typically having larger vocabularies than lower SES learners (Graves, 1986; White, Graves, & Slater, 1990). Most experts on children's vocabulary acquisition agree that due to the huge variation in reported size, it is probably more helpful to think in terms of the number of word families (e.g., transport, transportation, transportable) children will be exposed to while using printed school texts. One figure for which there is fairly wide agreement is that students in grades 3 through 9 could be exposed to as many as 88,533 word families in printed school texts (Nagy and Anderson cited in Baumann, Kame'enui, & Ash, 2003). This figure should not be interpreted to mean, however, that any individual student will meet or "know" that many words. It is simply the number of word families derived from a sampling of textbooks, workbooks, magazines, encyclopedias, and the like in use in grades 3 through 9 (Baumann et al., 2003).

Another complicating factor in determining how many words children know is that "knowing" a word is not an all-or-nothing proposition (McKeown & Beck, 1988);

there are degrees of word knowledge. For example, as Kameenui and colleagues (1987) pointed out, "It is conceivable that two students might know the same number of words, and possibly, even roughly the same words, but . . . have 'different vocabularies,' due to differences in the quality or extensiveness of their knowledge of particular words" (p. 133). Cultural knowledge of words may also affect meaning. For example, *cricket* in an Anglo–North American context may conjure up images of an insect that makes noise on hot summer nights. In England and other countries formerly of the British Empire, *cricket* denotes a sport where players run between wickets after the ball has been bowled. Given these complications, it is helpful when considering the size and nature of a child's vocabulary to be specific about the *type* of word knowledge one means.

For instance, is it the individual's expressive vocabulary (words used in speaking and writing) or receptive vocabulary (words understood when reading and listening) that is of interest? Being able to produce (use in conversation or in writing) the word *glue* to mean a substance that is sticky and holds something together is an example of expressive vocabulary. Being able to associate a word's meaning (sticky substance for holding things together) with its label (*glue*) while reading or listening is an example of receptive vocabulary. Thus, the size of a child's vocabulary will depend on whether it is the expressive or receptive vocabulary being considered.

As you no doubt have experienced for yourselves, word knowledge tasks that involve associating meanings and labels are typically easier to complete than those that require producing a specific label in order to communicate a particular thought. For that very reason, it is common for people's receptive vocabularies to be larger than their expressive vocabularies. This is fortunate, too, for children need not "know" a word —in the sense of being able independently to produce a label or meaning for it— to make meaning of it (Baumann et al., 2003). To get a feel for how children may derive meaning for words in their receptive vocabulary that are virtually unknown to them, read the following letter from a man traveling to the New World on the *Mayflower* to his wife in England. Context clues are embedded deliberately to help you understand the meaning of *shallop* and *brazier*, words we use infrequently today. As you read excerpts of the letter, try to determine the meanings of these two words.

November 4, 1620

My Dearest Diana,

The living conditions on the Mayflower are less than ideal but I did not expect the luxuries of home. Our sleeping arrangements leave much to be desired. Some people sleep on the deck of the ship, which is no different than sleeping on the floor. Others sleep in hammocks. I prefer to sleep in the shallops. They are fairly comfortable, but I look forward to losing my make-shift bed. Crew members will use these small boats to row to the shores of the New World.

The food cannot be compared to the delicious meals you prepare for our family. It is barely edible most of the time, but no one complains because there is so little to eat. The braziers that we brought on board to warm our food are rarely used. We are afraid the hot charcoal fires will spill out of the metal boxes when the ship is tossed and turned by the waves.

Now think back on the meaning you made of the two words in question. Did you infer that a shallop is a small boat? And a brazier? Did you think it's a metal box with a charcoal fire used for heating food? If so, you used your inferencing skills to determine the general meanings of the words. The author didn't come out and tell you explicitly what a *shallop* and *brazier* are, but instead gave you clues, which you were able to use in unlocking the words' meanings. If you could not make inferences, you would probably not comprehend what Diana's husband was talking about; in other words, you wouldn't understand the letter.

Although your ability to visualize a word's meaning and make connections between what you know about how authors arrange words and use descriptions to explain a particular word in context—those self-to-text, text-to-world, and text-to-text connections that you learned about in Chapter 2—may have helped you to infer the meanings of *shallop* and *brazier*, it is also the case that had you encountered several more unknown words in the same letter, it is likely you would have become frustrated. That's what happens to young children when they find themselves lost in a sea of words for which they have little or no immediate recognition. Teachers need to be aware of this possibility, especially when requiring learners to read subject matter texts that are filled with unknown words. Even known words can present problems when they take on specialized meanings within certain content areas (e.g., a water *table* in geography; a multiplication *table* in math; to *table* a motion, and so on).

All of which brings us to idioms, a type of vocabulary that is more difficult to teach in many respects than the expressive and receptive vocabularies just described. If you understand that the words *draw* and *dress* in phrases such as *draw the drapes* and *dress the hen* are not to be taken literally, then you are able to use figurative language, which is part of our everyday vocabulary. Idioms are especially troublesome when speakers of other languages first encounter English. Because of their difficult nature, idioms are treated at length in the last section of this chapter. For now, however, we think you will find the boxed-in Web resource a helpful reminder of just how prevalent idioms are in the English language.

Idioms for English Language Learners on the Web

Check out the *ESL Idiom Page* at http://www.eslcafe.com/idioms/id-mngs.html for a colorful and accurate rendering of some of the most common idioms in the English language. Phrases such as *hit the hay* and *easy as pie* are illustrated in sentences that are fairly obvious and helpful in determining meanings for these nonliteral expressions.

Reflecting on the Size and Nature of Students' Vocabularies

Think back to the statement that "knowing" a word is not an all-or-nothing proposition. Can you think of specific words in your expressive and receptive vocabularies that would be examples of this? What is it that determines the degree to which you "know" a word? Are you monolingual, bilingual, or multilingual? What impact might your facility with a language other than English have on your degree of word knowledge? How would the use of idioms in content area texts likely affect the students you teach (or children you know, if you are not presently teaching)?

What the Research on Vocabulary Instruction Can and Cannot Tell Us

Although it is the case that you will be expected to make decisions about content area vocabulary instruction based on your school's curricular goals, the needs of your students, and the type of words being taught, it is also the case that research-based guidelines derived from over twenty years of work can provide added insight throughout the decision process.

As with any body of research literature, of course, there are limits to what the following four guidelines (Blachowicz & Fisher, 2000) can tell you. Our recommendation is that you read the information presented with a critical eye; that is, ask yourself what assumptions are being made about effective content area vocabulary instruction? What kinds of students do the researchers who constructed these guidelines seem to have in mind? Whose needs are not being addressed? To what degree do the guidelines mesh with your personal beliefs about teaching content area vocabulary?

Guideline 1: Students Should Be Active in Developing Their Understanding of Words and Ways to Learn Them

Involving students in word-grouping activities, such as semantic mapping (Figure 4.2), can help them discover the related meanings of various words. This is an effective method for engaging youngsters in actively processing content area vocabulary. It also helps them develop strategies for independent word learning. Because there are more content-related words than you could ever hope to teach directly, the development of students' independent word-learning strategies is critical to their success in comprehending what you expect them to read in their content area texts. Independence in developing word meanings is sometimes made difficult, however, by the fact that some commonly known words take on specialized meanings in different content areas. An example of what we mean follows.

Try This:

Group the following words into two categories—those whose common meanings do not change in math and those whose meanings do change when applied to particular math processes or concepts: *table, curve, line, angle, minus, degree, square,* and *point.* The same is true for other content areas, such as music. Try the exercise again, this time using the following words: *sharp, flat, score, pitch, chord, scale,* and *note.* When you compare your groupings with those of a classmate, do you find you have differences of opinion? Might you both be right? Why? What does all of this have to do with a social constructionist perspective on learning?

Other approaches to semantic relatedness instruction that have a solid backing in the research literature include concept definition maps and semantic feature analysis charts. Both of these are illustrated in the next section of this chapter. In addition to teaching students to unlock vocabulary meanings by analyzing how words relate to one another, it is important to teach them to use context clues. However, the research is mixed on the effectiveness of using context. Because naturally occurring context does not always provide the necessary clues for figuring out word meanings (and in fact may be misleading at times), Blachowicz and Fisher (2000) recommend that teachers offer instruction that is "explicit, well-scaffolded, and provides practice and feedback" (p. 506). Their recommendation seems to fit well with the gradual release of responsibility instructional model described in Chapter 2.

Think back to earlier in this chapter when we asked you to infer the meanings for the words *shallop* and *brazier.* Although we did not model inference making explicitly, we did scaffold the task by first alerting you to the presence of two content words that we thought you'd be unfamiliar with and then we gave you time to practice using context clues before providing feedback on what we imagined might have been your responses. Of course, in an actual classroom, you wouldn't need to imagine your students' responses, which would make the feedback loop more useful in spotting any misconceptions they might have about the words in question.

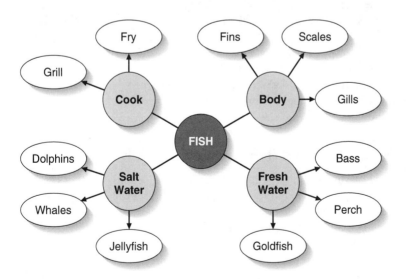

FIGURE 4.2 First Graders' Semantic Map on Fish

Speaking of misconceptions, it is important to note that the research literature is relatively silent on how to teach students to consider alternative explanations for certain conceptions that they hold. Although we know from a large meta-analysis conducted by Guzzetti, Snyder, Glass, and Gamas (1993) that it is important to help children confront potential misinterpretations of content area concepts (e.g., the concept of *force* as it is used in the study of simple machines), research to date has not been helpful in giving guidance on how to handle children's so-called misconceptions in social studies. We agree with Blachowicz and Fisher (2000) that it is far simpler to confront alternative understandings about science and math concepts than it is about value-laden concepts in social studies or children's literature, for instance.

Guideline 2: Students Should Personalize Word Learning

Encouraging students to take responsibility for selecting words they want to study can personalize vocabulary learning for the students in your classroom. It can also alert teachers to the vocabulary that students think is important or interesting. As Jimenez's (1997) research with English language learners has shown, vocabulary self-selection can provide especially useful information to teachers who are uncertain as to which concepts and word labels these learners already know. In content areas where it is crucial that particular concepts and their labels not be overlooked, teachers may want to join students in the selection of vocabulary to ensure that important words are taught. Collaborative word choice also provides an opportunity for teachers to model the criteria they use in selecting words for study.

Although research shows that students who are allowed to have some say in vocabulary selection remember the words they choose better and longer than the words their teachers choose, it is still unclear as to how selecting words of minimal importance affects comprehension and conceptual development overall. For example, knowing the meanings of *shallop* and *brazier*, while undoubtedly helpful in comprehending the letter that Diana's husband wrote—and perhaps to understanding something about the conditions and everyday routines aboard ships in the 1600s—will still not contribute to a child's overall understanding of what led people to settle in the New World. Additional resources would need to be explored to develop such an understanding.

Guideline 3: Students Should Be Immersed in Words

Learning words incidentally through reading or listening to others as they read aloud is known to play a role in children's general vocabulary development. However, the extent to which such learning favorably impacts children's knowledge of content area vocabulary is disputed in the research literature. What is not disputed is the need for literacy-rich environments in which children develop a love of language as they engage in word play through puzzles, word games, riddles, poetry, and puns. Fostering word consciousness, according to Graves (2002), develops a curiosity in children that can lead to noticing the uniqueness of words (e.g., the subtle distinction between *traitor*

and *spy*, which is useful in their own speech and writing) or to exploring what's behind a word (the following box provides a website for interesting word origins in various content areas).

Web Link on Word Play

Enjoy language and word play? Check out "A Word with You," a daily on-line column featuring little known facts about well-known words. At http://www.wordwithyou.com/ you'll find a cartoon panel and short article that play off one another. You can search through more than 300 past columns or you can look up a particular word or phrase using the alphabetic word finder. As the website says, "There's a whole etymological library at your fingertips."

Guideline 4: Students Should Build on Multiple Sources of Information to Learn Words through Repeated Exposures

Just as literacy-rich environments provide opportunities for enlarging children's general vocabulary (and to some extent their knowledge of content-specific vocabulary), so, too, do repeated exposures to the same word. The research is clear on the need to use multiple sources of information (e.g., textbooks, primary source documents, trade books, CD-ROMs, videos, the Internet, children's writings, charts compiled by the class) and various sensory inputs (visual, oral, tactile, olfactory, auditory, emotional) when teaching content area vocabulary so that learners meet the same word in different contexts repeatedly over time (National Reading Panel, 2000).

For example, the teacher whose first graders brainstormed what they knew about fish for a class science unit (see Figure 4.2) used the same semantic map to delve deeper into children's understanding of the word *scales*. They knew that fish had scales on their bodies. The teacher showed a video in which the scales of reptiles were compared to birds' feathers and human body hair. He also planned a class trip to the neighborhood fish market where the first graders were able to touch the scales of fresh fish (and smell them). One child observed a person behind the fish counter weighing a fish on the *fish scale* and pointed this out to her friend. Overhearing the girl's comment, the teacher made a mental note of the different use of the word *scales*, and the next day he engaged the entire class in a discussion of the new meaning. He also asked if anyone had ever helped *scale a fish*. Later, the class drew pictures of the fish they had seen at the market and labeled the scales on the body of the fish. A few of the children drew the fish scales used for weighing and labeled them as well.

These repeated exposures to *scale* accomplished more than simply introducing the word in different contexts. Each time the students came in contact with the word, there were slight manipulations of its meaning. As Blachowicz and Fisher (2000) noted in their review of the research literature on vocabulary instruction, when children meet the same word in different contexts and engage in discussions that focus on its different meanings, they are one step closer to knowing the word fully—to making it their own.

English Language Learners Socially Construct Meaning

The use of cognates is a powerful learning strategy for children whose first language is other than English. It helps them construct conceptual knowledge of vocabulary in their mother tongue as well in the language of the school. For example, *escala* in Spanish is a cognate of the word *scale* in English. However, *escala* does not mean fish scale, which is *escama*. Instead, *escala* is used in mathematics (price scales), music (scale of notes), and cartography (draw a map to scale). In encouraging children to explore the connection between cognates, you also encourage them to make conceptual linkages across different languages. Of course, there are many languages that do not have many English cognates. In such instances, you may want to encourage children to think of how English relates to their first language, and vice versa.

Reflecting on Vocabulary Instruction Research

Recall that we asked you to read the research on vocabulary instruction with a critical eye. What classroom activities have you observed or taught that support one or more of the guidelines? Did some of the activities go over better with some students than with others? Why do you think this was the case? Whose needs were not addressed? Which, if any, of the guidelines would you like researchers to elaborate further? Why? Would you ask different questions if you were researching children's word knowledge? What might they be?

Strategies for Teaching Vocabulary in Content Areas

Deciding which vocabulary strategy to teach is an important instructional consideration that you will need to make many times over as a classroom teacher. As you might expect, different strategies accomplish different things. We agree fully with McKeown and Beck (1988) that "the choice of the kind of instruction to use in specific instances depends on the goal of the instruction, the kinds of words being presented, and the characteristics of the learners" (p. 44). In short, we believe there are costs and benefits involved when selecting strategies to teach content area vocabulary.

> For example, if one's objective were to teach the meanings of a relatively few specific words in a content subject like science [or social studies], the least costly approach might be to use a definitional method. However, if one wished to teach meanings for

many words, or if the goal were to enhance passage comprehension, another method, perhaps a semantic relatedness procedure, would be preferred. If one's goal were long-term, expansive, independent vocabulary learning, regular independent reading combined with instruction in use of contextual and morphemic analysis would be the logical approach. (Baumann et al., 2003, p. 27)

In choosing the following strategies, we were guided by the research discussed earlier and by our own experiences, formerly as classroom teachers, and now as teacher educators. The categories—teaching new meanings for known words, teaching new words for "old" concepts, and teaching new words for new concepts—are fairly representative of the ways in which a teacher can help learners continually refine their vocabulary knowledge and grow conceptually in the content areas (Blachowicz & Fisher, 2002; Graves, 2002).

Teaching New Meanings for Known Words

When common words that most children know and use daily take on specialized or technical meanings in the content areas, they can cause confusion and lead to problems in comprehending information. For instance, let's say that Jenny, one of the first graders who drew a picture of a fish she had seen at the market during the class field trip, were to encounter the word *scale* in yet another context, one that was unfamiliar to her. Perhaps she observed her older brother poring over a geometry assignment at home and muttering something about not being able to draw an object to *scale* as the assignment called for. It is likely that Jenny would be momentarily confused, especially if she could not associate what her brother was muttering about with her understanding of fish scales, scaling a fish, or the fish market's scales.

Moving from the typical to the technical, as Pearson and Johnson (1984) phrased it—or from the technical to the *more* technical, as we see it in the Jenny example in the preceding paragraph—requires clarifying differences between what students already know about a particular word's meaning and the new meaning. In Jenny's case, let's assume her curiosity is raised to the point where she asks her brother what he means by "drawing an object to scale." She might even share with him what she knows about fish scales and her trip to the fist market. If her brother were an extraordinarily patient person (and perhaps headed for a career in teaching!), he might sketch a side image of a fish whose eye is out of proportion to the rest of its body (see Figure 4.3). If Jenny questions this oddity, her brother might tell her to "fix" the picture to make it look like the fish she saw at the market. Assuming she does what her brother suggests, he could tell her that she has just drawn an object (the eye) to scale.

Pretty far fetched? We agree, but it serves to illustrate several points. First, teaching new meanings for known words is best accomplished when children's curiosity about language is sufficient to lead them to question something that doesn't fit with their current understanding of a word. Second, linking new meanings to known words by capitalizing on children's real world experiences (in this instance, Jenny's fish market experience) taps into their ability to make text-to-self and text-to-world

**FIGURE 4.3   A Fish With an Eye Out of Proportion
to the Rest of Its Body**

connections. Third, involving children actively in word learning makes it possible to move beyond the printed text to include visualizing, drawing, talking, and so on. Finally, demonstrating to children that they indeed can learn new meanings for known words fairly painlessly makes it all the more probable that they'll never give up on wanting to learn new things.

Teaching New Words for "Old" Concepts

Refining students' knowledge of known or "old" concepts involves helping them develop the ability to discriminate among similar but sufficiently different words for describing membership in the "old" concept. An excellent strategy for teaching students to do this is semantic feature analysis. It takes little preparation time, but it is particularly effective in involving students in making decisions about which distinguishing features are associated with a particular concept and which are not. For example, in Figure 4.4, a fifth-grade class worked in small groups to complete duplicate copies of a semantic feature analysis chart on *Explorers of the New World* that their teacher had prepared for them. After assigning plusses, minuses, and question marks to indicate their agreement (plus signs), disagreement (minus signs), or uncertainty (question marks) about certain distinguishing characteristics of the *explorer* concept, the groups reassembled for a whole-class discussion to share the reasoning behind their choices.

Although you may disagree with the choices students made, it is important to keep in mind that the reasoning they used for rating a feature as being present, absent, or questionable for membership in a particular category or concept is what is important. Acknowledging this is equivalent to viewing children's learning from a social constructionist perspective. It focuses on children's interpretations and warranted justifications, not just on what you deem to be a "fact" or "the truth."

FIGURE 4.4   Semantic Feature Analysis Chart on Explorers of the New World

	Acquire Land	Write Books	Establish Missions	Build Trade	Acquire Riches
Prospectors	–	+	–	?	+
Missionary	–	+	+	–	–
Traveler	–	+	–	?	?
Voyager	?	+	–	+	?
Surveyor	+	?	–	+	–
Plunderer	+	–	–	–	+
Fur trappers	–	–	–	+	+

Teaching New Words for New Concepts

Children who do not have a sufficiently well-developed concept of a particular event or phenomenon will have difficulty understanding words used to define it. They are also likely to be confused about what a definition should include. To assist them in acquiring new words for new concepts—the most difficult of content area vocabulary learning tasks—teachers can introduce them to the concept of definition map (Figure 4.5). This strategy was developed by Schwartz and Raphael (1985) to draw learners' attention to the category to which a particular word belongs, the defining characteristics of the word under study, and some examples of it. To make the strategy

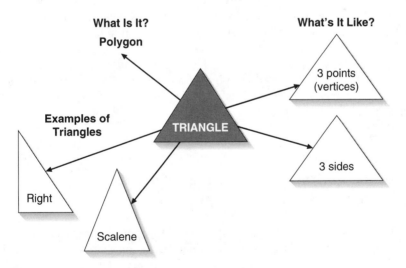

FIGURE 4.5   A Concept of Definition Map

more user-friendly for young children, Blachowicz and Fisher (2002) recommend that teachers substitute "What is it?" when discussing the category to which the word belongs, and "What's it like" when referring to the characteristics that define the word.

In the example from a fourth-grade math lesson used here (Figure 4.5), the teacher stated that her objective was twofold: she wanted students to learn some of the defining characteristics of a triangle and she wanted them to talk about the things that go into a definition (its parts) so they would have a better idea of how to construct a class dictionary on the shapes they see and use everyday. To illustrate what she meant by the everyday use of triangles, she read aloud from Ifeoma Onyefulu's *A Triangle for Adaora: An African Book of Shapes*.

Standards-Approved Practice: Reading Aloud and English Language Learners

The language arts standards adopted jointly by the International Reading Association and the National Council of Teachers of English advocate reading aloud to students in all content areas. It is especially helpful in building English language learners' concepts of definitions and receptive language.

Reflecting on Strategies for Teaching Content Area Vocabulary

As you think back to the strategies we suggest you try when working with children to increase their knowledge and use (both receptively and expressively) of content vocabulary, is there a common thread among them? For example, did you infer the need to draw on students' background knowledge and real world experiences to make specialized meanings of content words understandable and memorable? Did you sense a need to engage them in word learning that involves a combination of visual, aural, oral, olfactory, tactile, and emotional stimuli? Now think of how you learn new words, even as an adult. How is your learning similar to (or different from) the strategies suggested here?

Instructional Adaptations for Assisting Learners with Special Needs

This section focuses on the vocabulary needs of English language learners and children who struggle with reading. Grouping them under one label (special needs) is not intended to communicate that we think English language learners and struggling readers are one and the same population nor does it mean that we think all English language learners are alike or that all readers who struggle are alike. As you know from your own experiences, people differ on any number of variables (and thankfully so). What this grouping does allow, however, is a relatively efficient way of highlighting the instructional adaptations necessary for assisting English language learners and struggling readers to learn content area vocabulary.

English Language Learners

Speaking of how people differ reminds us that we'd be remiss if we didn't emphasize the importance of finding out whether an English language learner in your classroom is already literate in one language (L1) and learning English as a second language (L2), or whether the child is learning to read in both languages (L1 and L2) at the same time. For children in the first situation, a review of the research suggests that "reading skills . . . transfer from L1 to L2 reading once a level of proficiency has been reached in L2 oral language" (Blachowicz & Fisher, 2000). Thus, for these children, it is largely a matter of learning new words for "old" concepts.

For children in the latter situation, however, the research is relatively silent on how best to proceed in building their vocabulary knowledge. Although they may be orally fluent in L1 and becoming increasingly fluent in L2, the fact that they are not able to read in either of their languages means that you will need to teach them a core vocabulary of high-frequency words (Coady, Magoto, Hubbard, Graney, & Mokhtari, 1993; Nation, 1990). Cunningham (2000), drawing on earlier work in a vocabulary study, claims that "ten words—*the, of, and, a, to, in, is, you, that,* and *it*—account for almost one-quarter of all the words we read and write. Once taught through direct instruction (see Chapter 6), core vocabulary words must then be committed to memory so that they can be recognized and comprehended immediately in running (continuous) text. You can help English language learners retain the meanings of new core vocabulary in several ways: through writing activities, discussion, visual images (e.g., illustrations, photographs, videos), and repeated readings of easy materials in which the core words appear.

Informational picture books containing high-frequency words and focusing on content that may be part of your curriculum are good sources for introducing previously taught words in new contexts. For example, *Digging Up Dinosaurs* by Aliki and *The Cloud Book* by Tomie de Paola are rich in content-related vocabulary and colorful illustrations that reinforce science concepts common to the elementary grades. You can also choose books to read aloud to English language learners that are fun to discuss because they feature interesting word origins (e.g., *What's Behind the Word* by Sam and Beryl Epstein), little known facts about famous people and events (e.g., *Freaky Facts* by Barbara Seuling), and humorous incidents involving idioms (e.g., *Amelia Bedelia* by Peggy Parish).

As mentioned earlier, idioms make learning the English language a bit tricky for a child who is unaware of the nonliteral meanings that are associated with them. You can make such learning easier if you use the following process with children who have a basic understanding of idioms and who have some acquired skills in reading and writing:

1. On a given day each week, have each student take a small notebook home and write down any idioms that they encounter. They can find examples from the radio, television, books, or even from conversations they hear.
2. The next day, take about ten minutes to have students write some of the idioms on the board, explain the context in which they found them, and provide tentative definitions. The other students may also want to contribute their ideas regarding possible definitions.
3. Have the students record the new idioms in their notebooks.
4. Divide the students into groups and have them discuss an idiom that you have written on the board. Read the idiom in the context of a couple of different sentences. Have the groups talk about the way the idiom is used as well as give a possible definition. Discuss the definitions with the entire class and comment on any possible situations where its use would be inappropriate.
5. If desired, the students could write short dialogues that incorporate these idioms and then read them to the class. (Strickland, Ganske, & Monroe, 2002, pp. 34–35)

An alternative and less difficult activity would involve orally presenting some common idioms in class and having children listen for them. You might also ask them to think about where they have heard these idioms previously. This information could be recorded and used as a reference point when the same idioms come up again.

Children Who Struggle to Read

Our search of the literature on teaching content area vocabulary to children who struggle to read turned up support for this number one cardinal rule: "Provide struggling readers a systematic and sustained program of vocabulary instruction that teaches them more important words and efficient strategies in less time" (Baumann et al., 2003, p. 26).

Because children who experience severe difficulties processing printed texts do not acquire knowledge of words through wide reading on their own, they are at a disadvantage when it comes to reading content materials that are many times written above their instructional level and include words they may have heard but cannot recognize in print. Frustrated, they soon turn away from most, if not all, activities that require them to read, which of course means fewer opportunities to increase their word knowledge and to learn the content of their subject area classes. Thus, the "rule" of providing struggling readers with vocabulary instruction that focuses on only the most important words in the least amount of time makes good sense. They need to catch up, and they need to do it quickly.

That said, what kind of instruction should you provide? Based on a comprehensive review of the research on vocabulary instruction, it seems that your best bet is to explicitly teach words that are essential to students' understanding of a particular content text. This means you would teach students to decode words using a variety of techniques, for example, phonetic analysis (matching sounds and letters), structural analysis (breaking words into meaningful parts), semantic analysis (using strategies such as those illustrated in Figures 4.1, 4.3, and 4.4), and contextual analysis (looking for clues to meaning in the surrounding text). Computer programs that highlight difficult words in context and then provide access to visual and aural clues are also effective, largely because of their motivational aspects (Blachowicz & Fisher, 2000). You would not, however, want to choose programs that emphasize rote learning of word definitions. This has not been shown to be effective in the research literature.

An alternative to computer programs for word study is Internet sites. In her book, *Stretching Students' Vocabulary*, Bromley (2002) offers a wealth of choices in sites that stimulate children's curiosity about content area vocabulary and develop their communication skills as well.

Website for Building Vocabulary

At the Internet site *Ask an Expert* (http://www.askanexpert.com), children eight years and older can contact real world experts when they have questions about particular content or want to know the meanings of specialized vocabulary.

Vocabulary learning should not be all skill and drill, however. In fact, as you work with readers who struggle, the last thing you want to do is provide instruction that is boring or lacks kid appeal. To enliven your teaching, why not try reading aloud *Miss Alaineus: A Vocabulary Disaster* by Debra Frasier. It is filled with word play and word meanings that illustrate how learning vocabulary can be fun even though it may involve making mistakes from time to time. Audiobooks are also excellent sources for readers who may feel challenged by print but won't pass up a good book on tape. The American Library Association offers synopses of recent award-winning books on audiocassette at http://www.ala.org/alsc/awards.html.

Standard Supporting the Use of a Variety of Technological and Information Resources

One of the twelve English language arts standards addresses specifically the need to engage students in the use of a variety of information resources (e.g., libraries, databases, computer networks, video, audio) to create and communicate knowledge (IRA/NCTE, 1996).

The importance of games and other fun-filled activities, such as word sorts, should not be underestimated when planning instruction for students who struggle to read content area materials. Brandi Blankenship, a kindergarten teacher in Texas, helped students expand their understanding of animals they had read about by categorizing

FIGURE 4.6   Pets: A Kindergarten Class Word Sort (*Photo credit:* Jeanne Swafford).

TABLE 4.1

Can Be a Pet		Cannot Be a Pet	
cat	elephant	tiger	lion
dog	dragon	duck	ladybug
goldfish	cow	giraffe	kangaroo
gerbil	sheep	butterfly	zebra
rabbit	bee	pig	goat
	worm	ram	

them and then organizing them into a web (see Figure 4.6). They also categorized animals into "can be a pet" and "cannot be a pet" in a two-column chart—another type of word-sorting activity (see Table 4.1).

Reconsidering

The challenges you face as a teacher are probably never more evident than when you work with children who for one reason or another find learning with content area texts difficult or well nigh impossible. As you've no doubt inferred from this chapter, word knowledge plays a very large role in determining what is learned, or not learned, as the case may be. With this in mind, what do you know about yourself as a word learner and teacher? Does what you already know (or do) match somewhat closely the research-based guidelines presented here? Where are the mismatches? Why might differences exist, and what should you do (if anything) about them?

CHAPTER

5

Mediating Expository Text Structures and Common Access Features

In Chapter 5, we discuss how understanding text structure will enhance comprehension. We examine common access features, such as a table of contents and index, and introduce you to common expository text structures often used by authors to serve as guideposts for the reader. We also discuss the "new brand" of informational texts that adopt nonlinear arrangements. Included in this chapter are many visuals, including children's work, graphic organizers, and websites, to show you how to help students take advantage of the internal and external text structures that facilitate comprehension. Finally, we provide helpful hints for scaffolding instruction and visit a first-grade classroom, where many of these hints are implemented.

Have you ever thought about how stories, textbooks, and informational trade books are alike and different?

> "No, but now that you mention it, stories are easy to read and enjoyable. Textbooks can sometimes be boring. Informational trade books? Hmmm. . . . I don't know. Informational trade books have facts in them but are not written like textbooks; trade books are usually more interesting. Sometimes they are even written like stories."

If you agree with this reflection, yours is probably similar to many others. Almost everyone enjoys reading stories, and textbooks have a reputation for being boring. (This book is an exception of course!) Informational trade books have a better reputation, but many people have little experience reading the "new and improved" informational books that have been published recently.

Actually, stories, textbooks, and informational trade books are alike in that their authors do their best to write in ways that readers can easily understand. They organize their ideas, choosing a text structure that best matches the content they wish to communicate to readers. Sometimes the structure is a narrative one because a story is the most effective way to communicate what the author intends. Other times expository structures are the most effective ways for communicating information.

Remembering

Have you ever read something in which the author seems to jump all over the place? First she or he writes about this, then that, then this again? How does this lack of organization affect your comprehension? Have you ever read a textbook chapter that you just couldn't follow? Perhaps the text was structured differently than what you expected.

Readers' knowledge of text structure helps them anticipate the author's purpose for writing, the strategies to use when reading, and how the writing will be organized. Although you might not consciously think about text structure when you pick up a book, you most likely have expectations about how a text will be organized.

In this chapter you'll read about research that links a reader's knowledge and use of text structure to comprehension. You'll go on a scavenger hunt for access features in different informational texts and then explore common expository text structures and cues for identifying these structures. Next, you'll try your hand at reading the "new, improved" nonlinear text structures that are popping up in magazines, trade books, textbooks, on the Web, and elsewhere. Finally, we leave you with examples of how to scaffold instruction for teaching text structure.

Text Structure as a Framework for Writing

Can you imagine what it would be like if authors did not use common text structures to organize words, phrases, sentences, paragraphs, and chapters in books? Sentences would be randomly organized (that's an oxymoron!) in paragraphs. Paragraphs would be randomly placed in chapters. Chapters would be randomly placed in books. Written text would be utterly incomprehensible! Chaos would reign and written communication would cease to exist—no more novels, no more magazines, no more newspapers, no more email messages, no more textbooks! (Oh dear, we can't have that!)

The organizational structure of a text serves a similar purpose as the structural features of a building: the frame, the floor joists, and roof trusses work together to provide structural support for the entire building. Without these supports, the building would collapse. Likewise, a text structure provides the frame within which information or story elements are organized. Without it, a text would be incomprehensible.

Authors use both external organizational (access) features and internal structures to guide readers toward a better understanding of the content. External organizational features, such as a table of contents, index, glossary, headings, and subheadings, are built into a text to provide readers with easier *access* to information. Without these features, reading would be a more laborious process; there would be no signposts to help you navigate your way through a text.

Internal structure refers to how ideas are organized within paragraphs, sections, chapters, and so forth and provides coherence to texts. You're undoubtedly familiar with elements of internal structure. Remember your English lessons about writing topic sentences and supporting details? Perhaps you're also familiar with the five-paragraph essay, a structure often taught in elementary school and beyond. In the first paragraph, you introduce a topic and your "angle" on the topic. Next, you write three paragraphs explaining, in more detail, ideas introduced in the first paragraph. Then in the last paragraph, you restate what you said in the previous paragraphs and draw conclusions of some sort. Although this organization does not necessarily exemplify great writing, we use it to demonstrate how ideas can be linked systematically and deliberately. Sometimes lack of cohesion in a text may contribute to comprehension difficulties. Other times readers may not recognize the links among ideas, resulting in seeing many distinct parts rather than the "big picture."

Researchers such as Kintsch (as cited in Weaver & Kintsch, 1991) and others determined that expository texts are typically organized in a few basic ways, such as description, sequence, comparison/contrast, cause/effect, and problem/solution. We describe these structures later in this chapter. Other ways expository text structure are described include enumeration, chronology, procedural, definition/example, and categorical.

Stories also have an internal structure; they begin with a rendition of "Once upon a time" and then introduce the setting and characters. Then comes an initiating event—something that causes a problem for the characters. A series of twists and turns take place as the character works to resolve the problem. Finally, it is resolved and "they all live happily ever after." A table of contents and chapter titles are common external features used in narrative text.

Research: Text Structure and Reading Comprehension

Research has demonstrated a relationship between text structure and comprehension. A synthesis of the research on text structure (Dickson, Simmons, & Kameenui, 1995) revealed the following:

1. Well-written and designed text promotes reading comprehension. A well-written text enables readers to identify relevant information, including important ideas and relations among ideas. Visual cues, such as headings and subheadings, signal words, explicit statements of ideas' importance, and spacing, divide text into meaning units and contribute to well-written text. Semantic cues (such as topic sentences) and syntactic cues (such as signal words) help readers understand how ideas are related.

2. A text's structure and a student's awareness and use of that structure are strongly linked to reading comprehension. When reading well-written text, students who were aware of a text's structure were more successful identifying and remembering important ideas and supporting details. They were also better able to summarize texts than students who were not aware of text structure.

3. Explicit and systematic instruction related to the physical features of text and to the organizational structure promotes comprehension.

English Language Arts Standards

The importance of student knowledge and the use of a wide range of strategies, one of which is related to understanding textual features, is reflected in Standard 3. Relatedly, to meet Standard 1—to read a wide range of print and nonprint materials—students must have a knowledge of varying text structures.

Readers Who Struggle with Content Text

Comprehension difficulties can sometimes be attributed to students' lack of experience reading expository texts. Students who experience learning difficulties traditionally also have the least access to expository text. Making sure that students of varying reading proficiencies are exposed to well-written text *and* explicit instruction with text structure is essential to facilitate comprehension.

Access Features as Your Guide

Although you are undoubtedly very familiar with access features, you may not call them by this name. The purpose of access features is just what the name implies: to help readers gain access to ideas in print and in visual images such as photographs and diagrams (Kerper, 1998). Figure 5.1 lists common access features found in informational texts.

FIGURE 5.1   Access Features

Features at the beginning and end of books	Title page
	Acknowledgments
	Dedication page
	To the reader
	Foreword
	Photo credits
	Table of contents
	Afterward
	Bibliography
	Index
	Author index
	Glossary
	Pronunciation key
	Appendices
Features within chapters	Chapter title
	Chapter introduction
	Headings and subheadings
	Graphic organizers
	Charts, graphs, tables, figures
	Maps
	Illustrations
	Captions
	Photographs
	Sidebars
	Boxes
	Chapter summary
	Review questions

Web Activity: Access Features in Electronic Text

Check out www.dinodictionary.com. Use the website's access features to determine the size of dinosaurs compared to humans, interesting facts about your favorite dinosaurs, and even an audio pronunciation "key." You'll find scale drawings and easy to read information about your favorite dinosaur. Also, check out www.nationalgeographic.com/kids. Go to the "Creature Feature" section (see the headings in the sidebar). Then use the buttons to choose your favorite wild animal. You can examine a map to see where it lives, hear its "voice," send someone an email postcard with the animal's photo, and, of course, read some fun facts.

Try It! An Access Feature Scavenger Hunt

Meet with three of your peers. Each of you select a different kind of informational text (e.g., textbook, informational children's trade book, newspaper, magazine, website). Now go on a scavenger hunt with your text of choice, looking for access features. Share your findings with your group. Did some texts include features that were unique? What features do you like the best? The least?

Reflecting

How do you use the access features in this book to help you understand the content? Do you read the information in the figures and boxes? If you do, how do you make decisions about when to read information set apart from the text? How effective is this strategy for comprehending this text?

Common Expository Text Structures

This section describes five common text structures used to organize expository text. Examples of children's writing and visuals are incorporated throughout to illustrate and support our explanations.

Description

Authors use descriptive text structures when their purpose is to describe the characteristics, features, or traits of a person, place, or thing. Note how we use examples in this section to highlight characteristics of different text structures. This is a common occurrence in descriptive text.

When we think of descriptive texts, we envision three distinctly different, yet related structures. First, authors use *lists*, which provide characteristics, features, or traits. Consider the following description.

> All mammals have similar characteristics. Their babies are born alive; they are covered with hair and they are warm-blooded. Some mammals fly in the air (bats), others walk on the earth (humans, dogs, and elephants), and still others swim in the sea (whales and dolphins). Can you think of other animals that are mammals?

In the aforementioned example, we *list* common *characteristics* of mammals and then provide *examples*. We even use *signal* words—characteristics and similar—to give you clues that we're going to describe mammals. (See Figure 5.2 for a list of signal words used with expository text structures.)

FIGURE 5.2   Common Signal Words

Description	for example characteristics most important also in fact	
Definition (a type of description)	means defined is called definition	
Sequence (chronology)	first, second, third on (date) now next	not long after before finally after
Comparison/contrast	Alike as well as similarly	similarities same as
	differences yet however	but in contrast although
	not only . . . but also on the other hand either . . . or as opposed to nevertheless	
Cause/effect Problem/solution	reasons why as a result because thus consequently accordingly due to therefore	if . . . then therefore since so that because this led to then, so

Sometimes authors use a descriptive structure to *define* a concept. For example, in *A Drop of Water* (1997), Walter Wick defines molecules in this way: "Like every other substance in the world, water is made of very tiny particles *called* molecules" (p. 7). Note that the word "molecules" is defined before the term is introduced. Wick uses this signal throughout the book. Some authors signal definitions by using words such as *is, means,* or *defined as.* For example, "surface tension *is* . . ." or "democracy can be *defined as.* . . ." (See Figure 5.2 for more signal words.)

Finally, rich description (our favorite) provides readers with fodder for creating sensory images. (Remember the description of the diver in Chapter 2?) If you notice that an author is appealing to your senses, it is likely a descriptive text. Authors also use metaphors and similes in rich descriptions. One of our favorite children's nonfiction authors, Seymour Simon, uses rich description in his books. In *Whales* (Simon, 1989), Simon compares the weight of a blue whale's tongue to the weight of an elephant and the length of a humpback whale to a large bus.

Poetry: The Epitome of Descriptive Text

Poetry is sometimes considered to be the most descriptive of all texts. Poets choose just the right words to help readers experience a text. Children enjoy experimenting with poetry using cinquains, for example. To write a cinquain, they need background knowledge about a topic, exposure to examples, and, of course, guidance for considering different ways to use language in a cinquain. We include an example of a cinquain written by a second-grade boy in Figure 5.3.

Visuals are often used to support descriptive text. For example, Simon uses vivid, full-color photos of whales to help readers better appreciate what they look like.

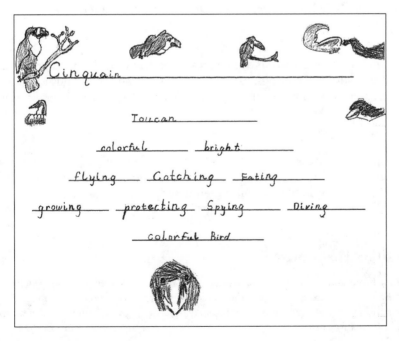

FIGURE 5.3 Cinquain

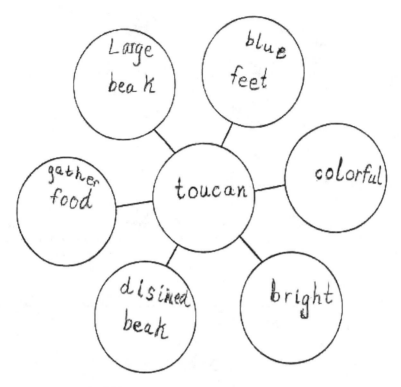

FIGURE 5.4   Bubble Map: Organizing Descriptive Information

Although his descriptive words communicate clearly, the book's photographs are "worth a thousand words!" Drawings, cartoons, paintings, and other kinds of graphic representations, such as bubble maps (see Figure 5.4), are also used to support print text.

Reflecting

Did you notice that we used a list and examples to describe the three ways authors organize descriptive structures? Consider your favorite authors of children's informational books. How do they organize their descriptions?

Try It! Writing Descriptively

Select a topic you're interested in knowing more about. (Perhaps you're curious about what *baleen* is, for example.) Surf the Web for information about the topic. Using the information you find, write about the topic, using a descriptive structure. Try writing the same information in two ways, one using a list of characteristics and examples and the other using rich description. Trade your descriptions with a partner. Which structure is more engaging? From which description did you learn more? What conclusions can you draw about the kinds of text structures that may be most meaningful and engaging to your students?

Riddles are another form of descriptive text. If authors want readers to solve a riddle, they provide explicit, telling clues: In what sport do players use a bat, a ball, and a glove? If, however, they want to "stump" the reader, the clues are more obtuse: "What's red and green and blue all over?"

Even very young children love to read and write "riddle" books. When Jeanne's son, Isaac, was in kindergarten, his class wrote several riddle books when they studied different sports. The following simple steps can be used for constructing "riddle books."

1. Fold a sheet of paper in half, horizontally or vertically. (To make a big book, use two pieces of paper and tape them together at the spine. To make a riddle anthology, fold several pieces of paper together and staple along the fold.)
2. Plan your riddle backward! Decide what your riddle will describe, an elephant for example. Then decide what characteristics or traits to include in the riddle—wrinkles, big ears, and a trunk.
3. On the front cover of the book, write your riddle using a frame such as "What is . . . ?" or, in the case mentioned previously, "What has . . . ?" Then write the answer on the inside page. (In pre-K–2, use shared or interactive writing for modeling and writing the text. In the higher grades, model the planning stage on a transparency before asking students to write riddle books independently.)
4. Decide how to illustrate the riddle so that visual clues are available to readers on the cover and inside page. Students may choose to draw full-color illustrations, use magazine photos, download clip art off the Internet, or create collages from found objects. For "big books," groups can create the illustrations.
5. Congratulations, you have just created a riddle book!

Sequence

Did you notice that the directions just given were written using a sequential structure? (How's that for a *segue*?!) Authors use a sequential organization when information *must* be presented in a particular order. How-to books, such as *Draw Insects* (DuBosque, 1998) or *Electric Gadgets and Gizmos* (Bartholomew, 1998), are written sequentially, step by step. Numerical lists of the steps are sometimes used. Visuals often include photographs to depict what "to do" first, second, and third.

Science texts related to the growth of plants and animals are typically organized sequentially. For example, phases in the life cycle of a plant or animal—eggs, tadpole, frog—must be organized in a *particular* order. Oftentimes, a cycle is represented by arrows forming a circle. Additionally, scientists often record their observations in dated logs (or journals) to reflect changes over time. Second graders in Judy Roger's class used such a log to write and sketch their observations as they watched caterpillars change into butterflies (see Figure 5.5).

Related to sequential structure is chronological structure, which denotes the passage of time. Biographies and history texts are often organized chronologically—from the past to the future. To intrigue readers, sometimes biographers start with the present, "flash back," and then proceed chronologically from the past to present. Time lines are sometimes used to visually depict chronological order. In the *Voyages of Discovery* series, each book includes a time line documenting events—related to theater, visual arts, literature, science/nature, and history—from antiquity to the twentieth century.

Signal words used in sequential texts are similar to those used in descriptive text (see Figure 5.2). To distinguish between the two structures, readers should consider whether the details must be presented in a particular order or not. If so, the text is organized using a sequential structure.

Alphabet books and counting books are also organized using a sequential structure, albeit a different kind of sequence than described earlier. As their name implies, alphabet books proceed sequentially from "A" to "Z" and include illustrations and words related to each letter. Some alphabet books represent variations on this theme, such as *Q Is for Duck* (Etling, Folsom, & Kent, 1985). Similarly, sequentially organized counting books begin with "1" and proceed to "10," for example, typically with illustrations that represent each number. Sometimes counting books follow a different, yet sequential pattern, such as skip counting (5, 10, 15, 20) or counting down (10, 9, 8, . . .). Although it may seem obvious what elements signal order in counting books, you'll need to be explicit about these signals with pre-K and kindergarten students and others who have had limited exposure to books.

Comparison/Contrast

Authors use a comparison/contrast structure when they wish to discuss similarities and differences related to people, places, things, or concepts. Like other structures, authors may use particular words to signal the structure. (Note that we use some signal words in this paragraph, such as similarities, differences, like, differentiate, comparison, and contrast). In the preceding paragraph, we compared the structure of alphabet books and counting books and compared and contrasted them to other books that are organized using a sequential structure.

The use of visuals is especially effective for comparing and contrasting characteristics. *How Big Is a Whale* (Johnson, 1995) uses a unique style. To show the weight of a Siberian tiger, the illustrator, Michael Woods, superimposes sixty-five house cats on the side of a Siberian tiger. The caption reads: "Did you know that a Siberian tiger weighs more than 550 pounds—as much as 65 pet cats?" (p. 23). Similar visuals are used throughout the book, always comparing larger animals with smaller ones that are likely to be familiar to readers.

Sometimes authors use diagrams or matrices to compare and contrast characteristics. In Gail Gibbons' book, *Frogs*, she uses a labeled diagram of a frog and a diagram

FIGURE 5.5 Butterfly Observation Log

Subject apples	Looks	Feels	Smells	Tastes	Sounds
Southern rose	red-yellow Hurt in middle Small star	Jucy	good	Sweet, gucy	crunchy ②
golden deicious	spots green-yellow	bumpy soft	same	tart	Lest crunchy ④
royal gala	red-gold	smooth	same	sweet tart	very crunch ③
Granny Smith	green loaf wh. dots	hard smooth	diferent	sour	crunchy ①
Fuji	gold-brown	smooth bumpy	Same	seet	
Mcintosh	green red	soft	Same	tart jully	quiet

FIGURE 5.6   Semantic Feature Analysis Chart: Comparing and Contrasting

of a toad to illustrate how the amphibians differ. A semantic feature analysis chart is a useful graphic for comparing and contrasting characteristics. Figure 5.6 shows an example of this kind of chart, used, in this instance, to organize students' notes as they examined different kinds of apples. Later in this chapter, we compare and contrast linear and nonlinear texts using a visual because we think the information will be most comprehensible in this form.

Try It! Peruse, List, Determine Purposes, and Compare!

Survey this book with a partner. List all the access features you find. Why do you think we included each feature? Organize your findings, using a semantic feature analysis chart, as suggested in "A Teaching Toolbox" of this textbook. List features vertically and their purposes across the top. When you compare and contrast features in this way, what do you notice? Are some purposes more prevalent than others? Why do you think this is?

Cause/Effect and Problem/Solution

We describe cause/effect and problem/solution structures in the same section because they are oftentimes intricately related. They are the most complex and the most difficult to understand. Authors use a cause-and-effect structure to explain how actions or events cause something to happen. Sometimes, several causes result in a single effect and vice versa. For teaching text structure, initially use a simple text, and then gradually move to more complex texts. We include the following simple example of information organized in a cause/effect structure.

> I was walking down the street and stepped on a nail (cause). It went through my shoe and into my foot (effect). I hobbled all the way home (effect), went to the emergency room (effect), and had to get a tetanus shot (effect). My foot was sore for a week (effect).

The following paragraph shows a text organized around a problem and solution. The simple text is illustrative of texts that could be used initially to introduce a problem/solution structure.

> You want to ride your bike to the library to check out the newest *Orbis Pictus* award winner. However, when you get out your bike, the front tire is flat (problem). The *solution* is to fix it by locating the leak, patching the tire, and then pumping air in the tire—(oops, we lapsed into a sequence of steps! More on combined structures later.)

Several disciplines lend themselves quite naturally to address problems and solutions. Mathematical word problems are organized in this way. The "problem" is typically identified in a question at the end of a problem. Students determine how to solve the problem, using the information explicitly stated and inferred in the problem, their knowledge of mathematics and the world, and other factors.

Try It! Read to Solve the Problem

Together, Jeanne and Donna have 6 large dogs and Kristiina has none. Each dog eats 3 cups of dry dog food daily and 2 of them eat a half a pound of green beans too. Jeanne and Donna typically purchase Canine Deluxe food in 50-lb. bags, which cost $20.00 apiece. How much does each woman need to budget per month for feeding her dogs?

What information is explicitly stated in the text? What is inferred? What information should you use? Which information is irrelevant? What information do you need to find out from other sources?

Science is all about causes and effects and related problems and solutions. For example, the problem is there's too much pollution. What causes pollution? Scientists hypothesize about the causes and possibilities for solving the problem. Then they carry out experiments to see what actions solve the problem. Historians also write about problems and solutions, but not in isolation. Many times causes lead to effects and then the effects become a problem that needs to be solved. Sound complicated? Perhaps, but the complex nature of problems and solutions, causes and effects, reflects reality.

Combining Text Structures

Authors use a combination of structures more often than a single structure. In fact, rarely is information in a chapter of a textbook or an entire trade book organized using only one structure. Sometimes there is a dominant structure—for example, many history books are organized chronologically—but within that structure, an author may *describe* the government, write about the *causes* and *effects* of a war, and *compare* and *contrast* the roles of men and women before women had the right to vote. An example of a book that uses an overall chronological structure to order the chapters, yet uses a compare/contrast structure within each chapter, is *Christmas in the Big House, Christmas in the Quarters* by Patricia and Fredrick McKissack (1994). The chapter titles *describe* the happenings of each day and include a date (like a diary), which denotes *chronology*. The authors then use a comparison/contrast structure to describe the Christmas celebration of slaves who lived in the Quarters and owners who lived in the Big House of a Virginia plantation in 1859, before the War Between the States. A pen-and-ink icon separates and denotes a shift of description from the Big House to the Quarters, and vice versa. The illustrations, by John Thompson, also clearly depict the contrasts between the families' lives and celebrations.

Mixed Genres: Informational Stories

Not only do authors mix organizational structures, they also mix genres. Some authors of informational books choose to embed facts into a narrative (story) structure, which results in an informational story. Criteria for choosing informational storybooks for content instruction change little from that described in Chapter 3 for other informational books. An additional element does need to be considered, however. It's important to help students differentiate between fact and fiction in informational storybooks. (This issue is also important to consider when utilizing historical fiction.) Sometimes authors speak to this in a note at the back of the book or preface. When they do not, use it as an opportunity to teach students how to differentiate between fact and fiction—what a perfect teachable moment to model how you investigate the credibility of information in books, magazines, newspapers, and the Internet.

One of the most popular series of informational storybooks is *The Magic School Bus* by Joanna Cole. The focus of the majority of these books is science content. One of Cole's most recent books, *Ms. Frizzle's Adventures: Ancient Egypt* (2001), features social studies content. The Magic School Bus series can be used in all elementary grades, for read alouds in the primary grades, and for student research in the intermediate grades.

The *Magic Tree House* series by Mary Pope Osborne also uses the informational storybook structure. These easy-to-read chapter books focus on adventures related to history, for the most part. Children in the primary grades love this series. Jack, one of the main characters, is a great model for reading and writing information because he writes important and interesting information in a notebook! During a visit to Jamie Duncan's second-grade classroom in Lubbock, Texas, Jeanne noticed José was taking notes in his own research notebook, keeping track of what he was learning about ancient Egypt, just like Jack!

Technology Try It! Turn on the Tube

What? You want us to watch TV?! Yes! Go to your local TV listings and find the Magic School Bus cartoon. (If you don't have cable, some episodes are available at local video rental stores.) Get your pencil and paper out, sit back, and watch cartoons! As you watch, jot down information you learn from the cartoon. You'll probably need to watch the episode more than once to learn everything; it's amazing how much information can be packed into a thirty-minute cartoon!

Nonlinear Structures

A new "breed" of text structure made a strong showing in the 1990s and continues to evolve today. This structure is often referred to as nonlinear. You would undoubtedly recognize this "new" text structure because it looks very different from traditional linear text. Short chunks of text describing visuals of all sorts are scattered across the pages. Sound familiar? If so, you know that reading these texts is quite different than reading linear texts. In fact, it's almost like surfing the Web and navigating through hypertext. Readers move from one "link" (chunk of text or visual) to another, making decisions about what to read, when to read particular text, and what not to read.

Perhaps the easiest way to describe nonlinear text structure is to contrast it with linear texts. Figure 5.7 uses a comparison/contrast graphic organizer to depict the similarities and differences.

Reflecting

What did you think about the effectiveness of using a graphic to communicate the similarities and differences of linear and nonlinear text? What are some of the advantages of viewing information in this form rather than as running text? If you could have your choice, how would you organize this information?

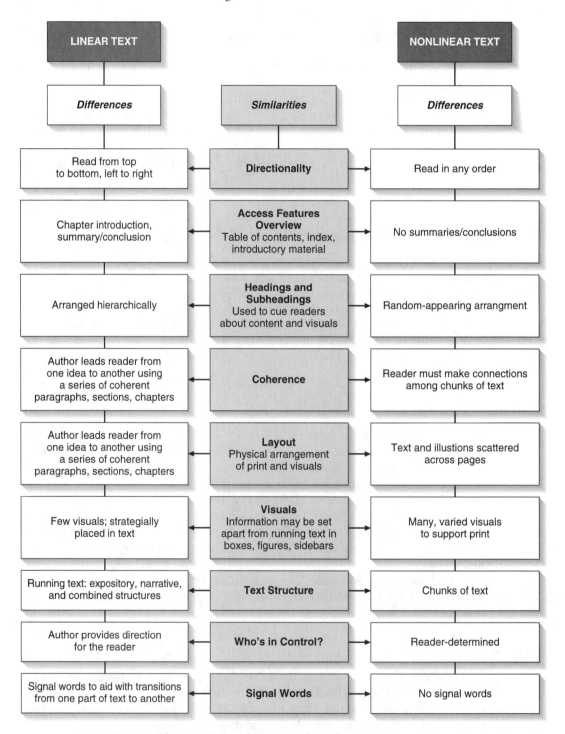

FIGURE 5.7   Characteristics of Linear and Nonlinear Text

Web Activity: Take a Look at Nonlinear Text

Log on to www.kidsdiscover.com. Click on "Explore." Then "Take a Tour." The "tour guide" will show you examples of nonlinear text on two-page spreads from back issues of *Kids Discover* magazine.

Based on hundreds of observations in elementary schools, we have noticed that texts with nonlinear structures seem to fascinate children. They often sit for long periods of time examining and discussing illustrations and captions with their peers. Nonlinear texts are definitely engaging. What is not clear is how students make decisions about what information is and is not important to read.

Walpole (1998–1999) found that fourth-grade students she interviewed did not necessarily understand how to use the features of "new" science texts. For example, some students reported they read nonlinear text just like linear text. Others read only the parts that were most interesting to them. Some students skipped chapter titles, captions, running text, and even some of the illustrations. Still others flipped through books, from the back to the front, selectively reading what they considered to be intriguing text. Based on Walpole's work, she postulated that nonlinear texts may increase interest and attention, lead to more active thinking during reading, help students build their knowledge base, and examine texts in more flexible and interactive ways than traditional textbooks. Even so, teachers need to teach students strategies for reading and learning with nonlinear text.

Try It! Examining Nonlinear Text

Select a children's informational book that is organized using a nonlinear structure. (If you need some ideas, check with the librarian and/or look for books published by Dorling Kindersley—DK.) Before you begin reading, consider what you know about reading nonlinear texts. Next, browse through the book, recording the strategies you use (see Chapter 2 for ideas). How do you determine what information the author deems most important? What strategies do you use to link ideas across chunks of text? How do you synthesize information from a book that moves from one two-page spread to another and seems to change focus every time you turn the page? How do your reading strategies change when you read nonlinear text compared to linear text? Why? Why not?

Graphic Organizers

Throughout this chapter, we have employed graphic organizers (or graphic representations) to help you visualize more clearly how expository text structures organize information. Graphic organizers are also useful for organizing notes during reading and for planning writing; they're like an outline but use a visual format. Examples of graphic organizers include semantic maps, flow charts, time lines, cycle charts, semantic feature analysis charts, and so forth. All are used for representing ideas and their organization visually. In a synthesis of reading comprehension research, Pearson and Fielding (1991) reported that systematic instruction about text structure with graphic organizers—designed to highlight relationships among ideas—enhances comprehension.

Readers Who Struggle with Content Texts

Readers who have difficulty comprehending content area texts often need assistance differentiating between the more important ideas and those that are less important and seeing how ideas relate to one another. Using graphic organizers helps readers sort and organize information. Similarly, less dense text and visible links between ideas make text organization more apparent. In addition, ideas presented in graphic organizers are often more memorable than those explained in linear text.

Web Activity: Graphic Organizers

There is a plethora of graphic organizers available on the Web. Check out www.google.com and search for "graphic organizers." Which organizers do you think would be most useful for your students? Choose a text that's clearly organized using one of the structures described earlier. Create a graphic to represent the content of the text.

Evaluating Texts in Regard to Organization

In their book *Checking Out Nonfiction K–8: Good Choices for Best Learning*, Bamford and Kristo (2000) suggest the following guidelines for evaluating text in terms of its organizational structures, including access features and visuals.

1. Generally, how is the information in a book organized?
2. Is the organization consistent with the nature of the content? Is it consistent with the author's purposes? Is it logical?
3. Does the internal structure (expository structure) clarify relationships among facts?
4. Do the headings, subheadings, and visuals make the text easier to follow and understand?
5. Do the access features make a text easier to use?

Teaching Students to Use Organizational Features

Research has shown that students need to be taught explicitly how to use internal text structures (expository and narrative forms) and external organizational (access) features of text to enhance comprehension. Likewise, it is important to teach students how to use and create graphic representations of text. A teaching model, like the gradual release of responsibility, has been recommended as an effective way to teach children to use text structure as they read (Pearson & Fielding, 1991). To review from Chapter 2, explanations of the how's, when's, where's, and why's of using text structure, along with teacher modeling and thinking aloud, are essential elements of instruction. Likewise, guided practice in large and small group contexts and independent practice are important to give students opportunities to apply their knowledge of text structure, yet have access to teacher support. As necessary, the teacher may extend or pull back the amounts and kinds of support she or he provides, depending on students' developing strengths and needs. Instruction occurs with a variety of texts, including different genres, content areas, text structures, linear and nonlinear texts, and so forth. Ultimately, the goal is that students will apply their knowledge of text structure to their independent reading. Figure 5.8 provides guidelines for scaffolding explicit instruction about text structure (Rhoder, 2002).

Teaching Text Structure in the First Grade

Several years ago, Julie Rogers, a first-grade teacher taking a graduate class with Jeanne, decided she wanted her students to better understand and appreciate informational books and become nonfiction authors. One aspect of instruction focused on explicit teaching about expository text structures. Julie employed trade books with clear structures for reading aloud, modeling, and explaining how text structure works. She also used graphic organizers and writing frames to scaffold student learning.

Here, we describe a series of lessons she taught about the comparison/contrast structure. Julie chose the book *Fire! Fire!* by Gail Gibbons (1993) for reading aloud, modeling, and demonstration purposes. She began the lesson by reviewing why and how understanding text structure aids comprehension and helps writers organize their ideas. She read the book aloud and then went back and modeled her thinking about its structure. She and her students discussed similarities described in the book and, using shared writing, constructed a Venn diagram.

The next day, Julie chose to use information from their "ocean" K-W-W-L chart (Bryan, 1998) to continue their study of the comparison/contrast structure. Because there was lots of information in the "K" column about whales and sharks that could be compared and contrasted, she chose to guide students in constructing a Venn diagram about those animals. Collaboratively they made decisions about information for the diagram. Next, she modeled the use of a paragraph frame (Cudd & Roberts, 1989), which provided students with scaffolding for their writing. The frame was simple and included the essentials for introducing students to writing about similarities

FIGURE 5.8   Hints for Teaching Text Structure

1. Introduce the concept of text structure as an element of text that strategic readers use. Explain and model how recognizing that an author is describing an object or explaining the steps in a procedure, for example, can help them better understand what they read.

2. To introduce a particular structure, use examples students can relate to. For example, introducing sequence after making no-bake cookies from a recipe provides a shared experience and introduces authentic sequential writing with its purpose. This memorable experience and related reading and writing will serve as links with similar tasks.

3. Examine texts with the same organizational structure. List elements that are the same across a particular text structure. For example, elements of cause/effect in their simplest form are something happened (effect) and someone or something made it happen (cause).

4. Introduce questions students may ask themselves to aid in identifying text structure (Rhoder, 2002).

    Cause/effect: Have I found . . .

                                what happened? What will happen? (effects)
    why it happened? Who/what made it happen? (causes)
    any signal words?

    Compare/contrast: Have I found . . .

                                what/who is being compared?
    facts that are the same?
    facts that are different?
    any signal words?

    Sequence: Have I found . . .

                                events that happen in a specific order?
    events that should happen in a specific order?
    signal words?

    Description: Have I found . . .

                                who/what is being described?
    characteristics?
    signal words?

    Problem/solution: Have I found . . .

                                something that has happened or is likely to happen?
            (problem)
    suggestions for possible solutions to take care of a problem?
    signal words?

5. Develop a class list of signal words, cautioning students that the words do not always guarantee a particular text structure.

6. Introduce and model the use of graphic organizers depicting clearly how ideas are organized in a text. Later, students develop their own graphic organizers for texts they read. Students can also create graphic representations to organize their writing.

7. Introduce and model the use of a writing frame. Then give students opportunities to practice writing within the context of a frame.

8. Continue providing students with practice, using texts of varying genres, structures, and content. Gradually turn more and more responsibility over to students until they apply their knowledge of text structure as they read independently.

and differences. Then students used information from the Venn diagram and completed a text frame similar to the one that follows:

> Although whales are mammals and sharks are fish, they are similar in many ways. First, _____. Second, _____. Last, _____.

The next day, Julie distributed Venn diagrams to each student and asked them to compare two ocean animals they had read and written about previously. Students completed their diagrams either collaboratively or independently. Finally, they used a paragraph frame to compare and contrast the animals.

English Language Arts Standards (ELA)

Julie's lessons, outlined earlier, addressed several ELA standards.

Standard 1. One of Julie's purposes for the lessons was that students would better understand and appreciate a variety of texts. Standard 1 is reflected in the different texts she chose to read aloud to the students.

Standard 3. Students collaborated as they discussed the content of texts, made decisions about information to include in Venn diagrams, and selected information to include in their writing frames.

Standard 4. Students were introduced to the characteristics of various text structures to expand their knowledge, which can facilitate comprehension.

Standard 6. As students composed paragraphs, they applied what they knew about text structure to create their own texts.

Constructing Paragraph Frames

A paragraph frame (Cudd & Roberts, 1989) is a tool that helps students learn to organize their writing using different expository and narrative text structures. To construct a frame, first compose a topic sentence or introduction; it provides students with a general direction to follow. Then include signal words (refer to Figure 5.2) relevant to the text structure. Finally, provide a concluding sentence.

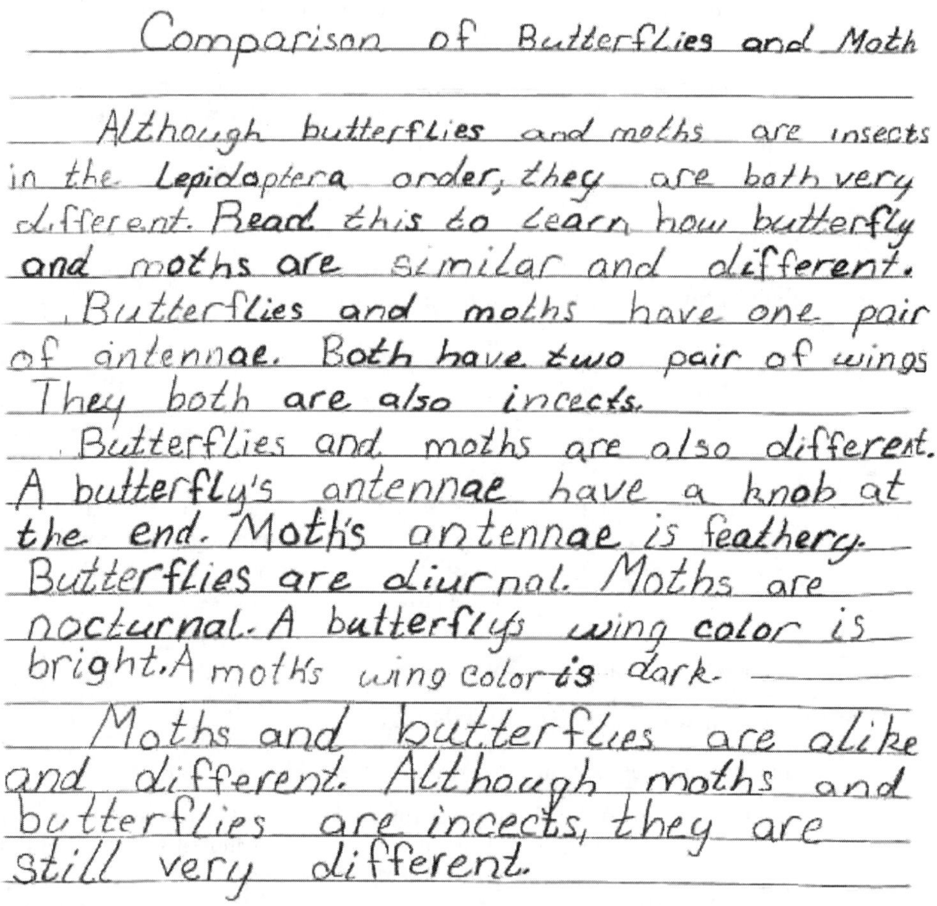

Comparison of Butterflies and Moth

Although butterflies and moths are insects in the Lepidoptera order, they are both very different. Read this to learn how butterfly and moths are similar and different.

Butterflies and moths have one pair of antennae. Both have two pair of wings They both are also incects.

Butterflies and moths are also different. A butterfly's antennae have a knob at the end. Moth's antennae is feathery. Butterflies are diurnal. Moths are nocturnal. A butterfly's wing color is bright. A moth's wing color is dark.

Moths and butterflies are alike and different. Although moths and butterflies are incects, they are still very different.

FIGURE 5.9   Paragraph Frame: Comparing Butterflies and Moths

Figures 5.9 and 5.10 include examples of two young girls' writing in which paragraph frames were used. In Figure 5.9, you'll read about how moths and butterflies are similar and different. Can you identify the components of the frame? The example in Figure 5.10 illustrates how frames can be used to scaffold students' *responses* to informational text. This kind of frame is referred to as a reaction frame.

Caution: Paragraph frames are for teaching children to better organize their writing. Frames should be used only as an instructional scaffold and withdrawn gradually so that students do not become dependent on them.

... If You Lived During Colonial Times

Although I already knew that _the colonial people_
talked   differentley, and dress
differentley.

I learned some new things from reading about Colonial times. For

instance, _they could not talk at the_
table.

I also learned _at school if they bite there_
nails they would have to ware a sine
that says finger nail biting baby.

However, the most interesting thing I learned was _they could_
not hug or kiss there parent.

I have a question about Colonial times   I would like to know

why did they do different stuff
then us?

FIGURE 5.10   Reaction Frame

Try It! Construct Paragraph Frames

Find examples of children's informational books that illustrate different structures. Design (or locate graphic organizers on the Internet or other resources) to accompany five books, one for each organizational pattern. Then prepare writing frames that include an introductory (or topic) sentence, signal words, and a concluding statement.

Reconsidering

Perhaps you never really considered how internal text structure and external organizational (access) features can help you understand a text. After reading this chapter, what have you learned about text structure that you were not aware of before? Do you prefer reading linear or nonlinear text? What do you think elementary school students prefer? Why? How do you think electronic text has affected the design of print text?

CHAPTER

6

Teaching Media and Visual Literacy in the Content Areas

In Chapter 6, you will learn about the importance of reading visual images as a way of becoming media literate. This is one of the newer forms of literacy to appear on many states' and professional organizations' lists of standards. You will also be invited to engage in an exercise aimed at showing you what it feels like to be media literate. Our hope, of course, is that you will find this a compelling kind of literacy and that you will share your expertise in developing it among your students. Toward that end, we offer examples of viewing and visual literacy activities suitable for content area learning. We also touch on the importance of play in developing children's media and visual literacy, and we offer ideas for helping you teach children strategies for reading and evaluating web sources.

> Already, some teachers are calling them the "video generation"—elementary school children who are thoroughly familiar with computers and even the Internet. A *Newsweek/Kaplan Poll* of parents with children in kindergarten to eighth grade shows that 75 percent of them have computers at home and that 62 percent are connected to the net. As might be expected, computers get more use from older kids than from little ones. Even so, more than half of the children in grades K–4 use computers at least a few times a week according to their parents. (*Newsweek/Score*, 2000, p. 26)

For the *Newsweek/Kaplan Poll*, Princeton Survey Research Associates interviewed 400 parents with children in grades K–8 by telephone. The survey group reported a margin of error of +/–5 percentage points. Two years later, we have results of the following study in which children themselves informed a different group of researchers about their media preferences.

Press Release:

More Kids Say Internet Is the Medium They Can't Live Without

Westfield, NJ and Menlo Park, CA; April 5, 2002

> If they could only have one medium, more children would choose the Internet with television placing second and the telephone third. These are among the findings of a newly released, in-depth study from Knowledge Networks/Statistical Research Institute. Given a choice of six media, 33 percent of the 8- to 17-year-olds in the study said the Web is what they would want if they couldn't have access to any other medium; 26 percent said television; 21 percent picked the telephone; and 15 percent said the radio. (Knowledge Networks, 2002)

Remembering

We remember hearing not too long ago that the Internet would be the wave of the future. If these two studies are representative of the population at large (and we believe they are), the future is now. Although data from the K–4 subgroup of the *Newsweek/Kaplan Poll* (2000) indicate that children in these grades spend most of their time playing computer games and using educational software, as many as 8 percent send and receive email at least once a week, and 10 percent use computers for word processing and doing research on the web. In grades 5–8, 33 percent of the children use computers to do homework. These figures suggest to us that in heavily wired households, at least, children are developing critical skills in media use at an early age and that those who have had access to computers will have an advantage over those who have not.

What do you recall about the two studies of children's media use that seems to hold true for children you know? Can you think of children who are exceptions to these findings? What does media use have to do with literacy or with being visually literate? Do you remember teachers talking about media literacy before now?

This chapter begins by defining media literacy in relation to reading *visual images as texts* (e.g., photographs, videos, films, TV, maps, graphs, diagrams, websites). Next, it provides examples of viewing and visual literacy activities suitable for content area learning. It then moves to a discussion of the role of play in developing children's media literacy in the content areas. It ends with a section on teaching children strategies for reading and evaluating web sources.

Accessibility of Visual Texts for All Readers

"One of the great advantages of visual texts, such as maps or diagrams, is that most of the information they provide is readily accessible to all readers, including very young children who are not yet fluent readers of words and older students whose first language is not English. Similarly, students who are judged to be 'poor writers' (when asked to write exclusively in words) are sometimes discovered to be excellent communicators if they are allowed the option to write the same information in a visual form, for example, as a diagram, graph or map." (Moline, 1995, p. 1)

Media Literacy: Learning to Read Visual Images

Visual texts in all their many forms can often communicate content area information more efficiently and clearly than the printed word. They are also media friendly in that they complement both older and newer technologies, frequently combining the two.

A Definition of Media Literacy

The Alliance for a Media Literate America (AMLA)—a national, grassroots membership organization committed to bringing media literacy education to all sixty million students in the United States—defines media literacy in terms of what it accomplishes:

> Media literacy empowers people to be both critical thinkers and creative producers of an increasingly wide range of messages using image, language, and sound. It is the skillful application of literacy skills to media and technology messages (http://www.amedialitamerica.org).

That's the short version of a definition of media literacy. A longer version, according to AMLA, takes into account four key communication competencies, which include the ability to access, analyze, evaluate, and communicate information using print and nonprint messages from a wide range of media, such as sound recordings, videos, books, websites, films, and television. Although we see each of these competencies as being vital to teaching and learning in content areas, we also recognize that the ability to analyze media messages presumes that one is visually literate.

What It Means to Be Visually Literate

Becoming visually literate involves expanding print literacy skills by developing a greater awareness of how things come to have the meanings that they have (and why those meanings vary from one individual to the next). As Muffoletto (2001) puts it: "Being 'visually literate' means more than having the ability to produce/encode and read/decode constructed visual experiences; it . . . is to be actively engaged in asking questions and seeking answers about the multiple meanings of a visual experience."

In the following "Try It" exercise, you are asked to envision a photograph that is ingrained in many people's minds in the United States following the events of the September 11th attack on the World Trade Center in New York City. The purpose of this exercise is to introduce you to the types of questions that are associated with making multiple meanings from the same image and with reading critically.

Try It! Developing a Sense of Media Literacy

Imagine in your mind's eye the photograph of the three firefighters raising the American flag at Ground Zero following the September 11th attack and then ask the following questions of the photograph:

- Why were you made?
- Who made you?
- Why do you show me what you do?
- Who benefits from your existence?
- What is the meaning of this?
- Is there another way of representing what you represent?

Discuss your answers to these questions with a friend. Did you and your friend differ in your answers? How might this difference relate to the social constructionist perspective on learning described in Chapter 1? Describe the text-to-self, text-to-text, and text-to-world connections that you made as you "read" the photograph—a visual image that is a text even though it contains no printed symbols.

It is often said that we currently live in a world saturated with media texts of all kinds. They are often hybrids (or mixes) of audio, visual, and tactile images, language, and sounds that are joined together to evoke certain emotions and meaning among us. They are commonly associated with television, video, multimedia, the Internet, and with other forms of new communication technologies, such as instant messaging and emailing. Less commonly thought of as media texts are the symbolically rich texts through which people make meaning when they engage in music, film, dance, drama, painting, and other nonprint forms of communication.

A Standard that Speaks to the Widening Definition of "Text"

One of the twelve standards for the English language arts approved by the International Reading Association and the National Council of Teachers of English is this one: Students need to "read a wide range of print and nonprint texts to build an understanding of texts, of themselves, and of the cultures of the United States and the world." (http://www.reading.org/advocacy/elastandards/standards.html)

To understand how all this affects what is taught and learned in content area classes, imagine yourself in the shoes of the fourth-grade teacher who collected the following materials to help students become visually literate as they simultaneously learned about the intricacies of desert life. For each of the media sources described (Table 6.1), ask yourself this question: How will reading this particular image contribute to my fourth-graders' understanding that while desert plants and animals have their own ways of coping with the hot, dry climate, each needs the other for survival?

TABLE 6.1

Media Sources Selected by the Teacher

1. A video, *NatureWorks* (Environmental Media, 2002), uses an entertaining and informative style to explore a variety of concepts for understanding ecological and environmental issues. Natural footage, animation, and a lively soundtrack make it an engaging experience for children between the ages of eight and fourteen.

2. A ten-page heavily illustrated print text titled "The Living Desert" from a book that was part of the school's curriculum (*Images*, 1995). One image is of a yucca moth collecting pollen from a yucca. A paragraph in the passage explains that only the yucca moth can pollinate a yucca and cause it to bloom. Similarly, only yucca seeds can feed the moth's larvae.

3. Coolmath.com (http://www.coolmath.com) is one of nine 2002 Notable Children's Websites selected by the Association for Library Service to Children. The site is fully interactive and allows users to play math-related games. The teacher plans to develop a math game related to surviving (and thriving) in a desert climate. Students will have to access the Coolmath site in order to play the game.

4. A brochure from the Arizona-Sonora Desert Museum that stresses conservation and teaches visitors about the interdependency of plant and animal life.

5. A recent issue of the news magazine *Time for Kids* that features a "Desert Fact File" and an invitation to continue the search for facts online at http://www.timeforkids.com/goplaces.

Viewing and Visual Literacy Activities

The communication and visual arts in a school curriculum emphasize the verbal, non-verbal, and visual processing of meaning. They include expanded definitions of "text" such as television, painting, drama, music, and dance (Harris & Hodges, 1995). Many informational trade books rely primarily on visual elements to convey their content. For example, *The Eyes of Gray Wolf* by Jonathan London (1993) uses pictures and symbols as well as printed words to communicate the precarious life style of an endangered species. *Biggest, Strongest, Fastest* (Jenkins, 1996) and *How Big Is a Whale?* (Johnson, 1995) use scaled comparisons and comparison overlays to help children estimate size—resources that Jenny's teacher in Chapter 4 might make good use of in helping her learn the meaning of *scale*.

A Standard for Using a Variety of Technological and Information Resources

Standard #8 of the English language arts standards approved by the International Reading Association and the National Council of Teachers of English explicitly calls attention to the need for students to "use a variety of information sources (e.g., libraries, databases, computer networks, video) to gather and synthesize information and to create and communicate knowledge." http://www.reading.org.advocacy/elastandards/standards.html

Visual Texts in the Classroom

Among the many reasons for using visual texts in your classroom on a regular basis include opportunities to:

- integrate literacy with other curriculum areas such as science and technology . . . and other key learning areas;
- motivate students judged to be "non-writers" and "non-readers";
- develop initiative and independence in learning, especially in the areas of research and writing;
- give support and confidence to those students whose strengths lie in visual perception . . . or who communicate well by drawing objects, mapping concepts and organizing content using graphic design;
- develop thinking skills such as selecting and combining strategies to solve problems . . . [and]
- combine verbal and visual literacies to make an integrated text. (Moline, 1995, pp. 3–4)

Viewing: The Fifth Language Art

Jeanne has conducted many professional development workshops on the use of viewing to facilitate comprehension across the content areas. One of her favorite strategies is an adaptation of Kathy Short's "Sketch to Stretch" (Short, Harste, & Burke, 1996) activity. The original and the adaptation of "Sketch to Stretch" appear in Table 6.2.

Five other visual literacy strategies that Jeanne has developed and used with teachers to facilitate children's comprehension of content area texts include "Picture This" (Table 6.3), "What's Your Story?" (Table 6.4), Teaching Questioning (Table 6.5),

TABLE 6.2 Original and Adaptation of "Sketch to Stretch"

Original "Sketch to Stretch" (Short, Harste, & Burke, 1996)

Purposes: To provide students with an opportunity to (a) respond visually to texts and (b) expand their thinking about, and interpretations of, texts.

1. Read a selection to students without revealing the illustrations.
2. After reading, ask students to sketch what the book means to them—something it reminds them of—or other such questions that require them to go beyond illustrating the literal text.
3. Each student shows her/his sketch to a small group of peers. Students in the group try to interpret the sketch and its relation to the text.
4. After everyone in the group has had a chance to share interpretations, the sketcher shares her/his interpretation of the sketch.

Adaptation of "Sketch to Stretch" (Swafford, 2001)

Rather than reading a text aloud to students, show them a painting, photograph, or other intriguing visual. (Wordless picture books are great for this strategy. Reproductions of art prints on calendars are also a good source. Don't forget about alphabet books and other picture books with intriguing illustrations.) Ask students to communicate their interpretation of the visual in any way they wish. Some students may write, some may draw, and others may use a combination of the communicative arts (e.g., drama, music, dance, painting).

TABLE 6.3 *Picture This* (Swafford, 2001)

Purpose: To help students access their background knowledge about a particular topic or concept through the use of visual prompts.

1. Select photographs, paintings, sketches, objects, or other visuals that relate to a text or unit of study. (Try to choose visuals that represent different aspects of the text or unit of study.)
2. Display one item at a time and ask students to brainstorm about what the visual makes them think of as they view it. The teacher records students' responses.
3. When students get "stuck" on a particular idea and offer variations on the same theme, introduce a new visual. This will help students to broaden (or narrow) their thinking.

TABLE 6.4   *What's Your Story?* (Swafford, 2001)

Purpose: To promote discussion and logical writing by interpreting photographs.

1. Take photographs of an activity that occurs in a sequential fashion.
2. Provide small groups of students with the photographs. Ask them to write the text to accompany the photographs after viewing and discussing them.
3. Students who write the text create cover art for the book.
4. Add a spiral binding and place in the classroom or school library.

TABLE 6.5   *Teaching Questioning* (Swafford, 2001)

Purpose: To introduce the self-questioning strategy to students who do not ask themselves questions as they read.

1. Choose photographs, paintings, sketches, or objects that are not easy to interpret.
2. Provide pairs of students with sticky notes and ask them to record questions they have about the visuals as they view them. They place the sticky note on the page that generated the questions.
3. Share with other pairs who may have the same visuals.

TABLE 6.6   *Visual Dictionary* (Swafford, 2001)

Purpose: To engage students in constructing a visual text (a visual dictionary) that includes more than one type of visual.

1. Share the *Visual Dictionary of Everyday Things* (1991) with the class.
2. Students collect visuals from a variety of sources (e.g., students' own drawings, photographs, magazines, catalogs, web pages, CD-ROMs).
3. After viewing *What's Inside? Insects* (1992) and *The Amazing Book of Insect Records* (Woods, 1999) to get an idea of how authors and illustrators "label" their texts, students label the parts of their entries.
4. Students arrange entries in alphabetical order.
5. Add a spiral binding.
6. Students can create visual dictionaries for different units of study or for difficult vocabulary they are expected to learn in the various content areas. (When words are not easily illustrated because of their abstract nature, be creative. Find ways to illustrate concepts so their meanings are memorable.)

TABLE 6.7 *The Sky's the Limit* (Swafford, 2001)

Purpose: To provide opportunities for students to create their own visuals using the Internet and a word-processing software program.

1. Students experiment with different fonts, font styles, special effects, colors, sizes, borders, and symbol systems.
2. After experimenting, they choose a style that best communicates the meaning they want to convey (could be an emotion, a response to a written or visual text, or some other stimulus).
3. Students view each other's choices in style and discuss what makes them work.

Visual Dictionary (Table 6.6), and "The Sky's the Limit" (Table 6.7). Each of these strategies can be taught using one or more of the beautiful (and free) photographs offered by Beryl (see the following box).

A Web Tip

Looking for *free* photographs to download and use with your class as part of the visual literacy activities described in Tables 6.3–6.7? Then go to http://www.berylsphotographs.com/index1.htm. At this website you will also find fascinating links to sites that will engage your students in solving on-line jigsaw puzzles, sending postcards to family members and friends, and much more. Choose from photograph categories such as animals, flowers, birds, butterflies, historic events, mountains, and ships to enhance your content literacy instruction through visual images.

Reflecting

Teaching students to read visual images is part and parcel of teaching them to be media literate. As you think back on your own schooling and your experiences outside of school, what are some things that have prepared you for teaching students to use media as learning resources? In what ways are you ill-prepared for this responsibility? Would you describe yourself as a visually literate person? Why? Why not?

Playing to Learn in the Content Areas

The word *play* often conjures up images of frivolity and a sense of abandonment that are made to seem at odds with the idea of what school work, such as content area learning, should involve. From our reading of the literature on school culture, play is typically relegated to the time and spaces in a day when children are allowed to take a break from an adult's direct supervision. In contrast to this rather pervasive view of play is one put forth by Buckingham (1993) and others (e.g., Dyson, 1997; Hull & Schultz, 2001) whose research demonstrates why educators need to take seriously the informal and playful media literacies that children develop outside of school. Despite their urging that we not dismiss such literacies as antieducational (and thus a questionable use of children's time), it is the case, as Luke (2002) has documented, that the tendency is to blame the media for undermining traditional forms of school literacy.

Treating Play Seriously

A growing realization is that everyone—young children, adolescents, and adults—is experiencing fewer opportunities for play these days. Adults, in ever greater numbers, are choosing to work out of their homes, with the consequence being undifferentiated spaces for work and play. More parents are placing more youngsters in more structured after-school programs than ever before, and schools themselves are becoming workplaces where fun is frowned upon, especially if it interferes with back-to-basics teaching methods "guaranteed" to raise test scores. The notion of play is under full frontal attack by certain segments of society, according to Tapscott (1998), author of a bestselling book on the rise of the net-generation.

However, in the midst of this feverish activity to raise the bar and institute high-stakes testing at national, state, and local levels, researchers from all walks of life are reminding us that we have underestimated the productive nature of play. For instance, John Seely Brown, chief research scientist at Xerox Corporation (cited in Tapscott, 1998), argues that play enables the kind of free-form thinking needed in today's highly technical world. To his way of thinking, new information communication technologies are tapping into an inner source of creative power and opening up the kid in each of us.

Learning across the Curriculum with a Computer Adventure Game

Before taking a more detailed look at how one teacher of a mixed year 3/4 class introduced a computer adventure game into the school curriculum and taught a number of media literacy skills using content related to life in space as contrasted to life on earth, you may be interested to learn that even as kindergarteners, children's play with computer software can lead to some serious learning. For example, in Labbo's (1996) study of eighteen kindergarteners enrolled in a low-SES neighborhood school, she found patterns in their play with write and draw software that rivaled the kind of literacy learning typically associated with more traditional forms of early literacy instruction. Just as the adult in Labbo's study played an important behind-the-scene role in orchestrating the computer-based activity, so, too, did the adult (in this case the teacher) in the example that follows.

FIGURE 6.1   A Computer Adventure Game

In a small rural school the mixed Year 3/4 class has spent this half of the term investigating 'Space World', a computer adventure game in which each group of children plays the role of the crew of a spaceship which has landed on a new planet. Their various curriculum activities connected to this adventure have involved life on earth as well as life in space—for example, planning real investigations into how things grow on earth and the variety of creatures to be found in various habitats. The space focus has provided many opportunities for the children to use their imaginations to the full by paralleling in the space dimension the idea of habitats and related life forms, which has allowed them to invent monsters, plants, and small furry inhabitants for their new world. In both dimensions the children have had to grapple with many problems while thinking about themselves, their team members and fellow players. Pupils have been working in small similar ability groups, each group engaged in one of several activities related to Space World which span many dimensions such as aesthetic and creative, scientific and technological, linguistic, moral, social and personal learning. Looking around the classroom we can see three children following screen directions using a map they are building up of the imaginary planet, and another group using boxes, batteries, wires and assorted bits to build a robotic guard. Others seem to be developing a piece of impromptu drama. The teacher is talking to a group who are searching through information book indices checking out bog-loving plant species. (Cook & Finlayson, 1999, p. 25)

Note, for instance, how the teacher designed a cross-curricular range of activities that involved students in map making, model building, problem solving, role playing, drama, and conventional searches of informational print texts similar to those described in Chapter 3. At the same time, this teacher extended their learning by using interactive communication technology to generate interest in the content and to tap their creative energies (Figure 6.1).

However, is this "really" a content area reading activity you might ask. We believe it is. Although playing the computer adventure game *Space World* provided the class with numerous opportunities for fanciful flights of imagination, it was nonetheless a meaning making activity. By definition, reading is a meaning making process involving both print and nonprint texts in which children make text-to-self, text-to-world, and text-to-text connections (see also Chapter 2). It is a process that no one to our knowledge has labeled as belonging purely to the "serious" student (at least not yet). Of course, "serious" is one of those mischievous terms that can be challenged simply by asking the following question: serious in whose eyes and by what standards?

Reflecting

Have you ever had someone say to you, "Play with computers? Sure, that's okay, but children spend enough time doing that after school. When they're in class, they don't need to be playing on computers." How would you answer? Would you reply that computers provide children with opportunities to develop their own games, their own visuals, and so on? Would you also allude to the fact that so-called computer "games" can be relevant, meaningful, and challenging for learning and developing critical thinking and reasoning skills in the content areas?

Would your reply also include something about access to computers after school? Consider, for example, the very real possibility that not all students in your classroom will have equal access to computer technology and on-line Internet connections. This unequal access is sometimes referred to as the "digital divide." How might such a divide widen still further the gap in opportunities available to upper- and lower-income families? Although we recall reading several articles debunking the notion of a digital divide—the latest one arguing that the divide is spontaneously shrinking as computers have come down in price and more low-income families are buying them (Samuelson, 2002)—it is still the case that most such families cannot afford Internet access. How might this factor into your use of computers in your classroom?

Teaching Children Strategies for Reading and Evaluating Web Sources

This last section focuses on web literacy and the strategies students need to evaluate web sources for their credibility. Based on a comprehensive review of the research literature, Leu (2002) argues that teaching children to become web literate is every bit as important as teaching them to read printed texts. We agree fully and would add that it is doubly important when teaching in the content areas.

Web-Reading Strategies

Navigating the web requires strategies that are quite different from those involved in reading traditional texts. Consequently, you will want to prepare students in advance of giving them homework or research assignments that involve web searches. In a growing number of school districts, curriculum standards mandate that teachers help students become web literate. Although we've seen several lists of ideas for how teachers might accomplish this task, we believe that the one developed in Australia by Sutherland-Smith (2002) in collaboration with students from two grade 6 classes and their teachers is the most helpful and explicit in its recommendations. Although the list (Figure 6.2) is not exhaustive, it offers strategies that worked in Sutherland-Smith's study, which spanned a ten-week term and involved 48 ten to twelve year olds from multilingual backgrounds.

Strategies for Evaluating Web Sources

Teaching children to be effective and efficient users of web sources in content area classes is an important first step. However, if you expect them to read the messages embedded in those sources with a critical eye, you will need to go further. We suggest

FIGURE 6.2   Strategies for Teaching Web Reading

- *Use the "snatch-and-grab" reading technique.* The objective is to read Web pages superficially: that is, skim to identify a key word or phrase, surf the relevant links, bookmark sites, and compile a grab-bag of references. It is important to remind students, however, that once they've gathered a sufficient number of potentially helpful references, they will need to read the accompanying texts in a much more careful manner.

- *Focus on refining keyword searches.* Once students have identified a keyword or phrase (e.g., printing press), teach them how to narrow the scope of their search by refining the original keyword or phrase. For example, if they were interested in the history of the printing press, they might search under *history of* or *invention of the printing press*.

- *Provide clear search guidelines.* Providing students with clear statements of the purpose for a search, giving them an approximation of how many sites they should search, and offering tips on how to use the toolbar for efficient searches are a few of the ways you can prevent panic from setting in when you require them to do an online research assignment.

- *Use the "chunking technique."* This involves teaching students who have poor organizational skills to break a complex topic into smaller, more manageable bits of information. For example, if they were searching on the topic of *September 11*, they might brainstorm keywords and phrases related to that event, such as *terrorists, rescue workers, location of buildings*, and *clean-up*. By focusing on one chunk at a time, students are less likely to feel overwhelmed or waste time getting "lost" in cyberspace.

- *Develop teaching mechanisms to overcome frustration with technology.* Students can become frustrated when the topic they're searching on involves a good deal of moving back and forth between links. One mechanism for alleviating some of their frustration is to model how you would ignore certain links but click on others. Talking through your reasons for doing so and letting them predict which ones will be useful to you are ways of handling this problem.

- *Provide short-cut lists to sites or search engines.* Give students in advance a list of bookmarks to reliable sites (e.g., those least likely to have broken links). Or, prepare a simple step-by-step handout that explains how to use search engines, and then model the process one step at a time.

- *Evaluate nontextual features (images, graphics).* Visual elements can distract some readers, while others may think the visuals are merely "illustrations" of something in the written text. Teaching them to become what Leu (1997) describes as "healthy skeptics" of Web site information and modeling for them how you know certain kinds of drawings, photographs, and graphs can manipulate what you see are helpful evaluation techniques. (Sutherland-Smith, 2002, pp. 665–667)

you begin by showing them how the web influences, for example, what they buy, where they look for information, who they believe is an authority on a topic, and so on, but that is only half the story. The other half involves helping them develop an awareness of how the particular meanings they make of a website's message may depend, among other things, on who they are (e.g., child, preteen, male, female, African American, European American, Hispanic, Native American, Asian American) and the context (e.g., at home, in class, with a friend) in which they are reading (Luke, 1997). It is important that children begin to experience, even at a relatively young age, why a text does not mean the same thing to all people, and why it does not necessarily reflect the intentions of its author.

One way you can provide children with this experience is to show them that a website's message may seem more believable or "real" to some readers than to others. For example, a teacher who was in one of Donna's content area classes at the University of Georgia was disturbed when she found that a group of boys in her fifth-grade class were using websites sponsored by the Ku Klux Klan to find information for their social studies report on bigotry. When this teacher approached the boys about their choice in websites, she learned that they valued sites for their visual and sound effects over their content, per se. This prompted a discussion in which she and the boys talked about the need to consider the source of a website's content and how the use of certain content could lead to serious consequences.

Once youngsters appreciate the fact that not all websites are credible, at least not according to the criteria they use in judging credibility, you can move to another level of evaluating web sources—one that helps users limit their searches. For example, you might share this short list of extension domains:

.com	commercial site (something is being sold)
.edu	educational institution (a university or college site)
.gov	government agency or department (U.S. Department of Education)
.org	professional organization (American Library Association, Girl Scouts)

Knowing which site is likely to offer what kind of information can cut down a child's search time considerably. It can also cut down on "information overload" by signaling which sites are likely to be appropriate (or inappropriate) for any given search (Gardner, Benham, & Newell, 1999).

Finally, making judgments about how "real" or authentic a website's information is may take considerable skill and practice. In the elementary grades, youngsters are still formulating their own ideas about what makes a story authentic. To expect them to apply criteria for judging authenticity of a website's message is probably not practical. However, teaching children to compare sites for inconsistencies, errors, and useless data is a step in the right direction. Hobbs (2001), a noted authority on children's Internet use, recommends that teachers not hand out checklists for determining website quality and authenticity. For example, checklists with questions such as "Does this page take a long time to load?" "Is the spelling correct?" and "Does the information appear biased?" give a false sense of security. According to Hobbs, such lists have "the disadvantage of being highly reductionist, transforming the complex process of making judgments about quality, relevance, authority, and authenticity into a series of yes-or-no questions about the format and structure of Web pages." However, at the present time such lists often comprise most of what is available for teachers' use.

Try It! An Opportunity to Develop Your Own Assessment

Develop a custom-made assessment with your students. Invite them to contribute ideas about what makes a website "real" and useful to them. Ask them to describe briefly what attracts them to a particular website. Then, using that website as a visual, call attention to the features that suggest it gives reliable information, that it is not overly biased, and so on.

Reconsidering

We began this chapter by recalling how quickly the Internet has worked its way to the top of some children's preferences in media. Our definition of media literacy and its relation to reading visual images suggests a broadening of what counts as reading and writing in the content areas. You might think from that definition and from the importance we attach both to web reading and to playing to learn using various media resources that we believe a change in how students learn in the content areas is imminent. You would be correct if you inferred as much. However, we also believe that teachers will have a big say in just how imminent this change may be, and that's why we want to hear from you. How do you interpret the situation? What would you have us reconsider if we were to rewrite this chapter? E-mail your responses to Donna (dalverma@uga.edu), Jeanne (js331@colled.msstate.edu), or Kristiina (kmontero@coe.uga.edu).

PART THREE

Learner Differences

7 Diversity in Content, Language, and Children

In Chapter 7, you will have several opportunities to explore the importance of attending to diversity in content, language, and children, especially as it relates to selecting content for teaching and learning in multilingual/multicultural classrooms, building community in these classrooms, and giving students choices in how they use reading and writing to learn content. As was true for the preceding chapters, this one draws on children's multiple literacies and interests in learning with texts of various kinds (print, nonprint, and digital). It also speaks in practical ways about opportunities for giving students choices within standards-based instruction that makes use of project-based content literacy and learning activities.

What do a repeating star pattern on a woven mat, the game of tic-tac-toe, a counting system based on parts of the body, and a knotted cord used for record-keeping have in common? The answer is that they are all examples of ethnomathematics, and they can all be used as classroom activities to help students appreciate mathematics in their own cultures and in cultures worldwide. (Lane, 2002, p. 22)

Web Tip for More Information on Ethnomathematics

If you are intrigued by the possibility of teaching math concepts such as counting, measuring, and calculating in a way that uses your students' lives and experiences as a starting point, then check out the following websites: http://www.rpi.edu/~eglash/isgem.dir/links.htm and http://www.ethnomath.org/. These sites provide links to other sites that will give you ideas for teaching from the premise that mathematical concepts develop in response to a culture's everyday activities. For example, you will find sites listed by ethnicity/geography, such as African mathematics, African American mathematics, Native American mathematics, math in European artifacts, Latino mathematics, Middle Eastern mathematics, Pacific Islander mathematics, and Asian mathematics. Sites are also listed by social categories, such as mathematics and gender, mathematics and economic class, and multicultural mathematics.

Remembering

Try to remember how you learned math in elementary school. Did any of your teachers take into account the diversity represented in your class? Perhaps you or some of your classmates spoke a language other than English as a first language, or maybe everyone spoke English but in a variety of dialects. Were there different ethnicities and social classes represented in your elementary school? Did you know that "research has shown that when mathematics is taught solely from a western European perspective, it often makes no sense to ethnically diverse children?" (Lane, 2002, p. 22).

An educational organization called Pacific Resources for Education and Learning (PREL) is using this finding (and others like it) to develop materials that help teachers understand why math—if it is to be taught meaningfully—must be embedded in children's cultural understandings. Similar materials are being developed for other content areas. For example, a book titled *Village Science* by Alan Dick and published by The Alaska Native Knowledge Network (http://www.ankn.uaf.edu/VS/index.html) is in its second edition—the first edition having worked its way across Alaska and parts of Canada for over fifteen years.

This chapter considers more than simply diversity in the content and form of the materials that elementary school children read and write. Because today's classrooms are places where languages vary widely, as do the children who speak them, it is important to take into account how such variation influences teachers' instructional decisions. In particular, we focus on content, community, and choice—the three C's for motivating content area literacy and learning (Kohn, 1993). The first section is on selecting content for teaching and learning in multilingual/multicultural classrooms; the second is on building community in these classrooms; and the third is on giving students choices in how they use reading and writing to learn content.

Selecting Content for Multilingual/Multicultural Students

Unless students find the content of your curriculum interesting, relevant, and worth knowing, they are not likely to engage with it, at least not in substantive and meaningful ways. This is not surprising, of course, but finding ways to match students' interests with your curriculum and available resources is no small task. Equally challenging is the task of keeping state-mandated standards and accountability measures in mind while simultaneously looking for ways to motivate all students to learn in a particular content area. What we propose here is not necessarily an easy solution to accomplishing these tasks, but it is, we believe, workable and within the guidelines of current thinking and research on teaching and learning in multilingual/multicultural classrooms (Delpit, 1995; Echevarria, Vogt, & Short, 2000; Strickland, 1994).

Genre, Content, and Visual Features

The use of trade books to enhance content area learning is a well-known way of matching students' interests with teachers' curricular goals. However, before using such books in the classroom, it is advisable to evaluate them on several levels. For example, according to Donovan and Smolkin's (2002) analysis of the different aspects of stories and informational books that can enhance science learning, there are three major categories deemed important in the selection of these texts: genre, content, and visual features.

Genre can refer to the type of text (e.g., a fictional storybook, an informational storybook, or an informational book). As a specialized term used by linguists, genre can also refer to the distinguishing linguistic features that constitute a particular text's structure and that make it suitable for a particular purpose. An informational science trade book, for example, is put together in such a way that the language conveys an authoritative stance on the content it presents. This would be in direct contrast to a poem, say, in which the playful use of language is meant to convey alternative (not authoritative) stances.

Other linguistic features that convey an authoritative stance include the author's choice of verb tense, vocabulary, syntax (or word order), and sequencing of events. Consider, for example, the excerpt in Figure 7.1, which is reproduced from a page in a science information book titled *Never Kiss an Alligator!* (Bare, 1989). What features do you recognize in this excerpt that give it its authoritative stance?

Did you notice, for example, that the author's language sounds authoritative? The alligator is defined as being ancient and living in the age of the dinosaurs, which is also defined as being "about two hundred million years ago." Did you also notice how the author further defined the alligator by tracing its name to the Spanish word for lizard (el lagarto), an animal that the alligator is said to resemble? Providing good

FIGURE 7.1   Sample of Authoritative Language from *Never Kiss an Alligator!* (Bare, 1989)

"Alligators are ancient, and lived when the dinosaurs lived about two hundred million years ago. The name alligator is from a Spanish word 'el lagarto,' which means 'the lizard.' Lizards do look like miniature alligators." (not paged)

definitions, then, is one way that authors can use language to make what they say sound authoritative.

Try It! Writing Authoritatively

Choose an animal that is of interest to you and write a scientific description of it. Try to use language in a way that conveys an authoritative sense but that differs from a definition (see Figure 7.1). For example, if you choose to write about a German shepherd, you might include information about your experiences as a show-ring judge to convince your readers that you are an authority on the standards that define the breed. You may also want to illustrate what you describe. Then share what you wrote in a small group discussion. Were others convinced that you wrote authoritatively? How do you know?

A second factor to consider when you select trade books to enhance science learning (or learning in other subject matter areas as well) is how accurate is the text's content. Unfortunately, as Donovan and Smolkin (2002) point out, "many books suggested for science instruction deliver incorrect information" (p. 508). They suggest checking out an author's background to determine if he or she has the requisite knowledge for writing on a particular topic, and if not, whether a content specialist checked the book for accuracy.

A Web Tip for Determining the Accuracy of Texts

At http://www.appraisal.neu.edu you can read reviews of books by librarians and scientists who evaluate the accuracy of selected texts. The appraisals contain reviews of individual books, series, science activities and experiments, reference books, photographic essays, picture books, science biographies, and educational software.

Checking for the accuracy of content also involves verifying that the author of a trade book demonstrates an awareness of the need to convey a sense of "oneness" with the culture and language in which he or she writes. For example, trade books bearing the seal of the Coretta Scott King Award, such as *The Skin I'm In* (Flake, 1998), provide an assurance that the text is free from verbal and visual images that may negatively affect the self-esteem of African American children (Joshua, 2002).

In instances where no such seals of approval are evident on a book's cover, you may want to consult one or more external review sources. For example, in the science informational storybook *An Algonquian Year: The Year According to the Full Moon*, author Michael McCurdy writes about the Native American custom of assigning descriptive names to each month's full moon. In checking on McCurdy's credibility as an author of Native American customs, we found positive reviews in three of the leading review journals: *Publisher's Weekly*, *Children's Literature*, and *School Library Journal*. In the latter journal, we also learned that this book, which is intended for children in grades 2–5, has some limitations:

> Unfortunately, the use of present tense throughout the narrative dilutes the historical focus and becomes confusing when phrases like "the game we now call lacrosse" or "what will someday be called New Brunswick" accompany descriptions of events and activities. Similarly, McCurdy's map of the tribes provides only subtle outlines of the current northeastern states, but the presence of contemporary geographic names in the text suggests that the pre-contact Algonquians used terms like "New England" and "Massachusetts." Despite its shortcomings, this is a beautiful book that would be best used in a classroom or with adult intervention (http://search.barnesandnoble.com/booksearch/isbnInquiry.asp?isbn=0618007059#reviews).

Web Tip on Literacy in Multicultural Settings

At http://www.readingonline.org/articles/ward.html, you can read Canadian author Angela Ward's commentary on her attempts at understanding the complexity of shifting from a mono-cultural to a multicultural view of literacy. In *Literacy in Multicultural Settings: Whose Culture Are We Discussing?*, Ward elaborates on the view that one's knowledge of several languages and cultures is a distinguishing mark of the educated person. Compare and contrast this view to your own thinking about English language learners whom you've known and/or taught.

Finally, a third category worth considering when you select trade books for use in content area instruction is the accuracy of their visual features. Research on this topic strongly suggests that pictures and photographs that illustrate a text's content can lead to improved comprehension, whereas visuals that serve merely to embellish the attractiveness of a book (and are unrelated to a text's content) can actually distract from learning. In light of this finding, Donovan and Smolkin (2002) recommend that in examining the illustrations of trade books (e.g., the drawings, paintings, photographs, maps, graphs, and charts), it is important to ask yourself these key questions:

- What is the relationship of the illustration to the textual content?
- Does it reinforce or elaborate upon the information in the text or does it simply serve as an embellishment unrelated to the information?

- Are there easy-to-read captions for the pictures and labels for diagrams?
- Do these captions help direct readers' attention to relevant elements, and prevent information from being overlooked? (p. 510)

Pulling It All Together: A Kindergarten Classroom Example

In the example that follows, your task is to look for the ways a kindergarten teacher demonstrates her awareness of the need to consider genre, content, and visual features in selecting trade books to use with her class. The example comes from a study in which Donald Richgels, a literacy teacher educator at Northern Illinois University, was a participant and an observer in Mrs. Poremba's kindergarten class for 164 school days. As a participant observer, he was interested in learning how the ten boys and eleven girls in her class engaged with informational texts to learn about dinosaurs and to explore the workings of written language. As you read the following excerpt from Richgel's (2002) study, try to imagine yourself in his role as an observer in Mrs. Poremba's classroom.

In mid-February Mrs. Poremba's class began studying dinosaurs. The block corner became the dinosaur corner. The children brought to school toy dinosaurs of every description and size. These perched on counter tops, windowsills, and shelves. In the reading center was a dinosaur library stocked with books children had brought from home and the school library. They included picture books, informational books, storybooks, and reference books about dinosaurs. Taped to the chalkboard was a dinosaur poster with a line drawing of a brontosaurus and the title, "What we know about dinosaurs!" The brontosaurus outline was filled with quotations from a discussion of what the class already knew about dinosaurs at the beginning of the unit. It was the kindergartners' first and most prominently displayed informational text about their new unit topic.

After the discussion that produced the dinosaur poster, Mrs. Poremba read to the class the informational book, *Story of Dinosaurs* (Eastman, 1989). This reading is an example of using more than one informational text (the student composed poster and the book) and of reading for a purpose especially suited to an informational text (to verify students' ideas). . . . Reading *Story of Dinosaurs* also encouraged the kindergartners to find complementary information to a second informational book, *Dinosaurs, an A to Z Guide* (Benton, 1988). When the students were uncertain about the name of a turtle-like dinosaur in one of the illustrations in *Story of Dinosaurs*, Mrs. Poremba asked, "What could we do to find out?"

Jason and Freddy provided an answer. They consulted *Dinosaurs, an A to Z Guide*, which Jason had loaned to the classroom library. They took this illustrated dinosaur encyclopedia to a table away from the group, found a picture of the same dinosaur, and returned to Mrs. Poremba, who read its name, *ankylosaurus*, to them. Then they reported their finding to the whole class. Jason and Freddy and their book served as valuable resources whenever *Story of Dinosaurs* raised further questions. . . .

Three school days later, Mrs. Poremba read to the class *Dinosaurs Dancing* (Connelly, n.d.), a big-book version of a dinosaur storybook. They would read the big book and smaller personal copies many times over the next several days. Mrs. Poremba's first reading provided an enjoyable experience with a new book and helped the class learn unfamiliar vocabulary and distinguish fact from fiction.

Mrs. Poremba began, "I'd like to read to you a different kind of a dinosaur story. And there are some words that I want you to be thinking about that you'll hear me use in the story as I read. These are words that you don't hear often, so I thought I'd write them down. I want you to look. . . ." Mrs. Poremba clipped to an easel a card with the words *morning dew* and a drawing of blades of grass with drops of water clinging to them. (Richgels, 2002, pp. 589–590)

Reflecting

As we leave the kindergartners and their study of dinosaurs, we wonder if you have any questions about what you observed. For example, do you agree with the way Mrs. Poremba delayed the start of *Dinosaurs Dancing* by introducing vocabulary that she wanted students to listen for in the story? Why might it have been preferable to read the storybook first just for the pleasure that students would get from it and then do word study prior to the second reading? What might students have learned about dinosaurs if they had tapped into the Internet rather than rely solely on conventional text forms? Is it even feasible to think of kindergarteners surfing the web for information on dinosaurs? What evidence do you have in support of your answer?

Building Community in the Classroom

The goal of establishing safe and caring environments is without a doubt one of the most compelling reasons for building community in the classroom. It is also one of the best motivators we know of for nurturing a community of learners in which children of diverse cultural and linguistic backgrounds, socioeconomic means, and ability levels can grow in their literate practices and content knowledge. Although all of this sounds fine in theory, what are some concrete ways for making it happen? One way is to draw from the existing research on culturally responsive instruction. The implications of this research are many, including the family photography project and the classroom story telling project, both of which are presented later. But first, what characterizes instruction that is culturally responsive?

Culturally Responsive Instruction

In the past, a deficit model of home–school relations assumed inappropriately that schools need to exert a good deal of influence on some parents' (typically those in the low-income brackets) literate interactions with their children in order to "compensate" for perceived inadequacies in the home. This manner of thinking has largely given way to one of mutual understanding and respect in which school literacy practices are adjusted to meet the needs of families, who in turn are encouraged to acquaint themselves with the kinds of literacy that schools support (Cairney, 2000). Accompanying this change in focus are several well-known intergenerational literacy programs that have implications for culturally responsive teaching.

For example, several carefully documented studies known collectively as the "cultural funds of knowledge project" (Moll, 1991) have demonstrated that Latina/o students are motivated to engage in school literacy tasks when the gap between school and home environments is bridged. Teachers in this project, who doubled as researchers, visited the working-class homes of their students' families for the purpose of tapping into certain cultural and linguistic resources that they could use in making classroom literacy instruction more relevant. These visits resulted in the teacher–researchers documenting the falseness of claims about working-class, language minority homes providing little in the way of background knowledge and experiences that are useful for literacy development in a second language. The teachers who participated in the project noted positive shifts in their students' attitudes toward school literacy and learning as they worked to revamp their instruction to make it more culturally responsive.

As shown in the cultural funds of knowledge project, teachers need not be "insiders" in a particular culture to engage in culturally responsive instruction. They can learn about another culture, respect its values, and view differences in their students' literacy practices as strengths, not deficits. Also, culturally responsive instruction need not match home and school literacies in grid-like precision in order for teachers to develop a heightened sensitivity of the need to connect *patterns* of participation and home literacy with the regular curriculum (Ladson-Billings, 1994).

Best of all, this attention to culturally responsive instruction means that students may no longer have to endure what Rosalinda Barrera, a researcher at the University of Illinois, Urbana Champaign, refers to as "culturalectomies"—her term for describing ill-conceived attempts by schools to excise all cultural differences among children of her generation who grew up under a deficit model of language and literacy instruction (Jimenez, Moll, Rodriguez-Brown, & Barrera, 1999, p. 217). In fact, in our observations in schools and in our interactions with classroom teachers, we are seeing more and more opportunities for students to introduce elements of their home literacies into classroom language arts activities. For example, in Figure 7.2, consider how Anthony, a second grader with an insider's knowledge about certain word meanings, is given an opportunity to share that knowledge with his peers and his teacher.

FIGURE 7.2   Planning for Learning That Values Privileged and Underprivileged Language Practices

The second graders gather in the rug area to share haikus written the day before. As students read their haikus, listeners think of questions or comments they would like to make regarding the patterned poem. When Chanae and Ture finish their poem, they call on the teacher who asks, "What does the word *dope* in your haiku mean?" Anthony responds for the authors, saying, "*Dope* means waterfalls are cool!" While it is not clear to the teacher that *dope* and *cool* are synonyms in hip-hop language, most of these second graders are aware of this word's current meaning. (Franquiz & de la Luz Reyes, 2000, p. 7)

Web Tip: Who Gets to Tell the Story of a People?

Visiting Joseph Bruchac's home page at http://www.josephbruchac.com/ will give you a number of insights into the importance of hearing about the Abenaki culture from an insider's perspective. As a professional teller of the traditional tales of the Adirondacks and the Native peoples of the Northeastern Woodlands, Joe Bruchac weaves language and traditional Abenaki skills into his stories. On Bruchac's home page you will also find information on how to schedule a school performance by him that features traditional and contemporary Abenaki music with the Dawnland Singers.

Family Photography Project

Culturally responsive instruction opens up opportunities for English language learners to acquire content knowledge by connecting home and school literacy practices. The importance of building on students' home language and culture has been documented repeatedly in the literature. For instance, the family photography project (Spielman, 2001) demonstrated the value of involving families and teachers in ways that made both parties more aware of how children's home experiences can become part of their content literacy learning. Here, in Jane Spielman's words, we have an overview of this project:

> In November . . . eight adults, two children, and one infant joined [two colleagues] and me. We met in a very small family room with three windows facing the inside concrete yard of the 100-year-old school, which was surrounded by scaffolding for renovations. The room had a very narrow table and a chalkboard for English lessons as well as left-over Halloween decorations.
>
> There were nine participant families, six from the Dominican Republic, one from Venezuela, one from Ecuador, and one from Argentina. The school is located on the upper west side of Manhattan. In the 1997–1998 school year, it had 665 students: 77.9% Dominican, 2.5% Mexican and Central American, 1.3% from other Latin American nations, 14% African American, 3.1% Asian, and 1.2% Anglo American or eastern European. All the participants were working class or poor, either unemployed or working part time. On a questionnaire, participants said they had lived in the United States from 3 to 21 years. They all lived within a mile of the school.
>
> At the first session, we introduced the project with the statement that "Schools need to hear what learning goes on in your homes so that teachers can build on that learning. We will be using cameras so you can show all the ways that your culture, your family, and your community are teachers for your children." We also shared our belief that children can acquire school literacies when their home literacies are recognized and developed in their classrooms. I then asked participants to introduce themselves to the group by talking about something that they remember having learned as children outside of school that is still important to them. (Spielman, 2001, pp. 763–764)

In the second session, the parents brought artifacts and shared with the group the ways in which those artifacts were linked to family stories about learning in their homes. For example, they brought items such as "a family *maté* (a kind of Latin American tea) cup, photos, and a pocket-sized Spanish–English dictionary" (Spielman, 2001, p. 764). Because most members of the group had had only minimal experience using cameras, Spielman planned a photowalk through the school neighborhood to acquaint them with the 35-mm automatic focus cameras.

Then, from January to May, the parents worked on the following photography assignments, with the general advice being: "Think about and watch when your children are learning at home:"

- Moments when your child is learning.
- Environments you create for your child to learn.
- Routines of your household ("A Day in the Life of Your Family").
- Learning in your community, outside your home.
- Values you are teaching your children. (Spielman, 2001, p. 765).

For a summary of the rest of the project, see Table 7.1.

TABLE 7.1   The Family Photography Project

Activities	Outcome 1	Outcome 2	Outcome 3	Outcome 4
Editing conversations	Each participant selected five photographs that best expressed what he or she was trying to communicate for a particular assignment	Each participant described to the group why he or she chose those five photos	Based on feedback from the group-sharing activity, each participant chose two photographs that best captured learning in his or her home	Spielman distributed a list of topics that participants had represented in their photographs along with an album in which they could organize the photos. Participants were encouraged to go beyond the list and include themes that they generated on their own
Distilling generative themes	Spielman meshed the participants' themes into seven categories that represented ways parents teach their children at home:			

TABLE 7.1   (Continued)

Activities	Outcome 1	Outcome 2	Outcome 3	Outcome 4
	(1) family, friendship, and love; (2) growing up to become independent; (3) culture (religion, ritual, and play); (4) literacy; (5) technology; (6) responsibility; and (7) learning outside the home			
Following through to partnership with teachers	Each teacher built a plan for incorporating what he or she learned from the photographs and conversations with the parents. For example, a second-grade teacher followed through on a girl's desire to read fiction and nonfiction books on the cycles of butterflies and to write about what she learned	Each teacher read current research on home–school partnerships	Each teacher kept a weekly journal that detailed the difficult issues entailed in building classroom learning communities based on relationships with the children's families	
Presenting photos as resources to inform teachers' instruction	Each participant presented his or her photo album as a teacher resource	Presentations were made to teachers in the school, to local graduate seminars, to an early childhood conference, and to a regional language arts conference		

Adapted from Spielman (2001).

Classroom Storytelling Project

In writing about her school's storytelling project, which makes use of the language experience approach as a way of building a community of learners, Dolores Bustamante, a fourth-grade teacher at River Oaks Elementary School in Houston, Texas, noted the following background information on the project:

> Our story begins with Vygotsky (1978), who reminded us that success with literacy is not just about skills and ability. Learning to read and write is a social task learned through relationships. Frank Smith (1988) brought Vygotsky a little closer to home by reasserting the role that social interaction plays in childhood development. Moreover, Smith encourages teachers to look at students and ask, "What's going on?" "What is the student doing to make connections for himself and others?" Smith asserts that teachers should read and write with children, modeling the behaviors of readers and writers. . . .
>
> Vivian Paley tells us that from children's stories come the myths of the classroom. As we've learned to work with children . . . we have learned to celebrate not only their stories, but also what we learn about the children *through* their stories. Children learn that their own voices are worth something and that we value what they have to say. Stories are listened to with affection and respect, and they bring the children together naturally, as their playing does. We watch this, we listen, and we learn. It is true, as Ms. Paley (1990) asserts, "the culture of a classroom can be discovered by listening to and exploring their stories." (Bustamante, 2002, pp. 2, 4)

Figure 7.3 lists the steps involved in helping children tell their stories.

Try It!

Ask your instructor to set aside a few minutes at the beginning of each class for a read aloud from Vivian Paley's (1997) *The Girl with the Brown Crayon*. As you listen to one of your classmates read from this book, think of the ways in which it connects to the English Language Arts Standard #9 on diversity. How does Paley's ability to get inside the inquiring minds of her kindergarteners help you think of ways to teach your own students about the need to respect diversity in terms of language use, ethnicity, gender, and an individual's identity in the classroom community?

Reflecting

Think back on the *family photography project* and the *classroom storytelling project*. How would you adapt those projects so that the focus is on learning content in social studies, science, health, or math, for example? What problems might arise in projects aimed at developing culturally responsive instruction? How would you handle them?

Figure 7.3 *Helping Children Tell Their Stories* (Based on recommendations made by Bustamante, 2002)

1. When children are in the storytelling area of your classroom, ask individuals if they have a story to tell. If so, write each child's name, date, and "First Story" at the top of a sheet of paper or on a laptop, and ask, "How does your story begin?"

2. If children ask if the story has to be true or made up, tell them it doesn't matter.

3. Record each story verbatim, stopping occasionally to clarify through prompts such as "And then what happened?" or "Do you mean the boy gotted or the boy got?" Usually children will choose the better of the two grammatical constructions, but if not, record the story exactly as they tell it.

4. When the story fills nearly a page, ask "How will you end your story?"

5. Once the story is completed, ask the child for a title.

6. Before reading the story back to the child, say "Let me know if you want me to change anything."

7. Move the storytelling project to the performance level by requesting that the child select a character (or an inanimate object) to role play. Assign other roles to other members of the class (or let the child do the assigning).

8. Give a copy of the story and the cast list to the storyteller.

9. Before children perform their stories, read aloud each child's story to familiarize the class with the storyline and to give actors a chance to think about how they will play their parts.

10. As the actors move to the "wings," read the story once again, going slowly enough to allow the actors to move to the "stage" as their parts come up.

Also allow time for children to ad lib dialogue.

Giving Students Choices in How They Use Reading and Writing to Learn Content

Proponents of choice typically favor classrooms in which content area learning is fostered through intrinsic rather than extrinsic rewards. It's a practical approach to take as well, for as Kohn (1993) aptly puts it,

> The irrefutable fact is that students always have a choice about whether they will learn. We may be able to force them to complete an assignment, but we can't compel them to learn effectively or to care about what they are doing. (p. 12)

Although the idea of giving students choices in how they use reading and writing to learn content is not new, the current emphasis on high-stakes testing, state-mandated standards, and "programs over people" (Wackerly & Young, 2002, p. 17) can make it difficult at times for teachers to follow through on what they know is good practice. In recognizing this possibility, we offer an example of an activity from the National Museum of American History and the Smithsonian Institution that gives students choices on how they meet both Standard #7 of the English Language Arts Standards and Standard #1 of the content standards approved by the National Council for the Social Studies (see the following box on standards). The name of the activity is "You Be the Historian" (Paisley-Jones et al., 2000).

Meeting the Standard for Student Research

Standard #7 of the English Language Arts Standards states: "Students conduct research on issues and interests by generating ideas and questions, and by posing problems. They gather, evaluate, and synthesize data from a variety of sources (e.g., print and nonprint texts, artifacts, people) to communicate their discoveries in ways that suit their purpose and audience" (http://www.reading.org/advocacy/elastandards/standards.html). The National Council for the Social Studies has a similar standard that applies to student research. It states that teachers should "use a variety of instructional materials such as physical examples, photographs, maps, illustrations, films, videos, textbooks, literary selections, and computerized databases" (http://www.ncss.org/standards/toc.html).

You Be the Historian Activity

This five-part activity is available online at http://www.si.edu/harcourt/nmah/history/00intro.htm. In part one, students are introduced to the purpose of the activity: "See if you can figure out what life was like 200 years ago for Thomas and Elizabeth Springer's family in New Castle, Delaware. At the same time discover what historians in the next century could learn about you if they found your house exactly the way it is today."

In part two, titled "Here is Your Evidence," they examine eight clues, each of which can be clicked on, and each of which gives hints as to the correct answer *before* a child resorts to a pull-down menu under each clue to find the answer. For example, Clue #1 consists of this question: "What are these objects?" (in reference to a Betty lamp and a candle mold). Two hints are given: "This is not a cooking tool" (the Betty lamp, which looks like a common soup ladle in the illustration) and "This used oil or grease" (the candle mold, which looks like a beverage stand of some sort). The question in large block letters under these two illustrations reads: "What do these tell us about life for the Springer family?" Students are given a choice as to whether they make educated guesses or use the pull-down menus to discover the correct answer. The answer also includes a definition of each of the objects.

In part three of the activity, students see a reproduction of a painting titled "Wethersfield Girls Weeding Onions, 1780" (courtesy of the Wethersfield Historical Society in Wethersfield, CT) and the following explanation of how the Springer family used the two items that were illustrated in Clue #1: "The Springers used betty lamps and candles for light, but these were not very bright sources of light. Their daily life was strongly affected by cycles of day and night because most of the work had to be done during the daylight." (This last sentence refers to the reproduction of the Wethersfield painting.)

In part four, students use a pull-down menu labeled "What about you?" and then respond to these two questions: "How does the availability of electric light affect your daily life?" and "What evidence of electricity would future historians find in your home?"

After answering these two questions, students have the choice of looking at more clues (in any order) prior to concluding their investigation. The remaining six clues have to do with spinning wool into cloth, obtaining medical information, harvesting crops, schooling, a list of the Springer family's worldly possessions, a tax sheet, and a last will and testament.

In part five, they conclude their investigation of the Springer family by answering the following questions:

1. What kinds of information did you learn from the objects and documents?
2. How is this information different?
3. What other sources of information might have helped you know more about daily life for the Springers?
4. What sources do we have today that did not exist in the 1700s?

Students are given a choice: they can either answer the questions for themselves or read an elaborated informational text about the Springer family. This elaborated text includes three additional illustrations reproduced from various museum collections to support the print information. Finally, students are asked to compare their conclusions about the Springer family with those made by historians (in the elaborated text).

An accompanying activity screen titled "For Teachers: Using This Activity in the Classroom" suggests that the activity can be "an excellent springboard for class discussion about primary and secondary sources and the historical process." It also suggests that inviting students to write in response to the "What about you?" sections of the activity encourages them to think about the study of history at a personal level. Similarly, the question "What can future historians learn about you, your school, your class, and so on?" invites students to reflect on the evidence they are leaving behind. (Donna, Jeanne, and Kristiina can imagine the myriad questions students might generate about conserving resources, recycling, and other ways their generation might see themselves being committed to preserving the environment. These student-generated questions are the grist of inquiry-based learning discussed in Chapter 12.) Finally, the teacher's guide suggests five related activities that students can complete on the Internet, plus two alternative activities for students who do not have Internet access.

What About the Less Proficient Readers in My Class?

Was this question running through your mind as you read the description of the "You Be the Historian" activity? If so, you aren't the first (nor will you be the last) to worry about those who struggle to read content-related materials, either on-line or off-line. In fact, full-length articles have been written addressing just this sort of question.

Consider, for example, the following excerpt from Anne Guillaume's (1998) article on learning with text in the primary grades: In her words, "Content area reading is not the sole territory of those who are already proficient readers. Teachers of children of all ages have the important job of helping learners interact with text to produce meaning" (p. 476). Guillaume makes the case that learning to read and reading to learn are not separate processes.

Indeed, as noted in Chapter 1, separating the act of reading from one of its functions—reading to learn *something*—makes no sense. Yet hardly a year goes by but what we (Donna, Jeanne, and Kristiina) can recall running across some reference to the outdated notion that children must first learn to read (supposedly in narrative or story-like materials) before they can be expected to read to learn from expository texts. Although it has no basis in current research, this notion lives on largely because so much emphasis is placed on the mechanics of learning to read narratives in the primary grades, despite the fact that even a cursory overview of the research literature on emergent and early reading (Baghban, 1984; Bissex, 1980; Richgels, 2002) shows that children as young as preschoolers and kindergarteners do in fact possess knowledge about (and interest in) the different forms that written language can take (e.g., nonfiction, fiction, poetry, and plays).

Putting a Face to the Label "At-Risk" or Struggling Reader

Paddy Lynch, a third-grade teacher in Hendersonville, North Carolina, looks for ways to avoid limiting so-called "at-risk" readers' opportunities to demonstrate their potential in content area learning. She writes:

> It is so easy to lump students together under a label like "at-risk." I wanted to resist the temptation to refer to my children as a collective 'they,' so in order to learn something about each of them, I created surveys to find out how the children perceived themselves as learners. . . . (Lynch, 2001, p. 18)

From information obtained through the survey, Lynch was able to see her so-called "struggling readers" as individuals with quite diverse talents and interests. She also learned a considerable amount of new information about her students' out-of-school literacy practices and their interests—information that she promptly connected to in-school experiences with content from her classroom science curriculum.

Web Tip on How to Avoid Limiting Struggling Readers' Opportunities to Learn Content

To find out how Paddy Lynch linked her knowledge of students' out-of-school literacy practices and interests with the school's curriculum, read "Salting the Oats: Using Inquiry-Based Science to Engage Learners at Risk," available at http://www.ncte.org. Click on journals, Primary Voices, August 2001, find Lynch's article, and click on full text.

Reconsidering

In terms of your own experience, do learning to read and reading to learn seem like separate processes or do the two seem like one—embedded in each other? Picture young children you may have observed who are learning to read. Are they separating the act of reading from reading to learn *something*? How do you know? How might a teacher influence this process? How might differences in children's background knowledge in a particular content area influence the process? For example, at the start of this chapter, we included information on ethnomathematics. What, if any, connections do you see between the cultural practices associated with particular content areas and giving children choices in how they use reading and writing to learn content?

CHAPTER

8 Readers and Writers Who Struggle with Content Area Learning

Chapter 8 focuses on readers and writers who struggle to learn in their content area classes. It is a topic that is of great concern to all teachers, no matter what their level of expertise or the number of years in the profession. This chapter is certain to interest you if you have ever asked yourself the question, "What causes some children to struggle with content literacy-related tasks more than others?" Here you will discover that there are three common approaches to teaching struggling readers. Although it might be argued that no one approach is better than another for all students, all three have distinctive features that vary in their responsiveness to children's developmental, cultural, and linguistic needs. Strategies for addressing these various needs and a discussion of the instructional modifications necessary for teaching children who struggle with reading and writing in the content areas are also included.

"My spelling is Wobbly. It's good spelling, but it Wobbles, and the letters get in the wrong places," Winnie the Pooh observes in A.A. Milne's classic story for children of all ages (http://www.geocities.com/EnchantedForest/Dell/4500/quo_pooh.htm).

Remembering

Does Pooh's observation remind you of children you've known who struggle to read and write? Can you recall children whose experiences with reading and spelling were similar to those of Pooh? Perhaps they were family members, friends, or children you taught. What do you remember about the way they read? For example, did they process texts fluently (with speed, accuracy, and appropriate expression) or was their reading slow and labored, perhaps marked by numerous stops and starts, so many in fact that their comprehension suffered? Was their spelling affected, too? Did their struggle to read contribute to difficulties in learning content?

This chapter explores factors that cause some children to struggle more (and longer) than others when reading in the content areas. We also consider three common approaches to teaching struggling readers and the degree to which these approaches are responsive to the children's developmental, cultural, and linguistic needs. Finally, we offer examples of instructional modifications to use with readers who struggle to learn in the content areas.

Factors Behind the Struggle

The *struggling reader* label is a contested term and one that means different things to different people. It is sometimes used to refer to children with clinically diagnosed reading disabilities, as well as to those who are English language learners (ELLs). The label is also used more broadly to include readers who are deemed "at risk," underachieving, unmotivated, disenchanted, or generally unsuccessful in school literacy tasks. As such, it tells little that is specific to a particular reader's instructional needs and much about the perceived "need" to categorize readers who struggle as belonging to a group of children who are achieving below their "full potential." Because the practice of labeling children is so firmly entrenched in schools today, our objective here is not to argue against it but rather to explore the complexity of what it means to be a reader who struggles in the content areas.

Who Struggles to Read and When?

Do all readers struggle? At some point? With certain texts? In different situations? The answer to all of these questions is yes. It would be rare, indeed, to meet anyone (child or adult) who has never met a print or nonprint text that did not prove too challenging a read, at least initially. What distinguishes that kind of reader from the reader who struggles daily to make sense of content area texts is a whole set of assumptions underlying how the latter came to be viewed as struggling, at least as portrayed in the research literature.

This literature covers a broad spectrum and varies in specificity according to the perceived reasons behind the struggle. For instance, reviews of research focusing on children with clinically diagnosed reading disabilities tend to view the struggle as having a cognitive or neurological basis (Shaywitz et al., 2000), whereas reviews of research on second language reading tend to focus on the social, cultural, motivational, and linguistic factors that may vary according to the population of English language learners being studied (Bernhardt, 2000; Garcia, 2000).

Another assumption underlying the struggling reader label is that school literacy is difficult to acquire and thus it is best learned in classrooms. This assumption works to reward children whose competencies in reading and writing measure up to certain school and district-wide standards. However, as McDermott and Varenne (1995) have argued,

- The more people believe that literacy is difficult to acquire, the more they find reasons to explain why some read better than others and, correspondingly, why some do better than others in the economic and political measures of the society; and
- the more people believe that literacy is best learned in classrooms, the more they ignore other sources of literacy. (p. 341)

Whether or not you agree with McDermott and Varenne's speculation, do you see why children who struggle to read in a society that insists on treating school literacy as something that is hard to acquire (and thus potentially beyond their reach) will indeed find it difficult to think of themselves as competent readers? Also, do you see why it may not work to a struggling reader's best interests when school literacy is valued over other forms of literacy? For example, picture a third-grade child who has recently immigrated to the United States and is learning English. Let's say this child struggles with reading in school but is the most competent reader in her family, which enables her to serve as an interpreter when her family goes shopping (Harris, 1988). Would the fact that she is a competent reader outside of school ever be known to her teacher? Even if it were, would her out-of-school competency be valued?

Web Activity on Literacy Outside the School

Search the web (www.google.com is a good place to start) for information on how common it is for immigrant children to serve as "interpreters" for the family and why they may grow to resent this responsibility, perhaps because of intergenerational conflicts over which culture will be emphasized (the new or the old). Share what you have learned with others in your class. What could you do as a teacher to help children value their interpreter roles? What could you do to help bridge the communication gap between home and school?

Fluency

The rate at which a child reads a passage and the accuracy and expression with which it is read all figure into what is known as the fluency factor. As someone interested in

FIGURE 8.1 Megan's Difficulty in Reading Fluently

In a flat, choppy voice, Megan began to read aloud: "Lit . . . tle . . . Chun ran down to . . . the big . . . yard Chun's . . . brothers and . . . sister . . . s . . . were making a dra . . . gon . . . boat There was . . . much . . . to be done before . . . the big . . . race began."

As Megan's teacher [Sarah] listened to her, many thoughts and questions began whirling in [her] mind: "I wonder . . . Megan knows how to decode all the words and reads at an acceptable rate; yet, she is not very fluent! Her reading does not sound like language. I tell my students to "read with expression," but do I really know what that means? How do I explain it to my students? How important is reading with expression? Will it help them be better lifelong readers who comprehend and enjoy what they read? How can I help my students read with the melodies and rhythms of language echoing in their ears?" (Dowhower, 1991, p. 165)

content area literacy, you may already know why these three elements of fluency deserve attention. You know from your own experience with reading textbooks for courses you've taken that they are typically packed with difficult concepts, many of which may be new to you. This density in conceptual load and the accompanying vocabulary demands make it unlikely that you will breeze along in these texts as you might if they were on topics you knew a great deal about. Also, if you read too slowly and don't group words into meaningful phrasal units, your comprehension is likely to falter. Consider, for example, what Sarah Dowhower (1991) remembers from her research and experiences as Megan's second-grade teacher (see Figure 8.1). Note in particular how Megan's difficulty in reading expressively contributes to your own difficulty in understanding the passage.

Are you perhaps thinking, as we once did, why does it matter if Megan reads haltingly and with little expression orally? Isn't it the case that most of the reading people engage in is done silently? Although the answer to the second question is yes, the first question is not answered so easily. Based on a review of the research dealing with fluency, the National Reading Panel (2000) concluded that fluency is a critical component of skilled reading and that fluency develops from practice in guided oral reading activities, such as repeated reading (see the last section in this chapter). It is important to keep in mind, however, that the panel did not reach consensus on whether fluency led to better comprehension or whether better comprehension ensures that children will read more fluently. Reminiscent of the chicken-or-the-egg dilemma, we are not sure which comes first, fluency or comprehension. What we do know, both from our experience as classroom teachers and the National Reading Panel's report, is that children who struggle to read their content area texts typically are not fluent readers and that there are ways of helping these children improve their fluency.

Self-Concept and Self-Efficacy

Children's perceptions of how competent they are as readers and writers, generally speaking, will affect how motivated they are to learn with texts in science, health, social studies, math, and other content areas. Whether or not they perceive themselves as good readers will make a difference in how competent they feel and how motivated they are to learn. Although the terms *self-concept* and *self-efficacy* are sometimes used interchangeably, they actually refer to different concepts. For example, you probably know children who have fairly good self-concepts of themselves as readers, but who would answer "not very" to the question "How sure are you that you can comprehend the material in your social studies book?" A "not very" answer would indicate low self-efficacy for that particular task. A statement of self-concept is domain specific, whereas self-efficacy is task specific (Pajares, 1996).

Self-efficacy is especially important to learning in the content areas. If children believe that they are likely to be successful in completing a particular task (e.g., comprehending information from their social studies text), they are apt to engage in the task, stay with it even when it becomes a bit difficult, and eventually gain satisfaction from having stayed with it. Readers who struggle often lack this kind of belief in themselves. When this is the case, a teacher's best instructional efforts may not be enough. For example, Guthrie and Wigfield (2000) concluded from their review of the research on teachers' instructional practices that such practices, while important, do not directly impact student outcomes (e.g., achievement on standardized tests, performance assessments, and beliefs about themselves as readers). Instead, it is the level of student engagement in a task—made possible by feelings of self-efficacy—that is the mediating factor, or avenue, through which classroom instruction influences student outcomes. Knowing this to be the case, we offer suggestions in the last section of the chapter for increasing struggling readers' self-efficacy in content area learning.

School Culture

Despite good intentions, reform-minded schools are coming to grips with the possibility that traditional school culture is *making* struggling readers out of some children by promoting certain normative ways of reading texts (e.g., reading from a textbook and answering questions at the end of a chapter) that may be disabling some of the very students they are trying to help. These students may know how to read, yet choose not to do so when the reading tasks they are required to do bore them or seem irrelevant. We do not mean to make excuses for why they don't read nor do we mean to suggest that certain normative ways of reading are necessarily wrong-headed. What we do want to emphasize, however, is that the reason for some children's struggle to read in the content areas may be a function of the tasks required of them.

Equally problematic is the possibility that print-based normative ways of reading are losing their usefulness, and perhaps to some extent their validity, in the wake of new media and interactive digital technologies and the changing literacies they evoke (Lankshear, Gee, Knobel, & Searle, 1997; Mackey & McClay, 2000). If you have reason to believe that this is the case and that other media (e.g., CD-ROMs, videotapes, the Internet) are viable means for learning content, then you are apt to agree that skills instruction in print-based school literacy tasks is necessary but insufficient for teaching struggling readers.

Finally, school culture can contribute to how children see themselves as either belonging or not belonging—as fitting in or not fitting in—to a way of learning and "doing" life in general. As James Banks (1993), an expert in multicultural education, points out, "school culture . . . communicates to students the school's attitudes toward a range of issues and problems, including how the school views them as human beings and its attitudes toward males, females, exceptional students, and students from various religious, cultural, racial, and ethnic groups" (p. 24). In parallel fashion, what students communicate to each other also affects their feelings of belonging, their values, and their actions.

English Language Learners and School Culture: An On-Line Article

To better understand how schools can consciously or unconsciously reinforce middle-class values and monolingual literacy practices regardless of their classroom populations, check out Margaret Cooney's (1995) on-line article entitled "Readiness for School or for School Culture?" To read it, go to http://readyweb.crc.uiuc.edu/library/1995/cooney95.html.

Reflecting

Think back to the statement we made at the beginning of this section—that is, "The *struggling* reader label is a contested term and one that means different things to different people." In what ways do you both agree and disagree with this statement? Do you think that instruction in content area literacy can be effective for readers who struggle? Under what conditions and taking into account what factors?

Three Approaches to Teaching Readers Who Struggle

A short story by H. G. Wells (1979) titled *The Country of the Blind* (Figure 8.2) offers a way to conceptualize (and to make concrete) how culture at large, not just school culture, can construct readers who struggle. Previously, Donna used the story, as she does here, to segue into the three approaches to teaching such readers: namely the deprivation approach, the difference approach, and the culture-*as*-disability approach (Alvermann, 2001).

The Deprivation Approach

This approach might be thought of in Nuñez's case as "I have eyes and you don't" or as explained by McDermott and Varenne (1995), "We have culture, and you don't" (pp. 333–334). This way of thinking about culture and the struggling reader buys into the argument that children develop so differently in their ability to read that they can

FIGURE 8.2   *The Country of the Blind* by H. G. Wells (1979).

Briefly, *The Country of the Blind* is a story about Nunez, a sighted man who miraculously survives a nasty fall from a peak in the Andes and lands relatively unharmed in an isolated valley populated exclusively by people who for generations have been born blind and have no words for "see" or for anything that can be seen. Nunez, being an opportunist of the worst kind, immediately senses he will have many privileges accorded him in a land where he alone can see. What he fails to consider, however, is that the people who live in *The Country of the Blind* have no need to see. They live a well-ordered life, moving about confidently in a culture that fits their needs precisely:

> Everything, you see, had been made to fit their needs; each of the radiating paths of the valley area had a constant angle to the others, and was distinguished by a special notch upon its [curbing]; all obstacles and irregularities of path or meadow had long since been cleared away; all of their methods and procedures arose naturally from their special needs (Wells, 1979, p. 135).

Time passes and the people of the valley grow weary of putting up with Nunez's pompous and clumsy ways. They turn to their surgeon to define the problem so that they may find a solution to this stranger's intrusive ways. After examining Nunez, the surgeon's diagnosis is *diseased eyes*: "They are greatly distended, he has eyelashes, and his eyelids move, and consequently his brain is in a state of constant irritation and destruction" (Wells, 1979, p. 142). Upon hearing this, the people decide that the only solution to the problem is to surgically remove his eyes—the thought of which sends Nunez scurrying back up the mountain from which he fell.

---

be classified into reliably distinct categories (e.g., struggling reader, good reader), at least as measured by standardized, performance-based, or informal tests and teacher observations. By buying into the deprivation approach, you are assuming that there is a stable set of tasks to which all children must respond if they are to qualify as competent or good readers. Being able to decode, comprehend, and summarize information would qualify as one such set of tasks. Poor performances on these tasks by some children would be viewed as evidence that they have not yet developed the requisite set of skills necessary for reading competently at a particular grade level or in a particular set of texts within a particular content area.

By unpacking some of the assumptions underlying this argument, it is possible to see a culture's influence on a reader's self-perception and identity formation. Children who recognize and are recognized by others like themselves as being struggling readers often end up the recipients of what Finn (1999) calls "a domesticating" education—that is, an education that stresses "functional literacy, literacy that makes a person productive and dependable, but not troublesome" (pp. ix–x). It is a second-rate kind of educational arrangement that typically leads to lower expectations and to social and economic inequalities. A further assumption of the deprivation approach is that children who struggle with reading will have lower self-esteem when they find they are unable to compete for the privileges that come with grade-level (or above) performance on reading-related tasks.

To partially offset the negative fallout from these kinds of assumptions, schools may offer small-group or one-on-one instruction by a reading specialist. Such instruction, while well intended, still has its critics. For example, there are teachers, administrators, and parent advocacy groups that deplore isolating students from each other in an effort to make up for their so-called "deficiencies." Consider, too, how a negative connotation associated with the deprivation approach might be used to apply to English language learners' linguistic abilities.

English Language Learners and the Deprivation Approach

The deprivation approach described by McDermott and Varenne might be equated to the way some monolinguals view English language learners when English acquisition is the benchmark against which ELLs are measured. Through this lens one can hear the words, "I have English and you don't."

The Difference Approach

Once again referring to the story of Nunez, the difference approach to thinking about culture and the struggling reader might be, as McDermott and Varenne (1995) phrase it, "We have culture, and you have a different one" (p. 335). This rather off-handed, tongue-in-cheek observation serves to point out one of the assumptions underlying the difference approach, namely that an arbitrary set of reading tasks deemed important for one group of children may have little or no relevance for another group. Translated into classroom practice, this assumption is often the underlying rationale for culturally responsive teaching, such as that described in Chapter 7 of this book.

Website for Culturally Responsive Ways to Teach Readers Who Struggle

Visit the *Reading Rockets'* website (http://www.readingrockets.org) and learn how to use home, school, and community support systems for identifying and helping children who struggle to read in the content areas. This site also offers a free newsletter.

The difference approach contends that the ways in which children develop competencies as literate beings will vary according to the demands of their particular cultures. Thus, if you were to use this approach to teaching struggling readers, you would likely introduce them to relatively few predefined reading tasks; instead, you would focus on the literacy activities that adults in their communities regularly perform as fully functioning members of that culture. An assumption underlying this approach is that teachers will have the resources necessary—both personally and professionally, in terms of their own experience and development—for instructing students from varying cultural backgrounds with varying literacy practices. A corollary to this assumption is that children exposed to such instruction will benefit from it in the long term. This is not a trivial consideration, for as McDermott and Varenne (1995) have pointed out, "despite a liberal lament that variation is wonderful, those who cannot show the right skills at the right time in the right format are often considered out of the race for the rewards of the larger culture" (p. 335).

The Culture-*as*-Disability Approach

This approach assumes that school culture (like the culture of one's home, community, and the like) is a historically evolved way of doing life. As such, it has certain norms that implicitly and explicitly teach students about what is worth working for, how to succeed, and who will fall short. In fact, society at large (made up of policy makers, publishers, journalists, news anchors, and educators like you, Jeanne, Kristiina, and Donna) mirrors school culture in holding up for inspection those students who succeed in literacy learning and those who do not. According to McDermott and Varenne (1995), "cultures offer a wealth of positions for human beings to inhabit" (p. 336). Each position requires certain things.

For example, to inhabit the position of "good reader," one must possess certain abilities that are verifiable and recognizable to others who occupy that same position. If you favor this approach to teaching children who struggle with reading, you are likely to subscribe to the notion that *how* some children end up inhabiting the position of "struggling reader" (as opposed to "good reader") is more a matter of extenuating circumstances—for example, differential treatment or fewer opportunities due to socioeconomic background—than of their innate or "natural" abilities.

One of the assumptions underlying the culture-as-disability approach is that unlike the deprivation and difference approaches, it does not isolate groups so that one group stands apart from another, nor is one group marginalized in relation to another group. Instead, all groups—good and not-so-good readers—stand in relation to the wider culture of which they are a part. Viewed from this approach, children who struggle with reading are perceived as part of the same cloth from which good readers come. This has implications for instruction.

For example, if you think of children who struggle to read in the content areas as being part of the same cloth from which good readers come, you are likely to observe them with new eyes. You may look for reading and writing activities that qualify them as competent under a different set of proficiencies (i.e., you may adapt your content area instruction in ways that are similar to those described in the last section of this chapter). You may also begin to question the fairly common practice of allowing struggling readers to rely on you, rather than on the assigned texts, as a source of information. Often it is a matter of simply expecting them to use their texts and then supporting them in their attempts to do so. Over and over again in our own practices as teachers, we have to curb the tendency to be "too helpful." Making students too dependent on us would work against our goal of gradually releasing responsibility so that they ultimately become strategic learners in their own right.

Reflecting

As you read about the deprivation, difference, and culture-*as*-disability approaches to teaching readers who struggle, what thoughts crossed your mind as an educator? If you saw these approaches as something more than just another means of categorizing or labeling people and their practices, how might this affect your views on teaching children to read content area materials? For example, what would count as reading materials in a deprivation approach? In a difference approach? In a culture-*as*-disability approach?

Examples of Instructional Adaptations for Struggling Readers

A Standard That Speaks Especially to Readers Who Struggle

This chapter section is focused on helping you adapt research-based strategies for improving comprehension. ELA Standard 3 calls for students to "apply a wide range of strategies to comprehend, interpret, evaluate, and appreciate texts"—something that all skilled readers do well and that struggling readers need to learn to do (with your help).

Students who struggle to learn content area material tend to experience difficulty in reading fluently and in understanding concepts that are expressed in new or unknown terms (see Chapter 4 for a fuller discussion of vocabulary learning). With their ability to comprehend what they read seriously compromised by these difficulties with fluency and word meanings, students often develop attitudes of low self-efficacy that prevent them from even trying to engage with the reading tasks their teachers assign. If you have observed this phenomenon in your own classroom or someone else's, you know how frustrating it can be for both the teacher and the student. Thus, we offer three instructional adaptations you can make that have research backing and that we know will work from our own experiences in using them. One such adaptation, repeated reading, involves altering any expectations that you might have concerning children's ability to read fluently; another, direct instruction in figuring out the meaning of the "big words" in content area materials, involves teacher modeling; and a third, applying fix-up strategies when meaning is lost during reading, involves teaching struggling readers to monitor their own comprehension.

Repeated Reading

Repeated reading is simply practicing a passage until you can read it accurately, at an acceptable speed, and with good oral expression. As noted by Jay Samuels (2002a, b), a long-time advocate of repeated reading as a technique for building fluency, the National Reading Panel (2000) found that this strategy had a clear and positive effect on struggling readers' fluency throughout the elementary and secondary grades.

Because children generally recognize the fact that it takes practice to get good in most of the things they do (e.g., riding bikes, playing sports), they are typically willing to give the repeated reading technique a try. Basically, it involves these steps:

1. Choose a passage containing between 50 and 300 words from a content text that the class is using. The objective is to keep the passage short so that it's possible for a child to demonstrate success in reading it, thus building a sense of self-efficacy when reading from content area texts. The passage we selected (Figure 8.3) contains 69 words and is from a selection entitled *Where's the Water?* (Banks & Weiss, 1995).
2. Set a predetermined mastery level for word accuracy (e.g., 85 percent word recognition accuracy) and speed (e.g., reading at a rate of 85 to 100 words per minute). Establish criteria for reading with good oral expression (e.g., observing punctuation marks or other appropriate cues for pausing; grouping words into meaningful thought units; raising and lowering of pitch; and emphasizing certain words. Note that if you set word recognition accuracy too high, a reader is likely to slow down for fear of miscuing on a word (Samuels, 1979/2002a).
3. The teacher reads the selected passage orally while the students read it silently. The purpose is to familiarize the students with the words and the concepts in the passage.
4. Assign students to work in pairs. If one member of the pair is slightly better in reading fluently, that is ideal. For each reading of the passage, the students take

FIGURE 8.3 *Where's the Water?* **A Passage for Repeated Reading**

Many farmers have trouble growing crops when rain is scarce. Yet the Hopi (hō' pē) people of Arizona and New Mexico have successfully farmed dry lands for more than 1000 years. How? For many centuries, they have carefully observed nature. Using what they learned, the Hopi have developed ways of growing corn, beans, and squash, even though their lands receive only eight to twelve inches of rain each year.

turns, with one person acting as the teacher and the other as the student. The student's role involves reading the passage, whereas the teacher's role involves listening while following along in the text. In this way, both students are getting practice reading the passage.

5. Tell students to reverse roles after the first reading of the passage, with each child reading the passage orally for a total of four times. Research has shown that most of the gains students make in word recognition accuracy, reading speed, and expressiveness are in place by the fourth reading (Samuels, 2002b).

Our experience tells us that during the first few sessions of repeated reading, you will need to offer considerable teacher guidance as the students work in pairs. However, after a few sessions (and with support from you to build feelings of self-efficacy), most pairs are able to follow through on the technique with minimal teacher guidance.

So that you get a feel for how repeated reading might work for your students, find someone who will pair with you. Then try the repeated reading activity that follows.

Try It! A Repeated Reading Activity

Take turns with your partner reading the passage *Where's the Water?* Make sure you assume the role of student reader (reading orally four times) and the role of teacher (listening and following along four times). After you have finished this exercise, try to answer the following questions:

1. Did you find yourself becoming more fluent each time you read the passage? If so, in what ways was this evident to you?
2. Recognizing that it was a relatively easy passage for you to read, you might want to try a more difficult one and see if you can explain why being "on automatic" as you decode words in a passage is necessary for good comprehension.

Although repeated reading has withstood the test of time as a strategy for developing struggling readers' fluency, it is not foolproof. For example, there is no guarantee that gaining fluency on one passage will transfer to another passage. In fact, research has shown that "if there is substantial overlap in the words, there is good transfer, but if the amount of overlap is minimal, transfer is not as good" (Samuels, 2002b, p. 170). Still, the technique of repeated reading is valuable if for no other reason than to demonstrate to the struggling reader that he or she can improve with practice.

Direct Instruction in Decoding "Big Words"

Modeling, or showing someone how to do something, is a common practice in everyday life. Consider, for example, how many times you've said to someone, "Show me how you did that." Typically, we don't want long explanations, at least not when we're first starting to learn something. We just want to get on with it; explanations can come later. Children who struggle with reading are no different, especially when faced with the task of learning to decode big words that are part of the content area curriculum. Like adults, they appreciate someone showing them how to do things that are not yet automatic or that are not easy to accomplish on their own. Patricia Cunningham (2000) understood this implicitly when she developed her method of teaching children how to decode multisyllabic words, such as *international*. Here's how she suggests modeling that method:

> Write on the board or overhead transparency: *The thinning of the ozone layer is an international problem.*
>
> "Today, we are going to look at a big word that is really just a little word with a prefix added to the beginning and a suffix added to the end."
>
> Underline *nation*.
>
> "Who can tell me this word? Yes, that's the word *nation*, and we know *nation* is another word for *country*. Now let's look at the prefix that comes before *nation*."
>
> Underline *inter*.
>
> "This prefix is *inter*. You probably know *inter* from words like *interrupt* and *internal*. Now let's look at what follows *inter* and *nation*."
>
> Underline *al*.
>
> "You know *al* from many words, such as *unusual* and *critical*."
>
> Write *unusual* and *critical* and underline the *al*.
>
> "Listen as I pronounce this part of the word."
>
> Underline and pronounce *national*.
>
> "Notice how the pronunciation of *nation* changes when we put *a-l* on it. Now let's put all the parts together and pronounce the word *inter nation al*. Let's read the sentence and make sure *international* makes sense."
>
> Have the sentence read and confirm that ozone thinning is indeed a problem for many nations to solve.
>
> "You can figure out the pronunciation of many big words if you look for common prefixes, such as *inter*, common root words, such as *nation*, and common suffixes, such at *al*."
>
> "In addition to helping you figure out the pronunciation of a word, prefixes and suffixes sometimes help you know what the word means or where in a sentence we can use the word. The word *nation* names a thing. When we describe a nation, we add the suffix *al* and have *national*. The prefix *inter* often means "between or among." Something that is *international* is between many nations. The Olympics are the best example of an *international* sports event." (Cunningham, 2000, pp. 151–152)

As you can probably guess, numerous other words would work well in teaching students to look for common prefixes and suffixes as a way of unlocking the meanings of big words. So many in fact that an extensive review of the research on the frequency of particular multisyllabic words at various grade levels turned up what Cunningham (2000) named her list of the "Nifty Thrifty Fifty." This list (Figure 8.4) contains the most useful prefixes and suffixes that students in the intermediate grades are likely to meet as they read content area materials. Cunningham (2002) estimated from her review of the research that two-thirds of fourth graders would know all but eight of the fifty words on the list.

FIGURE 8.4 The *Nifty Thrifty Fifty* (Cunningham, 2000, pp. 166–167)

Word	Prefix	Suffix or ending
antifreeze	anti	
beautiful		ful (y-i) (spelling change)
classify		ify
communities	com	es (y-i)
community	com	
composer	com	er
continuous	con	ous
conversation	con	tion
deodorize	de	ize
different		ent
discovery	dis	y
dishonest	dis	
electricity		ity
employee	em	ee
encouragement	en	ment
expensive	ex	ive
forecast	fore	
forgotten		en (double t)
governor		or
happiness		ness (y-i)
hopeless		less
illegal	il	
impossible	im	
impression	im	sion
independence	in	ence
international	inter	al
invasion	in	sion
irresponsible	ir	ible
midnight	mid	
misunderstand	mis	

(continued)

FIGURE 8.4   (Continued)

Word	Prefix	Suffix or ending
musician		ian
nonliving	non	ing (drop e)
overpower	over	
performance	per	ance
prehistoric	pre	ic
prettier		er (y-i)
rearrange	re	
replacement	re	ment
richest		est
semifinal	semi	
signature		ture
submarine	sub	
supermarkets	super	s
swimming		ing (double m)
transportation	trans	tion
underweight	under	
unfinished	un	ed
unfriendly	un	ly
unpleasant	un	ant
valuable		able (drop e)

Although direct instruction takes a good bit of time, it is time well spent. Readers who struggle with the vocabulary in their content area texts often need someone to show them how to make the struggle less onerous. By modeling how to decode big words and then providing students with lots of guided practice, you are also helping them to dispel lingering doubts about their self-efficacy in comprehending the content materials you assign them.

Fix-Up Strategies for Recovering Meaning

In Chapter 2, you learned that struggling readers often have difficulty keeping track of when they are comprehending and when they are not. Unlike skilled readers, they seem not to demand much from texts; instead, they read passively and appear to have few fix-up strategies they can employ when working with content area texts. Research on metacognition—that is, knowing when and how to recover meaning—has shown that three things influence how proactive readers will be in attempting to recover lost meaning: the first is self-knowledge; the second is task knowledge; and the third is the ability to monitor one's own comprehension (Brown & Palincsar, 1989).

An instructional adaptation that will allow you to take all three of these things into account simultaneously as you work with struggling readers in content area lessons involves embedding questions directly in the text using sticky notes so that students will be helped to think *during* reading. This strategy, an adaptation of Weir's (1998) efforts to jump start metacognition in struggling readers, is explained and illustrated in the toolbox of teaching and learning strategies found at the end of this textbook. Suffice it to say here that embedded questions in content area texts provide the kind of scaffolding needed for learning more about the self, the task, and the need to recover lost meaning while reading. In embedded questions, opportunities abound for predicting, self-questioning, and summarizing—skills that help struggling readers discover what good readers already know, namely, that meaning is *made*, not found. This is a cornerstone of the social constructionist perspective on learning.

Reconsidering

We wonder if your definition of the so-called struggling reader has changed as a result of reading this chapter or, if not your definition, then perhaps you have had reason to reconsider how the assumptions you make about such a reader can affect your approach to teaching her or him. In your own words, try to summarize what you have learned about the three approaches to teaching readers who struggle with their content area texts. What is it about one or more of those approaches that make them compatible with either the repeated reading method or the direct instruction method for decoding multisyllabic words? Do you sense any incompatibilities? What are they?

PART FOUR

Instructional Decisions

9 Organizing for Content Literacy Instruction

In this chapter, we make a case for providing literacy-rich classroom environments for students across the grades in elementary school. We take you on a tour of a bookstore and ask you to consider what elements you can borrow for your classroom. Then we examine various ways to organize content literacy instruction and suggest ways to integrate content into literacy instruction. Finally, we visit a second-grade and a fifth-grade classroom that are organized in different ways, yet both integrate content and literacy instruction.

Seated comfortably on the floor, leaning against the lockers, Ms. Casey, a parent volunteer, is reading *The Great Kapok Tree: A Tale of the Amazon Rain Forest* (Cherry, 1990) to a group of children. Some students snuggle around her while others recline on oversized pillows or sit cross-legged, leaning against the wall. They all listen intently as the story unfolds. As Ms. Casey reads, she occasionally stops to explain an unfamiliar term and pauses to provide a "space" for students to share their connections, make predictions, or ask questions. After reading and discussing the story, they go back to their desks and reflect on the story by writing or drawing in their response logs.

Simultaneously, the student teacher is moving about the classroom, stopping occasionally to conference with students about the books they are reading independently and helping others use the index of a book to find specific information about a particular plant or animal that lives in the rain forest. Some students sit with a buddy and examine photographs and captions in informational books about the rain forest. Another student, sitting in the respected "author's chair," practices reading aloud his most recent manuscript, an informational story that features Jake and Anna, a variation on Jack and Annie, main characters of the *Magic Tree House* series, informational storybooks by Mary Pope Osborne.

The teacher, sitting at the kidney-shaped table at the rear of the classroom, assists three students who need guidance understanding the life cycle text structure in *Life of a Butterfly* by David Drew (1989). Another group of students is seated at the science center observing a painted lady butterfly chrysalis. They discuss their observations and record them, using illustrations and written descriptions in their dated science logs.

Does this scenario sound realistic to you? Can you sense the students' engagement in reading and writing about the rain forest? Perhaps you teach in such an environment or were once a student in a classroom like this.

The scenario just given reflects the kinds of engagements that take place in Judy Rogers' second-grade classroom in Lubbock, Texas. Social studies and science instruction is not relegated to a short time each day. Rather, the classroom organization provides seamless opportunities for children to be actively involved in content learning and literacy instruction throughout the day. A classroom organized in this way provides opportunities for students to learn to read and write while they read and write to learn.

Remembering

Think for a moment about your elementary school days. What do you remember about your favorite teacher? What was that classroom like? Do you remember feeling free to explore literacy-related activities? Was there time to read and many books to choose from? What do you remember about how the teacher organized social studies, science, mathematics, and reading/language arts instruction? Did he or she integrate reading, writing, and content instruction?

Thinking back to our elementary school days, we (Kristiina, Jeanne, and Donna) cannot remember any kind of integration. To the contrary, a time was allotted for social studies or science; e.g., social studies was taught from 2:00 to 2:30 on Tuesdays and Thursdays, and science was taught for an hour on Wednesday mornings. Most times we read our textbooks at our seats and reluctantly wrote answers to the questions at the end of a chapter. Teachers sat at their desks and answered our questions only if we were bold enough to ask. If we weren't reading the textbooks at our seats, then we frantically copied information from the chalkboard into our notebooks. These notes served as another "text," one that we memorized for a test on Fridays.

Creating a Literacy-Rich Environment for Content and Literacy Learning

Now, let's take a look at ways to organize content literacy instruction. First we consider the "who," the "what," and the "how." *Who* are your students? *What* knowledge and interests do your students bring with them? *What* content, skills, and strategies do students need to learn? The question then becomes *how* do you go about creating an environment that encourages content literacy development? *How* do you organize for content area literacy instruction?

This chapter focuses on ways to organize content literacy instruction by building on familiar frameworks elementary school teachers use for organizing literacy instruction: the reading workshop and thematic units. We explain how a shift in focus within these frameworks can enhance both content learning and literacy development. We use classroom examples to demonstrate how two teachers organize content and literacy instruction in integrated ways.

Teachers and researchers have documented over the years the critical importance of creating literacy-rich classroom environments in the primary grades. Morrow (1997) has researched and written about how the physical design of the classroom impacts the ways in which young children interact with one another and engage in literacy use. She recommends that literacy materials, such as writing implements, paper, books, magnetic letters, and environmental print, should be easily accessible to students and work spaces arranged to encourage peer interaction. Furthermore, the classroom literacy environment should reflect how different sources of information may be accessed and used outside school.

We believe a rich literacy environment is as essential in grade 6 as it is in the primary grades. Designing a literacy-rich environment that meets the needs of all students is not a simple task. What constitutes a literacy-rich environment changes—sometimes subtly and other times drastically—as we move from one life domain to another and from one culture to another because literacy is a social process situated within different contexts (Barton & Hamilton, 2000; Gee as cited in Brock, 1997). When designing a classroom environment, it is important to consider the outside environmental factors that influence students' engagement with or disenfranchisement from literacy.

Bridging the Gap between School and Home

Children who have limited experiences with books and other literacy-related materials need an especially rich literacy environment at school. The classroom needs to be a safe place where students feel comfortable and encouraged as they experiment with varying uses of their developing literacies. Books with characters that represent different cultures and experiences are important for helping children feel "at home" with books. Also, it's important that a teacher is aware of culturally related literacy practices that can help bridge the gap between school and home—attempting to bring more of home to school, rather than the traditional practice of making home more like school.

Exploring Literacy-Rich Environments

In this section we take you on a guided tour of a bookstore, representative of establishments you may find in almost any midsize to large city in the United States and Canada. The purpose is to describe a literacy-rich environment outside a school context in which many people choose to spend their free time and simply "hang out." The bookstore's organization may help you think about ways to organize the physical environment of your classroom and choose literacy materials that promote active learning. As you accompany us through the bookstore, think about what makes these establishments so appealing and inviting. Use your senses to see, hear, smell, taste, feel, and imagine.

Upon entering the glass double doors of the bookstore, we find ourselves in a small foyer where flyers advertising upcoming events are posted on bulletin boards and heavily discounted hardcover books are stacked on wheeled book carts. We enter the second set of double doors and feel the cool air-conditioned air stroke our faces. The aroma of lightly scented candles, glossy magazine papers, newsprint, the pages of new books, and Colombian coffee blends infuse our senses. Slowly we begin to notice the sounds of Beethoven's *La Revoluntionnaire*.

We approach the "best sellers" table, which is strategically placed right inside the door. We look at the image on the front cover, flip to the back cover, quickly scan reviewers' comments, and then read the synopsis of the book. We are not in a rush. We can simply enjoy the surroundings and go wherever our minds desire. The music, the scents, the attractive displays welcome us.

As we walk down the aisle, we notice a plethora of materials that support and foster literacy. There are displays of colorful bookmarks, pens, pencils, day timers, diaries, photo albums, stationery, book bags, scrapbooks, bookends, greeting cards, postcards, reading lights, reading glasses, and magnets to hold notes on the fridge.

Wandering down another aisle, we arrive at a table with items that appeal to children: crossword puzzle and maze books, connect-the-dot books, word searches, tangrams with information explaining their origin, mobiles, card trick books, and chess and checkers games.

We shift our attention to shelves upon shelves of books. Each one is labeled with bold white lettering on a black background, announcing its contents. The themes are countless: mystery, reference, gardening, fitness, women's health, mythology, religion, spirituality, computer programming, field guides, European history, U.S. history, auto repair, science fiction, cookbooks, biographies, poetry, home decorating, science, psychology, young adult, and many more. If we want to find a specific book and know the author or title, we can look it up on one of the bookstore's many computers.

Next, we wander through a section dedicated to education and teaching aids, placed strategically beside the children's section (obviously marketed for parents and teachers). Hopping over our heads, a painted kangaroo beckons us to venture into the world found within the pages of books written for children. As we enter, we see a child-sized locomotive where a dad and two children are enjoying a book together. Seated in a cozy treehouse two young girls are reading *Verdi* (Cannon, 1997) and wondering aloud if there are real snakes like him.

As we browse through the children's section, we see books everywhere; some are placed on shelves where only the spines are visible, whereas others are displayed so that kids (and other children's book enthusiasts) can see the cover art. Various sections abound: picture books, board books, beginning readers, chapter books, juvenile fiction, Newbery winners, Caldecott winners, classics (*Pinnochio, Oliver Twist*), favorite series (including the likes of *Nancy Drew, Hardy Boys*, and *Series of Unfortunate Events*), audio books, nonfiction books, biographies, Disney books, alphabet books, and counting books. Tables and chairs also invite browsers to "come in and sit a spell." The environment is so inviting, it's hard to tear ourselves away. Nevertheless, we continue our tour.

Toward the rear of the store, we find different U.S. national and local newspapers and magazines. We are excited to see newspapers from various countries across the world: *El País* (Spain), *Le Figaro and Le Monde* (France), *The Observer* (United Kingdom), *Irish Times* (Ireland), *Corriere della la Sera* (Italy), and *Frankfurter Allgemeine* (Germany). While the news may be outdated by a week or so (due to the lag in delivery time), there is nothing as delightful as opening a newspaper to read about world events reported from different perspectives.

Before we leave the bookstore, we make our way to the café, enjoy a cup of *cafe con leche*, and chat about the books we found along the way.

Now that we've completed our tour, think about what ideas you could "borrow" from the bookstore and take into your elementary school classroom. Remember the reading and writing-related materials we saw early in our tour? Consider how books were displayed and organized. What was it about their arrangement that drew us to pick them up? Is your classroom environment conducive to book browsing and reading?

Try It!

Draw a two-column chart. In the left-hand column, list aspects of a bookstore's environment that you find appealing. In the right-hand column, list ideas you could easily implement in your classroom, ideas you've observed others incorporate, or ideas you presently use in your own classroom. Compare your list with a partner. What ideas did you learn from your partner? How do you think children's literacy engagements might change if you used some of these ideas to modify the classroom environment?

Organizing for Content Literacy Instruction

Reading and Writing Workshop

Much has been written about organizing for literacy instruction. Nancy Atwell (1994), Lucy Calkins (1994, 2001), and Regie Routman (2000), among others, describe a workshop format for organizing literacy instruction. Basal reading programs also provide guidelines for organizing literacy instruction.

In contrast, much less has been written about frameworks for organizing content area instruction in the elementary grades. The traditional, whole class textbook approach dominates much content area instruction—if content instruction occurs at all. Round robin reading, teacher questioning, and reviewing for tests are common, despite the fact that research suggests good content teaching reflects practices similar to good literacy instruction: teacher-led class discussions, collaborative small groups, and sustained time for individual learning.

In this chapter, we propose that content literacy instruction can be integrated into the daily literacy instructional routines teachers currently use by broadening the purposes for reading and writing and varying the types of texts used for instruction. In this way, content literacy instruction becomes an integral part of reading and writing instruction rather than considered as an "add on."

Figure 9.1 lists examples of how content-related literacy instruction can be seamlessly folded into a reading and writing workshop instructional framework. As you examine Figure 9.1, try to imagine how to develop a content literacy workshop.

FIGURE 9.1 Integrating Content into Reading Workshop

Reading Workshop Component	Purposes of Components: Content Focus
Read alouds (pre-K–6)	• Enjoyment, stimulate curiosity, sustain interest • Become accustomed to the "sound" of informational text • Learn the language of the discipline • Build students' background knowledge about particular content • Provide access to challenging concepts for all students, regardless of reading abilities • Familiarize students with organization of informational books, including access features • Highlight how authors use photographs and other visuals to communicate information • Demonstrate ways to read informational text: by section, cover to cover, browse, skim • Revisit familiar texts • Provide models for student writing • Model fluent reading and oral interpretation
Minilessons (K–6)	• Model comprehension strategies • Compare/contrast features of informational books • Examine characteristics of fiction and nonfiction • Introduce many kinds of informational texts, including posters, maps, charts, timelines, magazines, newspapers • Study author's craft

Figure 9.1 Continued

Reading Workshop Component	Purposes of Components: Content Focus
	• Demonstrate how to surf the Web • Model how to use the index and table of contents to search for information and get a sense of what information may be included in a particular book • Demonstrate notetaking • Model how to organize information • Teach word attack skills
Shared writing/ interactive writing (K–2)	• Write about a topic or theme based on efferent and/or aesthetic responses to read alouds • Write about structure of informational books • Scaffold writing tasks
Guided reading (K–2)	• Read informational texts on students' instructional levels (guided reading books, newspapers, magazines, and nonprint texts)
Collaborative student group work (K–6)	• Explore informational texts • Read texts and discuss texts (literature circles, book clubs) • Paired/buddy reading for supporting one another • Practice strategies introduced in minilessons
Learning centers (pre-K–6)	• Engagements for exploring various aspects of topic or theme (In the upper grades, "centers" may take the form of areas of the room: library, writer's nook, technology corner, science lab)
Independent reading (pre-K–6)	• "Read the room" in pre-K–K (environmental print, charts, graphs) • Read text written during shared/interactive writing in K–1 • Read self-selected books about particular content—classroom library and displays must contain many nonfiction choices (K–6)
Independent writing (pre-K–6)	• Journal writing • Efferent and aesthetic responses to informational texts • Drafting and revising presentation

Theme or Topic Focus

Probably one of the most common ways to organize literacy instruction with a content focus is to select a theme or topic that provides the *context* and *content* for literacy instruction. To quote Linda Delpit (1991): "You don't learn to read, you learn to read something, and you read something because you want to know something, enjoy a text or participate in a group. . ." (p. 542). We advocate that the "something" we give students to read can be related to the content areas.

Very young children come to school expecting to learn to read and write and bring with them curiosity and experience about the world—that is, content knowledge.

Before coming to school, their lives are full of "thematic" studies in which literacy and content learning experiences are integrated. When young children become very intrigued by rocks or bugs or plants (the content of their lives), they experiment, ask questions, share their ideas, and even write and draw about them. Everything they do revolves around content. Building on students' interests and background knowledge will certainly enhance content learning.

Students in grades 4 through 6 also benefit from integrated, thematic content and literacy instruction. In contrast to traditional textbook-centered instruction, which seems divorced from students' lives, integrated instruction, aligned with students' interests and questions, can help motivate them to engage in school-related activities.

How can a theme or topic help teachers create an environment for content literacy instruction? It provides direction for selecting books for the classroom library, for read alouds, and for guided reading. A theme or topic can also provide guidance for choosing other print and nonprint resources to bring into the classroom. For example, videos may be used to build background knowledge and provide common "experiences" for class members. The choice of photographs, postcards, maps, posters, and learning center engagements can also stem from a theme or topic.

We are not advocating that every literacy engagement, whether teacher- or student-initiated, should be linked to a content topic or theme. However, content-related engagements are very important. One reason for suggesting the use of a theme or topic is due to our belief that it is important to build students' background knowledge. Using a common theme around which to plan literacy engagements provides a thread that links information. The alternative is that students switch their focus every thirty to forty-five minutes: for example, they read about people who have changed the world; next they shift to studying the human body; then they write procedures for making a peanut butter sandwich; and finally they engage in spelling and grammar exercises about nothing in particular. Organizing instruction in this way provides no continuity and little time for learning about anything in any depth. Neither does it provide opportunities for students to engage in the use of new vocabulary in meaningful contexts, which is essential for developing content-related concepts.

Research supports integrated content and reading instruction. In Chapter 3, we described several studies that demonstrated the effectiveness of integrating reading and science or reading and social studies instruction. Researchers found that students in the integrated classes did as well, and usually better, on tests of reading and content knowledge than students who received separate instruction in each area. A theme or topic provides the content—the "what" that students read and write about. Consequently, as students become better readers and writers, they also become more content literate, *and* as they become more content literate, they also become better readers and writers.

Planning Considerations

Planning involves more than selecting enjoyable activities about a particular theme or topic. Planning considerations for units are listed in Figure 9.2.

Figure 9.2   Planning Units

Things to Consider When Planning a Unit

1. Familiarize yourself with state and national standards for which you and your students are accountable. Because of the sheer size of the standards documents, it's tempting to say "this is impossible!" However, in actuality, most of the standards are fairly general and can be made manageable if you take a few minutes with fellow teachers to examine them.

2. Choose a topic or theme. Themes are broader and more conceptual in nature than topics. "Change" is an example of a theme. If you are developing a unit for the first time, we suggest you choose a topic that's consistent with content standards. (Topics seem to be a bit easier to manage for novices.) Consider students' interests, their background knowledge (schema) for the topic, developmental levels, and skills. What do they know and what do you think will intrigue them? Can you think of ways to make the topic relevant to students' lives? Don't forget about your knowledge and interests. You need to be intrigued by the unit too.

3. What print and nonprint materials are available that will extend students' existing knowledge and build new knowledge? Are resources of varying genres and reading levels available?

4. Determine what kinds of assessments you'll use to determine what students have learned in relation to the topic and to literacy development.

Try It! Becoming Familiar with Standards

Go to the website of your state's standards for your grade level. If you don't know the address, try www.google.com and key in (your state) department of education. Then locate a link that mentions English language arts, reading, mathematics, science, or social studies standards. Print the standards. With a partner, develop a matrix in which you group similar standards together. (An easy way to do this is to actually cut the standards apart and organize them.) Notice how process standards in science, social studies, and mathematics are related to ELA standards. Share your developing matrix with another group and explain your thinking. (By the way, don't despair if you can't finish this exercise after sticking with it for an hour or so. Chances are you will have become very familiar with the standards after all of the manipulation, discussion, and thinking!)

Visiting Classrooms

In this section, we first share with you an outline of a topical unit about the rain forest. It demonstrates how science and literacy instruction can be integrated in a primary-grade classroom. Then, we outline how fifth-grade history and literacy instruction can be integrated and organized. Notice how we link the English language arts and science or English language arts and social studies standards to the teachers' goals or objectives.

The first classroom glimpse is into Judy Rogers' second-grade classroom in Lubbock, Texas. A few years ago Jeanne had the privilege of spending a year studying and researching with Judy and her students and participated in this rain forest study. It began in mid-November and continued until mid-February. Figure 9.3 demonstrates how the unit objectives were aligned with the national standards for science education and for English language arts. Figure 9.4 outlines several days' activities from the three-month-long unit.

FIGURE 9.3 Correlation between Second-Grade Teacher's Goals and National Standards

Teacher's Goals for Content Unit	NSES	ELA
■ Increase students' knowledge of tropical rain forests, its plants and animals, and their importance to the world	Standard B: Physical Science Develop understanding of properties of objects and materials Standard C: Life Science Characteristics of organisms Life cycles of organisms	**Std 7:** Conduct research on issues and interests by generating ideas and questions, and by posing problems. They gather, evaluate, and synthesize data from a variety of sources
■ Develop science observation skills and procedures for recording data	Standard A: Science as Inquiry Develop abilities necessary to do scientific inquiry Develop an understanding of scientific inquiry Standard G: History and Nature of Science Science as a human endeavor	
■ Increase students' understanding of their responsibility for protecting the environment	Standard F: Science in Personal and Social Perspectives Develop understanding of resources Develop understanding of changes in the environment	
■ Increase students' understanding of literary conventions (expository text structures, access and organizational features in print and nonprint texts; distinguish between informational texts and other genres)		**Std 1:** Read a wide range of print and nonprint texts to build understanding of texts and the world; to acquire new information. **Std 3:** Apply a wide range of strategies to comprehend, interpret, evaluate, and appreciate texts. Draw on understanding of textual features.

FIGURE 9.3 Continued

Teacher's Goals for Content Unit	NSES	ELA
		Std 6: Apply knowledge of language structure, language conventions, and genre to create, critique, and discuss print and nonprint texts.
■ Develop literacy skills, such as locating particular information to answer questions, integrating information to report new understandings, and further developing word attack skills and comprehension strategies		**Std 3:** Apply a wide range of strategies to comprehend, interpret, evaluate, and appreciate texts. They draw on their prior experience, knowledge of word meaning and of other texts, word identification strategies, and understanding of textual features. **Std 7:** Conduct research on issues and interests by generating ideas and questions, and by posing problems. They gather, evaluate, and synthesize data from a variety of sources to communicate their discoveries in ways that suit their purpose and audience.
■ Interpret visual information in maps, charts, diagrams, photographs, and scaled drawings		**Std 7:** Gather, evaluate, and synthesize data from a variety of sources (print and nonprint texts)
■ Communicate their learning in different ways (book, illustrations, Readers' Theatre)		**Std 12:** Use spoken, written, and visual language to accomplish their own purposes (learning, enjoyment, persuasion, and exchange of information)
■ Work with peers to support one another's learning and to solve problems		**Std 3:** Apply a wide range of strategies to comprehend. Draw on their interactions with other readers and writers.

FIGURE 9.4   Exerpt from Second-Grade Rain Forest Unit

Day 1	**Increase students' understanding of wide range of texts, communicate their learning in different ways** **Work with peers to support one another's learning**

- Book Talks: Ms. Frizzle (Jeanne).
- KWWL: What do you <u>K</u>now? What do you <u>W</u>ant to know? <u>W</u>here can you <u>L</u>earn it? What did you <u>L</u>earn?
- Teacher modeling: KWWL chart—teacher records ideas, thinks aloud about why and how to organize similar ideas into categories. Also models how to make a KWWL chart in learning logs.
- Teacher-led discussion: Students share what they <u>K</u>now about the rain forest.
- Minilesson: How to use the dictionary to check the spelling of orangutan.
- Independent work: Write and draw in personal learning log: what I <u>K</u>now.
- Pairs: Begin exploration of literature about rain forest, write one or two interesting facts.

Day 2	**Increase understanding of literary conventions in expository text, including access and organizational features; distinguish between genres** **Work with peers to support one another's learning** **Increase students' understanding of their responsibility for protecting the environment** **Increase students' knowledge of tropical rain forest**

- Pairs: Continue exploring texts, record a few more intriguing facts.
- Teacher modeling and teacher-led discussion: Distinguish between genres, using a poster as a visual cue. Model use of access features in informational big books: *In the Rain Forest* (Barth), *Looking at Insects* (Glover).
- Guided Practice: Game to practice using access features to identify and locate information in a text.
- Teacher modeling and think aloud: Conversational read aloud—*Great Kapok Tree* (Cherry). Model questioning, wonderings, observations, clarify vocabulary.
- Teacher-led discussion: Build background knowledge and raise consciousness about the environment and deforestation. Continue discussion of genre: informational storybook.
- Independent work: Locate rain forests on map.

Day 3	**Increase understanding of literary conventions in expository text, particularly access and organizational features** **Interpret visual information in maps, charts, etc.** **Work with peers to support one another's learning**

- Teacher modeling: Accessing information from posters and charts with varying formats.
- Model book browsing and how to organize learning log notes.
- Pairs: Shared reading—explore rain forest books.
- Teacher modeling and guided practice: Model writing a cinquain with rain forest-related content. Introduce parts of speech.

Day 4:	**Interpret visual information in maps, charts, etc.** **Communicate learning in different ways**

- Teacher modeling: How to read a chart with a numbered legion.
- Small group guided practice: Introduce mural, discuss audience.
- Small groups: Draft cinquains.

FIGURE 9.4 Continued

- Class share: Report progress on cinquains.
- Teacher modeling, think aloud, discussion: Read aloud—*Welcome to the Green House* (Yolen). Think aloud how Yolen uses descriptive language. Purpose: to model language use in poetry. Explain vocabulary and introduce alliteration, onamodepia, text-to-text connections, invite students to visualize.
- Teacher modeling and think aloud: Write a cinquain, thinking aloud about content, form, and ongoing revision process.
- Shared reading: Read cinquains aloud together.
- Guided practice: Whole group practice writing a cinquain.
- Individual: Compose a cinquain and illustrate it.

Daily   **Develop literacy skills**

Judy chose books for guided reading instruction* that were related to the rain forest study. Students learned to read and write with meaningful content. They developed their content knowledge about the rain forest, learned to read with informational texts, and used reading and writing to learn content.

*Appendix A includes a list of leveled books that can be used for guided reading and content instruction.

Informational Texts for *All* Readers

A plethora of informational (nonfiction) books designed for guided reading has been published in recent years by a number of companies. They include texts that are written especially for emergent readers, beginning readers, and fluent readers. Even readers who find it difficult to negotiate print can construct meaning with the detailed photographs and other visuals that illustrate the books. When informational books are used for guided reading instruction, it provides even less proficient readers with access to content text other students may be able to read independently. The former are not denied access to the content because they have teacher support for reading to learn and learning to read. Caveat: Any text can be used for guided reading. If you're concerned about how to level books, check out resources such as Weaver's *Leveling Books K–6: Matching Readers to Text* (2000) or Fountas and Pinnell's *Matching Books to Readers: Using Leveled Books in Guided Reading, K–3* (1999).

Readers' Theatre and Fluency

Readers' Theatre (RT) is a multipurpose strategy. It is "a natural" for developing fluency, especially when a "real" audience is in attendance. RT provides a purpose for repeated readings: to prepare for a "performance." It also provides a reason for students to attend to their oral interpretation of a text; adding stress, appropriate intonation and volume, and so forth are important for communicating the message of the

RT. Writing an RT script also provides a context for learning about the different structures of stories and scripts. Appropriate uses for quotation marks and colons can be taught in a meaningful context when translating a story to a script. Students of all ages can participate in RT. Jeanne has observed students in grades K–3, who have written *and* performed their own Readers' Theatre.

Steps for Readers' Theatre

1. Write a script. (You don't have to be creative! Simply choose a text that includes several characters and dialogue, change the dialogue to characters' parts, add a narrator, and there you have it! A script!)
2. Distribute parts to students and rehearse, rehearse, rehearse. Switch parts to provide students with more practice.
3. Read the script for an audience!
4. Readers' Theatre can be embellished with costumes, props, etc. but all that's required is a script, readers, practice, and an audience.

Readers' Theatre: There's Always Room for Adaptations

In Terri Nash's first-grade classroom in Lubbock, Texas, students adapted the Readers' Theatre concept to demonstrate and share what they learned about Egypt with parents, teachers, and other students. After much negotiation, students decided that instead of writing a narrative Readers' Theatre script, each child took the role of someone or something important to ancient Egyptians. Then, based on information they had learned during their earlier research, they wrote individual scripts. For example, two girls chose "makeup." They wrote: "I am makeup. I am green. Both men and women wear me. They wore me because I keep the sun from burning them." Another child was the Nile River and there was Tutankomen, a mummy, a sarcophagus, and even a cat! Students demonstrated what they knew about ancient Egypt in relation to each person's or thing's significance to the culture.

Try It! Write and Perform a Readers' Theatre Script

Choose a *content area-related* book or download a script from a Readers' Theatre website. (If you search for Readers' Theatre at www.google.com, you'll find many sites and great ideas.) One of your purposes for writing and performing the script is to communicate social studies, science, health, or mathematics content to elementary school students.

Write or adapt an appropriate script. Practice reading your script and videotape your performance to evaluate your oral interpretation of the script. How'd you do? What could you do to improve your reading? Later, perform your script for elementary school students and explain your process of writing and preparing for your performance.

A Fifth-Grade Unit

Now we turn to Laura Pardo's fifth-grade classroom where she and her students are studying about the War Between the States (Raphael & Hiebert, 1996). She organized instruction so that social studies and literacy learning were integrated, using what she called an inquiry book club structure. The organization differs from the previous example so that you can see how integrated units can take many forms. Figure 9.5 shows how Ms. Pardo's goals are related to national literacy and social studies standards. Figure 9.6 illustrates how her instruction is organized.

Figure 9.5 Correlation between Fifth-Grade Teacher's Goals and National Standards

Teacher's Goals for War Between the States Unit	NCSS Standards	ELA Standards
■ Develop knowledge of the War Between the States as it relates to U.S. development What led to the war? Key historical figures Lives of ordinary people and war's impact on them Impact of war on issues we face today	Theme II: Time, continuity, and change ■ Understand historical roots and locate selves in time ■ Knowing how to read and reconstruct the past allows students to develop a historical perspective	**Std 1:** Read a wide range of print and nonprint texts to build understanding of texts, of themselves, and cultures of the United States, to acquire new information **Std. 2:** Read a wide range of literature from many periods to build an understanding of the many perspectives of human experience **Std. 3:** Apply a wide range of strategies to comprehend, interpret, and evaluate texts **Std 7:** Conduct research on issues and interests by generating ideas and posing questions. Gather, evaluate, and synthesize data from a variety of sources **Std. 12:** Use spoken, written, and visual language to learn and share information

(continued)

FIGURE 9.5   Continued

Teacher's Goals for War Between the States Unit	NCSS Standards	ELA Standards
■ Increase students' knowledge of literary conventions (genre study, author's craft, text structure, literary elements of plot and setting, point of view)		**Std 1:** Read a wide range of print and nonprint texts to build understanding of cultures of United States, to acquire new information **Std 3:** Apply a wide range of strategies to comprehend, interpret, evaluate, and appreciate texts. Draw on understanding of textual features **Std 6:** Apply knowledge of language structure, language conventions, and genre to create, critique, and discuss print and nonprint texts

■ Increase students' knowledge of literary skills:
  Use response logs to facilitate reflection, explore ideas, and develop new understandings
  Make intertextual connections
		Std 3: Apply a wide range of strategies to comprehend, interpret, evaluate, and appreciate texts
		Std 12: Use spoken, written, and visual language to respond to, learn, and exchange information

■ Develop metacognitive knowledge		**Std 3:** Use a wide range of strategies to comprehend texts
■ Share information, ideas, responses, and connections to texts, self, and others		**Std 11:** Participate as a knowledgeable, reflective member of the classroom literacy community

Figure 9.6 Fifth-Grade: War Between the States Unit Outline

Weeks 1 and 2 	**Goal: Building knowledge of the War Between the States** **Build enthusiasm and pique curiosity**

- K-W-L-S (*Know, Want* to know, *Learned, Still* need to know) (see Teaching Toolbox, KWWL details)
- Teacher-led discussion: Students shared what they knew (*K*) about the War Between the States and where they learned the information
- Teacher modeling: As teacher recorded students' ideas on a chart, she modeled how to take notes using phrases and abbreviations
- Teacher guidance: To help students think about questions they had about the War Between the States, the teacher guided students to distinguish between "big" questions—important for understanding aspects of the War Between the States—and those of lesser importance or those that could be answered simply

Making decisions for initial class research and instruction

- Class-developed criteria, generated with teacher guidance: Stemmed from "big" questions discussion, class developed criteria for evaluating questions to determine research worthiness.
- Inquiry Chart
- Small groups: Listed top two questions they thought should be answered
- Whole class share and decision: Voted on top four questions that students thought were important to investigate
- Small groups: Each group was given a set of resources and, for two days, looked for answers to the four questions. Each group recorded their answers to the questions on the class inquiry chart
- Teacher modeling and think aloud of how to summarize: Because each group had different answers to each question, the teacher modeled how to summarize across answers. To do this, she used procedures like those explained in Chapter 2: checked duplicate information, listed additional key ideas, and then wrote summary that drew from key ideas
- Guided practice for writing summaries: Class divided into two groups and summarized information to answer each question
- Whole group share: Shared summaries to demonstrate that there is no single correct way to summarize information

Determining questions for personal research, additional instruction

- What students had read thus far: textbook, other informational books, and historical fiction (*Across Five Aprils* by Hunt)
- Individual free write: Students wrote everything they knew about the War Between the States
- Whole class discussion: Filled in "L" on K-W-L-S chart and compared it to what they had written initially in K and W columns. The discussion helped the teacher identify students' points of confusion and misconceptions
- Individual: Determining personal inquiry topic. Listed questions they cared about and possible resources
- Whole class: Teacher-led discussion of questions they *still* wanted to answer and listed them in "S" column on K-W-L-S chart

(continued)

Figure 9.6   Continued

- Individual: Listed their top three questions. Teacher drew questions from a hat to determine which of those questions each child would investigate
- Whole class: Developed criteria for good project
- Individual: Four days to complete inquiry projects
- Individual: Presentation of projects

Weeks 3–5   **Goal: Develop a better understanding of people's lives during the War Between the States**

- Book Club: Students chose to read one of four historical fiction novels (*Who Comes with Cannons* by Beatty, *Shades of Gray* by Reeder, *Turn Homeward, Hannalee* by Beatty, and *Behind Rebel Lines* by Reit)
- Related small group and individual activities: Reading, writing in response log (sometimes referring to prompts teacher provided for scaffolding more reflective responses), book club discussions
- Whole class: All book club groups came together to share what they were learning about the War Between the States, their sources, responses, intertextual connections, issues, points of view, etc.

Reflecting

What did you notice about the way Ms. Pardo organized the unit? How effectively do you think she integrated social studies, reading, and writing? Explain. How do the organizational structures of the second-grade and fifth-grade classes differ? How are they similar? What would you do differently (and similarly) if you were to plan a unit about the rain forest or the War Between the States?

Try It! Technology Integration and Much More!

Check out www.education-world.com. Ideas for integrating technology into units like those described earlier are available at this website. Go to the file folder labeled *Article Archives* and click on "Technology in the Classroom" or the *Subject Resources* folder and click on "Technology." With a partner, take the information you learn here (and from other sites) and add primary source documents to the War Between the States unit.

Reconsidering

Think back to the beginning of the chapter. If you had your choice, how would you design your classroom so that students choose to spend time reading and writing there? If you could redesign your content and literacy instruction, what would you change? How do you think these changes would affect your students? What do you consider to be the advantages and disadvantages for organizing instruction in this way?

10 Assessing Learners and Texts in the Content Areas

In Chapter 10 we will ask you to picture in your mind a typical classroom of today—one filled with linguistically, ethnically, and culturally diverse children. Keep this classroom in view as you read and think about the politicized nature of high-stakes testing. We provide some questioning tools that you may use to evaluate standardized tests. We also offer some examples of how you may use English language arts and content area standards to guide the assessment process in your classroom and school. Finally, we examine several approaches you may take to assess learners and texts and how to use this information to inform your teaching practice.

Una selección del Principito, escrito por Antoine de St. Exupéry. Por favor, lea la selección siguiente y identifique el secreto del zorro. ¿Cómo se relaciona el secreto del zorro a su filosofía de la vida, teniendo en cuenta la experiencia del lector? (Antes de poder continuar con la lectura de este capitulo, es necesario responder a esta pregunta).

> —Vete a ver las rosas; comprenderás que la tuya es única en el mundo.
> Volverás a decirme adiós y yo te regalaré un secreto.
> El principito se fue a ver las rosas a las que dijo:
> —No son nada, ni en nada se parecen a mi rosa. Nadie las ha domesticado ni ustedes han domesticado a nadie. Son como el zorro era antes, que en nada se diferenciaba de otros cien mil zorros. Pero yo le hice mi amigo y ahora es único en el mundo.
> Las rosas se sentían molestas oyendo al principito, que continuó diciéndoles:
> —Son muy bellas, pero están vacías y nadie daría la vida por ustedes. Cualquiera que las vea podrá creer indudablemente que mí rosa es igual que cualquiera de ustedes. Pero ella se sabe más importante que todas, porque yo la he regado, porque ha sido a ella a la que abrigué con el fanal, porque yo le maté los gusanos (salvo dos o tres que se hicieron mariposas) y es a ella a la que yo he oído quejarse, alabarse y algunas veces hasta callarse. Porque es mi rosa, en fin.
> Y volvió con el zorro.
> —Adiós -le dijo.
> —Adiós -dijo el zorro-. Y aquí mi secreto, que no puede ser más simple:
> sólo con el corazón se puede ver bien; lo esencial es invisible para los ojos.
> —Lo esencial es invisible para los ojos -repitió el principito para acordarse (de St. Exupéry, 2001).

STOP!

Did you follow the instructions written in the first paragraph? Don't forget, before you may continue reading the rest of this chapter, you must identify the secret revealed to the Little Prince and relate it to your present life philosophies and past experiences. If you have arrived at this point in the text and have not answered, or at least have not thought about this question, you did not follow the directions. You will need to go back to the beginning and figure out the secret. It may be necessary to place you in a lower ability level.

Imagine if we were somehow able to enforce this statement. What would you do? How would you react? What if reading and comprehending this text actually had high stakes attached to it, for example, entry into the next phase of your teacher preparation courses or a pay raise? What if you had to produce a text written in a language not considered to be your academically proficient language? Do you feel you would be adequately assessed? Why or why not?

Remembering

Think about your own experiences being assessed as a student—no matter what age. How were you assessed? For what purposes were the assessments used? How did you feel after you received feedback from an assessment? Did the feedback extend your learning? What did you learn about your learning from this assessment? How would you change the assessment, if necessary, so it would have positively impacted your learning and integration into a learning culture?

Thinking back to learning French as a second language in Ontario, Kristiina remembers one of the goals of the classes was to impart the skills to use and continue learning one of Canada's official languages, French. Since Kristiina lived in an English-dominant region of Ontario, schooling was conducted in English, with daily lessons in French. Learning the language was divided into four sections: *savoir lire* (reading), *savoir écrire* (writing), *savoir écouter* (listening), and *savoir parler* (speaking). The class was frequently assessed in each of these arts of language, for example, approximately once a week, the class would listen to the dreaded "*Savoir Écouter*" tape and check off boxes according to what was heard on the cassette with what was printed on the "*Savoir Écouter*" worksheet. At the end of the test, the test papers were passed to a classmate and corrected as the teacher rambled off the correct answers. "Question numéro un: A; Question numéro deux: B; Question numéro trois: B" and so on. The paper was then returned to the original test taker with a score of ten or twenty. The students looked at the score, either grumbled or smiled, and put the page in a notebook. No further mention was made of the assessment.

Now, let's get political as well as practical! As we move through the rest of this chapter, we will discuss some of the politics of assessment at national levels and then we will take you to the microlevel of the classroom where we will discuss assessing learners and texts in the content areas.

Considering Linguistic, Ethnic, and Cultural Diversity in Assessment

Students in U.S. and English-speaking Canadian schools are assessed via the medium of the English language, the gatekeeper of mainstream education culture. As we consider the discussion on assessment in this chapter, let's keep in mind the rising number of children whose mother tongue and/or home language is other than that of the mainstream (English in the United States and English or French in Canada). The U.S. Census Bureau (2000) reported 13.8 percent of the population or nearly 32 million people use a language other than English in the home. This figure comprises 6.3 million children, aged five through seventeen, of which 4.1 million use Spanish. The Canadian Census (Statistics Canada, 1996) reported 16.1 percent of the population or 4.7 million people using a language other than English or French in the home. The relevance of considering multicompetent English language learners goes without saying. Although the uses and misuses of formal and informal assessments used in schools, school districts, states, and provinces must be understood in regards to all students, they must be carefully considered in regards to English language learners if we are to break the figurative glass ceiling placed above many of their heads.

Assessing Linguistically Diverse Students Learning English

Web link: http://www.ncbe.gwu.edu/library/assess.htm#STUDENTS

This link will connect you with numerous up-to-date articles pertaining to the assessment of linguistically and culturally diverse students. The articles address relevant issues impacting students as related to research, practice, program evaluation, and the evaluation of teacher education programs.

High Stakes to *Leave No Children Behind*: Both Sides Considered

On January 8, 2002, U.S. President George W. Bush signed the No Child Left Behind Act of 2001 as a reform effort to improve academic achievement by making schools and teachers accountable for student learning. The act requires national testing in reading and mathematics for students in grades 3–8 (implemented at the state level) verified by the National Assessment of Educational Progress (NAEP) in an effort to publish the results at state and local levels and levy corrective sanctions upon schools that do not show adequate improvement in student test scores (North Central Regional Educational Laboratory, 2002). Similarly, education systems in Canada are also being restructured with the implementation of standardized tests. For example, in Ontario, all students in grades 3 and 6 are assessed in reading, writing, and mathematics. These new regulations affect all students, parents, and educators (at all levels) and are causing some to worry, some to rejoice, and others to remain indifferent.

Standardized tests, such as the Iowa Basic Skills Test, California Achievement Tests, and Ontario EQAO assessment for reading, writing, and mathematics, have been coined "high-stakes" assessments because of the decisions made about students, teachers, schools, and educational programs based on results provided. Many teachers believe that enforcement of these tests reduces their professionalism because they decrease a teacher's freedom to be a decision maker in the classroom. The perception is reinforced when teachers see these assessment results used to make decisions about student tracking, promotion, retention, and placement in certain programs—special or gifted education. Because many teachers do not want to fail their students they feel they are forced into a corner: teach to the test or perish. We have often heard teachers express that high-stakes tests cause stress and anxiety, in themselves as well as in students, and reduce the amount of time spent on quality teaching because too much time is spent on testing and preparing students for the tests, which in turn negatively impacts learning, achievement, and self-esteem.

However, advocates for standardized tests lobby for their value to achieve high standards for educational excellence and achievement. The tests are expected to demonstrate the academic progress of each student and school over the years of testing and measure how well teachers are meeting the expectations of the curriculum. The purpose of these assessments is to improve the learning of all students.

Paul Barton (2001), a writer/researcher for Educational Testing Services, cautions the public that standardized tests should not be regarded as a treatment for educational problems, but as a way to measure if implemented reforms are producing results. In addition, Barton notes that administered standardized tests must align with the curriculum; in other words, the tests must assess what the students are taught in the classroom. He warns that if tests are not aligned with the curriculum, then students, parents, and educators may lose faith in the implemented reform. Citing the National Research Council's warning, Barton (2001) writes "when the test use is inappropriate . . . [i]t can undermine the quality of education and the equality of opportunity" (p. 6). This is precisely the fear expressed by many who oppose standardized testing.

Considering Ethnic, Cultural and Linguistic Biases in Standardized Tests

Joseph Laturnau (2002), the ESL specialist for the Pacific Center, writes about his experiences working with English language learners and test taking. Often times the "correct" answer is not the "correct" answer because of the inherent cultural bias within a test. For example, he notes in Korea, when a child loses his or her tooth, a tooth fairy does not place money under the child's pillow, but rather throws it onto the roof so that the next one will grow in straight. Therefore, in response to the multiple choice question,

Her tooth came out so she put it:

- ☐ On top of the refrigerator
- ☐ Under the tree
- ☐ Under her pillow
- ☐ None of the above

the child answered on top of the refrigerator because no other option expressed the direction "up."

Terry Salinger (2001), a research associate at the Pelavin Research Center of the American Institutes for Research in Washington, D.C., and former project leader for the IRA/NCTE National Standards for English Language Arts, offers educators a series of ten questions they can ask to evaluate standardized tests:

1. Is there evidence of test validity? Is it adequate?
2. Were norming procedures adequate? For example, was the test normed against an appropriate population?
3. Is there evidence of adequate reliability?
4. How will the test be scored? How will the scores be reported?

5. What is the purpose of the test? Is it congruent with local purposes?
6. Is testing time appropriate for young children? Is the test divided into testing sessions in an appropriate way?
7. Do timing and tasks seem developmentally appropriate?
8. How are scores calculated? Will information be useful to teachers, parents, others? What do score reports tell about students?
9. How are reading and writing represented in the tests?
10. What is the focus of the test? What is the balance of item types? (p. 393)

As you can see, many important decisions are made about a student and his or her learning environment through testing. Many standardized tests assess a student's knowledge in the content areas, for example, the California Achievement Tests measure a student's educational development in mathematics, science, and social studies (Salinger, 2001). You may choose to examine the content area questions on standardized tests using Salinger's questions noted earlier in order to understand what the tests contain and how they assess reading in the content areas. As Salinger (2001) notes, "the more teachers and other stakeholders understand the standardized tests children take, the more they can interpret test scores and determine how accurately test scores correspond to their own interpretation of students' progress" (p. 393). As with all decisions, the best ones are informed decisions: those made after much research and reflection. The same is true with making decisions about students, teachers, and schools; therefore, the case for multiple assessments in a variety of educational contexts is made.

High Stakes Testing: Multiple Perspectives

To learn more about high-stakes testing from multiple perspectives, have a look at the following websites. Don't forget to look at the extension domains of the mentioned sites (as discussed in Chapter 6) to get some insight about the potential bias of the information presented on the website.

Highlights of the No Child Left Behind Act of 2001
    http://www.ncrel.org/policy/curve/part1a.htm

Introduction: No Child Left Behind
    http://www.nochildleftbehind.gov/next/overview/index.html

Standardized Testing and High-Stakes Decisions
    http://www.ctf-fce.ca/E/WHAT/OTHER/ASSESSMENT/high-stakes.htm

The Nation's Report Card: Reading
    http://nces.ed.gov/nationsreportcard/reading/

International Reading Association's position statement on high-stakes testing
    http://www.reading.org/positions/high_stakes.html

Reflection

What is your opinion about the role of state or provincial achievement testing in the classroom? What do you think about the fear of "teaching to the test?" Do you think standardized tests can impact student learning? How can you use standardized tests to your advantage?

Assessing Texts and Learners

Three crucial questions a teacher must ask herself or himself when thinking about evaluating texts and learners in relation to instruction are "why am I doing what I am doing?" (instruction), "what information do I need to gather about each student so that I can understand how each student is progressing?" (assessment) and "what information do I need to gather that will help improve my instruction?" (planning). A question often heard from preservice and inservice teachers alike when talking about content area literacy is "How do I know a student is learning and understanding the content?" Our quick answer would be that prior knowledge, background experiences, the ability to decode text, attitude toward reading, and motivation to read all impact the way a reader transacts with a text—that the reader makes meaning with the text. You may want to refer back to Chapters 1 and 2 where we talk in more detail about readers making meaning with text.

Consider the importance of knowing something about a text and its content. Recht and Leslie (1988) have studied the impact of a student's prior knowledge on comprehending the content of a written text. They demonstrated how high prior knowledge about the content positively impacted comprehension of the text, regardless of a student's reading ability. Using a passage about baseball, the researchers asked four groups of students to read it and answer a series of comprehension questions. Table 10.1 shows the composition of each group.

 Recht and Leslie (1988) found that low-ability readers with high background knowledge about baseball performed nearly as well as high-level readers with high background knowledge about baseball on comprehension questions relying on memory recall after reading a text about baseball.

An important question to ask at this point is how do we assess a student's prior knowledge about particular content? Informal prediction strategies such as the

TABLE 10.1 **Group Compositions in Recht and Leslie's (1988) Study on the Effect of Prior Knowledge on Good and Poor Readers' Memory of Text**

Group 1	Group 2	Group 3	Group 4
Low prior knowledge of baseball	High prior knowledge of baseball	Low prior knowledge of baseball	High prior knowledge of baseball
Low reading ability	Low reading ability	High reading ability	High reading ability

K-W-W-L are often used to assess a student's prior knowledge about a topic. By asking students "What do you know about . . . ?" we gain insight into their knowledge about certain content information. We may learn whether or not the student has detailed knowledge about the content or only superficial knowledge. If, for example, you find the students do not have enough prior knowledge about the content you are preparing to teach, then you may need to teach some of the important concepts embedded in the vocabulary before you present the text.

Informational Predict-O-Gram

Camille Blachowicz (1986) designed a predict-o-gram to present students with key words from a story before reading in order to elicit background knowledge and get students to start thinking about the story. In this activity, students are asked to place the preselected words into the following categories: setting, characters, goal or problem, action, resolution, and other things. During or after reading, the students move words if they think they incorrectly placed a word in a category the first time around. The strategy may also be used to informally assess the students' comprehension of the text as they manipulate the words originally placed in the categories.

The strategy, based on the same principles, can be used for informational texts with a little tweaking. Instead of categories typically found in narrative texts, create categories typically found in informational texts. In Chapter 5 you learned that descriptive texts describe characteristics, features, or traits of a person, place, or thing; sequential texts present information in a particular order; comparison contrast texts present information in terms of similarities and differences of related people, places, things, or concepts; and cause and effect texts explain the actions or events that caused something to happen. When creating an informational predict-o-gram, use this knowledge of nonfiction organizational patterns to guide you as you create six categories (this number, of course, can be modified if you deem it necessary). You may choose to present vocabulary directly appearing in the text and/or vocabulary associated with the topic of the text that may enrich the student's text-to-world as discussed in Chapter 2.

Getting started.   Let's make an informational predict-o-gram with the book *Meet the Orchestra* by Ann Hayes (1991). Hayes's book describes various orchestral instruments, examining their various sounds and physical characteristics (Table 10.2). The author also compares and contrasts the various instruments; for example, note in the following text how she compares the viola to the violin. The following excerpt from the text is provided to give you a flavor of the writing.

> Viola. As instruments get bigger, their voices get lower. The viola looks and sounds like a big brother to the violin. It has a deeper tone, reminding you of evening shadows, cloudy skies, and the color blue. (p. 4)
> Piccolo. The piccolo, little sister to the flute, loves attention and always gets it. This tiny flute is so shrill you can't help hearing it. Its high notes almost pierce your eardrums. Yet everyone loves the piccolo because it has such a great sense of fun. (p. 8)

TABLE 10.2 Example of Informational Predict-O-Gram Using Words from *Meet the Orchestra* by Ann Hayes (1991)

Type of instrument	Sounds instruments make	Size of instruments
Violin, French horn, Cymbals	Boom-boom-boom, tootles, soft, loud	Small, big
Instrument families	How instruments are played	Where instruments are played
Wind, strings	Mouth, fingers, lips	Stage, theater

Creating categories.   Instead of using the categories defined by Blachowicz in the pre-dict-o-gram, which work well with fictional text, we need to create new categories for the informational predict-o-gram. Let's concentrate on highlighting the words used to describe musical instruments. This way, after the text has been read, your students will be better able to engage in a conversation or activity comparing and contrasting different kinds of orchestral instruments. Let's consider using the following categories: type of instrument, sounds instruments make, size of instruments, instrument families, how instruments are played, and where instruments are played.

Choosing words.   Now let's choose some words that the children can place in the categories before the book is read: violin, lips, french horn, cymbals, mouth, theater, loud, stage, small, soft, boom-boom-boom, fingers, tootles, big, strings, wind. (Note that the words in this list were extracted from the entire text and not just the excerpt presented earlier. Also, the word *theater* does not appear in the text, yet it is included in the list in order to make a possible connection with the outside world.) As the students work through the text, not only will they learn about music, but also about the functions of words in text, vocabulary, and about descriptive informational texts.

Putting it all together.   Now you will need to present your students the words you chose and ask them to place them in the categories you created. Remember to give your students the option to move words to other categories as you read the book.

Now that you have a better idea of the importance of understanding the students' prior knowledge of a text's topic, it is important to consider the difficulty of the text in comparison with the reading ability level of the students. How do you assess the difficulty of varying text types you may ask your students to read and vary the instruction accordingly? How do you choose appropriate books for students that match their reading abilities for content area reading and learning?

Assessing texts

It can be difficult to make meaning from a content-specific piece of expository text because of the potentially conceptually dense, content-specific vocabulary, sentence structure complexity, and sentence length. In addition, if the author's writing style is unfamiliar to the reader, it may be more difficult for the reader to make meaning with the text. When you ask children to work with any text you will need to consider the difficulty of the text, as well as the students' reading abilities, background knowledge of the content, and motivation and interest to read the text.

In this section, assessing the readability of a text will be considered. The difficulty of the text must be considered, particularly when asking students to read independently, without the assistance or supervision of a more experienced reader. If children are asked to read a text that is too difficult to read for reasons mentioned earlier, then they are at risk of becoming overwhelmed with feelings of frustration and inadequacy about their reading abilities. When readers become frustrated with the text they are reading, then their attitude toward reading and motivation to read may spiral downward.

Readability formulas may help you judge a text's difficulty. Once computed, the readability formula attributes an approximate reading grade level to the text. Generally speaking, the formulas use the following two variables in the computation of a reading grade level: number of syllables in a word and number of words in a sentence. The formulas assume that monosyllabic words are "easy" and polysyllabic words are more difficult. This is true from a decoding perspective. It is much easier to decode the word *dog* as compared to *canine*. Conceptually, the two words indicate membership to the same animal species, the first word being more colloquial and the second more specialized and content specific. In addition, the formulas function on the assumption that one can make meaning from a short sentence more easily than from a longer sentence. Readability formulas are easy and relatively quick to use (many with computer-assisted technology) and yield estimates of a text's difficulty, which are useful to teachers who are trying to choose a suitable text for their students to read and from which to learn. However, the limitations of such tools must be acknowledged and professional judgment employed when making a decision about a text's adoption. For example, it would be necessary to consider the conceptually rich monosyllabic word and short sentence and the student's background knowledge of and interest in the subject.

Popular readability formulas used to evaluate text difficulty of tradebooks, textbooks, and content found on the Internet include the following: the Fry readability formula, Flesch–Kincaid readability formula (this is the formula used by Microsoft Word after you run a spelling and grammar check on a document), and the Dale–Chall readability formula. You may also want to consult our adaptation of Jennifer Connor's (2002) adaptation of the readability checklist designed by Judith Irwin and Carol Davis (1980). The checklist examines the organization of the text, the way vocabulary and concepts are presented, the compatibility of text and reader, and how the text uses visuals (Figure 10.1).

Try It!

Choose a text for which you would like to find an estimated readability level. Log onto Kathy Schrock's guide for educators at http://school.discovery.com/schrockguide/fry/fry.html and follow the clear instructions she has laid out for using the Fry readability formula. Then type the same passage you chose to assess with the Fry readability formula into a Word document, run a spelling and grammar check, and find out what the estimated Flesch–Kincaid readability level is. What are the similarities or differences? What are the limitations of these formulas? How can you use them to the advantage of your students and your teaching practice?

Figure 10.1   General Readability Checklist

Place a check mark in the column that best describes your impression of the text according to the questions asked. Use the following scale and record your answers to the questions asked in the checklist: A=Always or Yes; B=Sometimes; C=Never or No; N/A=Not applicable

A B C N/A   **UNDERSTANDABILITY**

☐ ☐ ☐   ☐   1. Do the authors of the text consider the developmental level of the students' current vocabulary knowledge?

☐ ☐ ☐   ☐   2. Do the authors of the text consider the students' prior knowledge of the content area?

☐ ☐ ☐   ☐   3. Do the authors consider the students' general background experiences?

☐ ☐ ☐   ☐   4. Do the authors explicitly link new concepts to the students' prior knowledge or background experiences?

☐ ☐ ☐   ☐   5. Do the authors support abstract concepts with concrete examples?

☐ ☐ ☐   ☐   6. Do the authors introduce new concepts one at a time, with examples?

☐ ☐ ☐   ☐   7. Do the authors provide understandable definitions at a lower level of abstraction than the concept being defined?

☐ ☐ ☐   ☐   8. Do the authors of the text avoid irrelevant details?

☐ ☐ ☐   ☐   9. Do the authors of the text state important complex relationships (for example, causality and conditionality) rather than always expecting the reader to infer from the context?

USABILITY: External Organization Aids

☐ ☐ ☐   ☐   1. How useful is the table of contents (if any) to accessing information in the main text?

☐ ☐ ☐   ☐   2. Do the chapter headings clearly define the content of the chapter?

☐ ☐ ☐   ☐   3. Do the headings and subheadings clearly highlight important concepts and help readers understand how information is related throughout the text?

☐ ☐ ☐   ☐   4. Do the topic headings and subheadings help chunk the text into meaningful sections?

☐ ☐ ☐   ☐   5. Are content area words presented in a glossary?

☐ ☐ ☐   ☐   6. Do the graphs and charts support the textual material?

☐ ☐ ☐   ☐   7. Is the print size of the text appropriate for the developmental level of the students?

(continued)

Figure 10.1   Continued

A	B	C	N/A	USABILITY: Internal Organization Aids
☐	☐	☐	☐	1. Are the concepts spaced appropriately throughout the text, as opposed to being too many in too short a space or too few words?
☐	☐	☐	☐	2. Do the authors strategically use internal texts structures (description, sequence, compare/contrast, cause/effect, and problem/solution) to help the reader navigate through the content of the text?
☐	☐	☐	☐	3. Is the author's writing style appropriate for the level of students who will be using the text?

VISUAL AND MEDIA USABILITY

A	B	C	N/A	
☐	☐	☐	☐	1. Do the media resources contribute to the understanding of the content area being addressed?
☐	☐	☐	☐	2. How well do the authors combine visual and verbal literacies to make an integrated text?
☐	☐	☐	☐	3. Are the photographs, pictures, and/or diagrams in the book labeled?
☐	☐	☐	☐	4. Do the photographs, pictures, and/or diagrams stand alone without the text or does the reader need to comprehend the content of the text in order to understand the visuals?
☐	☐	☐	☐	5. Is there a table of contents or index for the photographs, pictures, and/or diagrams?

INTERESTABILITY

A	B	C	N/A	
☐	☐	☐	☐	1. Are the chapter titles, headings, and subheadings concrete, meaningful, and interesting?
☐	☐	☐	☐	2. Does the text provide positive models for both males and females as well as for other racial, ethnic, linguistic, and socioeconomic groups?
☐	☐	☐	☐	3. Does the text avoid stereotyping?

Strengths of Text:

_____

_____

Areas of need of text:

_____

_____

How can I best supplement the areas of need of text?

_____

_____

(*Source:* adapted from Jennifer Conner's adaptation of the Irwin and Davis Readability Checklist available on-line: http://www.indiana.edu/~l517/readability.htm)

Try It! The Five-Finger Test

When children are in the library choosing books for independent reading, tell them about this test to see if the book they choose is too hard for them to read independently. Tell the students to flip to a page near the middle of the book and start reading. Each time they come to a word they do not understand, tell them to hold up one finger. If they put up five fingers before they finish reading the page, the book is too hard for them to read independently and they should choose another book.

Assessing Learners in the Content Areas

Matching texts with students can be complex. One way to match text with a student is to understand a student's reading level, reading interests, and reading attitude. Informal (unnormed) assessment tools such as student portfolios, anecdotal records, project-based learning, observation of students' interactions within authentic learning situations, and simply asking students to "think aloud" as they work through a text or activity are examples of ways teachers assess students' reading and writing abilities and content knowledge.

Many informal tools are available that yield volumes of information about a student's development in alphabetics, fluency, and comprehension, for example, informal reading inventories, running records, analyzing oral miscues, answering comprehension questions, and engaging students in story retellings. Understanding how a student feels when reading in different contexts (e.g., in the classroom, at home, or in the library) along with understanding the student's reading interests will help you choose texts the student may be more motivated to read than texts that are less appealing. You may wish to interview your students using questions you create yourself or with ready-made informal interest or attitude surveys.

Assessing Learners Working with Texts

Assessment is not all that bad! Barksdale-Ladd and Thomas (2000), interviewed teachers about high-stakes assessment and found that many of them felt strongly about the positive and useful information provided by informal assessment tools. Specifically the teachers appreciated how properly engineered assessment tools provided students with feedback about their learning and offered ways to continue learning. In addition, the teachers appreciated how information obtained from student assessments could also inform their teaching practice, therefore improving student learning.

As you consider assessment in the content areas, you need to question the purposes of the assessments you administer. Too often we hear teachers threatening students with a test if the work is not done appropriately, adequately, and in a timely fashion. Think about the implications. If such a threat is used, what message might you send to your students? How might you shift the focus of assessment?

When planning for assessment, consider the purpose of the assessment. Ask yourself some of the following questions: What is the test trying to evaluate? Does the test correspond with what I have taught in the classroom according to the curriculum? What information will the assessment tool give me to help improve my teaching practice? How will I record this information? How will I present this information to students and parents?

Try It! The Sticky-Note Anecdotal Record Collector

In today's classrooms and schools, sticky notes abound. Carry around a pack of sticky notes in your pocket and when you come across a note-worthy event, write the child's name, date, and description of what you observe on the note. Keep a three-ringed binder with a page dedicated to each student in your class. When you have time, attach the sticky note to the child's personal page. Each week, sit down with your binder and analyze the data you have collected on a few students per week. What learning patterns do you notice? How does what you observe align with other assessments you administer? You will begin to see how the rich, descriptive information you collect will help you better understand your students, their learning, and your practice.

The following anecdotal records were collected by Anne Goodrow, a preservice teacher at The University of Georgia, during her practicum in a second–grade classroom. Anne spent time observing Calvin (not his real name) interact with text at his school. What information about Calvin's literacy development, interaction with text, and attitude and interest in learning can you glean from these anecdotal records?

September 10

I am watching Calvin during today's social studies lesson. The students are reading about Native Americans. He is picking at his name tag on his desk and is obviously not following along with the book. I asked him to keep his eyes on the paper several times. He put his eyes on the book for a few seconds, but now they are wandering again. Now, he is taking out an index card and using it to keep his place as he follows along with the reading of the text.

September 19

Calvin is working on an anticipation guide about the Cherokee tribe. He is having problems reading the questions for today's assignment. He continuously asks me to read the statements on the guide for him. I asked him to try to read the questions himself, but he visibly became frustrated and anxious. When I read the sentences aloud to Calvin, he was able to give a logical answer.

September 24

Calvin and I read together today during free time. He chose to look at a book in the *Goosebumps* series, a book he selected from the library. I suspect the book is above his independent reading level. He started reading very quickly. He uses a lot of intonation; however, he seems to guess or skip over words he does not know. When he comes to a word he does not know, he stares at the page.

The BioPoem, for example, may be used as a unique way to assess a student's learning. The BioPoem can be an alternative to the standard biographical report or can be used for any content area, provided you change the categories to suit the needs of the subject. For example, learning about music, you may ask your students to study a famous musician or composer. You can begin the activity by asking students to work with the K-W-W-L chart. Students will write down what they know, what they want to know, where they will find (or think they will find) the information, and what they have learned. In this example, the students could represent their learning in the form of a BioPoem. As the students research their famous musician (using information found in books, magazines, newspapers, the Internet, for example) you can ask them to organize the information using any number of graphic organizers. The students can then be evaluated on the completeness and depth of the K-W-W-L chart, their representation of the chosen musician, the accuracy of the information, the quality of the language, and the style of writing (Penrose, 2002). In order to make the assessment work with planning and instruction, you may choose to create a rubric for assessing one or more English language or specific content area standards with your students. The following is an example of a general rubric you may wish to use or adapt to your own instruction and assessment of instruction (Figure 10.2).

Try It!

Take, for example, the second of three goals for grades pre-K to 3 as outlined in TESOL, the ESL standards for pre-K–12 students. Goal 2 states that students should "use English to achieve academically in all content areas." Standard 1: students will use English to interact in the classroom; standard 2: to obtain, process, construct, and provide subject matter information in spoken and written form; and standard 3: to use appropriate learning strategies to construct and apply academic knowledge." Keeping this goal and standards in mind, take a lesson plan you have already created or tried with your students in a content area and find areas where your English language learners might have opportunities to achieve each of these standards. What would you have to modify, change, add, or take away in order for English language learners to better achieve this goal?

Figure 10.2   Sample Assessment Rubric for Use with a BioPoem

	4	3	2	1
Content: The information in the BioPoem is accurate	Complete and accurate information	Accurate information	Some inaccurate information	Inaccurate information
Language: Frequently used words are spelled correctly	Most of the time	Some of the time	Almost never	Never
Word use: Student used descriptive words and phrases	Original descriptive words used	Some original descriptive words used	Few descriptive words used	Lacking original descriptive words
Visuals: Student used an appropriate visual to represent his/her BioPoem	Represents contents of BioPoem very well	Represents contents of BioPoem well	Represents contents of BioPoem marginally	Does not represent contents of BioPoem

Assessing Literacy at Play

Let's consider some work done by Baker and Swafford (2000) in which qualitative research methods were used to explore the kind of information a teacher could obtain from observing a child play in a literacy-rich play center. The following field notes were collected from the observation time.

One day at the block center, Amy and Katie were building a town with wooden blocks and road signs. Dennis pretended to be a dog and began knocking down their buildings. The girls asked Dennis to stop, but when he did not, they went to Michelle (Baker) for help. She asked them what they could do to keep Dennis from knocking down their blocks. Amy's first solution was that Michelle should tell Dennis to play in another center. Michelle, however, told the girls they needed to work out the problem themselves.

Katie and Amy proceeded to the reading center, sat in comfortable chairs, and discussed different ways they could stop Dennis. All at once Amy declared, "We need to make a sign, just like Mrs. Michelle did for the water!" (Michelle had recently put a "do not touch" sign on the water faucet in the classroom.) Amy and Katie decided to make a sign that said, "No Dogs." Katie was the scribe and Amy dictated. They wrote No with few problems. When they got to the word dog, Amy told Katie that the word dog stated with a d and has a g, but she could not help Katie write the letter g. Katie wrote the letter d, and Amy asked Greg how to write a g. Then she told Katie to look at the dog poster on the wall and copy the word dog. When the girls finished, Michelle asked Amy what the sign said. She replied "no dogs." Then the girls hung the sign in the block center. (pp. 282–284)

Baker and Swafford (2000) noted how the child was able to demonstrate an understanding of different functions of print. In this example, the student demonstrated her understanding that print is used to gain instructions, provide others with information, provide labels, test others' skills, organize, identify ownership, tell a story, entertain, be a resource for information, direct other's behavior, gain entrance or reserve space, convey feelings, and record information. (Remember, print is used in daily life as a functional tool, hence the reason why teaching with expository text is critical). The child also exhibited an understanding of eight concepts of print: print is made up of separate words, carries a message, has its own type of language, has directionality, orientation, and return sweep, holds a permanent message, includes punctuation, is related to pictures, and has special features.

Obviously, it would take much time and dedication to sit with children and just watch them interact with text or engage in similar scenarios as the one just mentioned. Baker and Swafford (2000) acknowledge that this method of assessment would not be appropriate as a sole means of assessing a student's emerging literacy development; however, they recommend this technique be used to understand how children use printed sources in authentic contexts.

Set yourself some realistic goals. Maybe you could decide that you will watch one group of children play per day and see what you discover. You can even record your observations on sticky notes, as mentioned earlier. Here are some guidelines for collecting anecdotal records suggested by Thorndike and Hagen as cited in Rhodes and Nathenson-Meija (1992) that may help you focus on the content of the situation being observed.

1. *Describe a specific event or product*—as you engage in kid watching, take a note pad and write down what you observe going on at a center, for example. Write down what the children do, what the children say, and how they interact with each other. What content learning is going on?
2. *Report rather than evaluate or interpret*—report only what you observe; do not engage in analyzing the situation just yet or you may miss out on some interesting information.
3. *Relate the material to other facts that are known about the child*—when you look back at your notes, relate the information you gathered to other assessments or other information you may have gathered about that child.

Now it is time to go out and "test" some "testing." To assist you in this activity, we offer a quote from Regie Routman (2000):

Whatever we do for the first time, whether it is small group guided reading, shared writing, integrating spelling, or holistic evaluation, we are bound to bungle it at the start. This is natural behavior for all new, comprehensive processes and procedures, and we need to be forgiving and patient with ourselves. The main thing is to begin, to give it a try (p. 4).

Reconsidering

In this chapter we have tried to address many complex issues pertaining to assessment at various levels of education. As you grow in your teaching career, whether you are just beginning or have been teaching for a long time, you will be assessing your own progress as well as the progress of your students. How will you use informal assessment tools to learn about the students you teach and about the material you present them in order to improve learning, (yours as well as theirs)? Have you thought about how standardized tests may be used to inform your learning and practice? How will you consider the needs of English language learners as you assess their learning? What do you still want to learn about assessment in the classroom, the school, and the country?

11 Integrating Literacy into the Content Areas

In Chapter 11, you will learn why we think integrating literacy into the content areas is crucial to support learning in democratic classrooms where life experiences are valued. Literacy demands for the new millennium are examined and how integrating literacy into content area instruction will help meet these demands. We examine the "what," the "why," and the "how" of integrated literacy instruction by providing you with an example using technology in the classroom, as well as offering you an example of a preservice teacher's first attempt to integrate literacy instruction into a science lesson in a third-grade classroom. We also examine how connecting home and school may help teachers integrate literacy instruction with content in powerful ways.

The Setting

Sitting in a second-grade classroom, the room still buzzing with the energy of children scrambling off to their homes, the playground, or their music lessons, I (Kristiina) sit waiting to chat with Sofia, the second-grade teacher, about her views and opinions of integrating literacy instruction into the content areas. The interview occurred in the springtime of the school year.

KRISTIINA: Tell me a little bit about what you are studying with your kids.

SOFIA: At the moment we are doing something very exciting! We are doing a story-book unit in which we are comparing and contrasting different versions of one story. I got the idea in a children's literature course I took that compared and contrasted the various cultural versions of the original French fairytale, *Cinderella*. I thought it might be interesting to do the same type of activity with my students.

KRISTIINA: Yes, this certainly sounds exciting. I have seen many teachers reading different versions of The *Three Little Pigs* with their students. There is a great version of the same story told from the perspective of the big bad wolf. I know the children enjoy this type of narrative fiction.

SOFIA: Definitely! A great writing activity I have used with my students is the "point of view study guide" found in Doug Buehl's (2001) book entitled *Classroom Strategies for Interactive Learning*. I find the activity not only pedagogically interesting, but also engaging for the students. The strategy recommends that the teacher provide the students (or the students may choose for themselves) a person or character, not an obvious main character though, through whose eyes to read the text. For example, to read the more traditional version of the folktale *The Three Little Pigs* from the perspective of the so-called villain of the story. A commercial example of this type of activity is told by Jan Scieszka (1996) in his book called *The True Story of the Three Little Pigs*. This activity challenges the students to consider different points of view.

KRISTIINA: Absolutely! I have also seen this activity used to guide readers to consider different perspectives in nonfictional or informational texts. For example, if students are studying about the life cycle of flowers and plants, they might consider looking at the material from the perspective of a bee, an insect responsible for pollinating many flowers. Speaking of nonfiction texts, I am very interested in learning about how you use these texts with your students. What content are you currently studying in your class and how do you integrate literacy instruction with your content areas?

SOFIA: Well, in the fall, we did a lot of work with nonfiction text. We studied many things in science like birds, sharks, and the coral reef. It was fun for a while, but I noticed my students were simply not engaged with the material and I don't exactly understand why. I tried getting the students to write sentences about the animals and their environment being studied, but they became tired and bored with the content. This semester I decided to do something different. I still have a writing center for the students and we still do whole group interactive writing, but not as much. I primarily use the writer's workshop strategy during literacy centers, when we read more narrative work. I think this might work better.

Sofia and Kristiina engaged in a reflective discussion about teaching strategies and what each considered important pedagogies. Sofia, taking the role of a practicing teacher, wondered why her attempt to use nonfiction text in her content area lessons was not being well received. In this instance, we ask you to think about why Sofia chose to abandon teaching science lessons using literacy centers. Think about Sofia's planning, her teaching philosophy, and the resources to which she might have had access. Can you try to imagine reasons why the children were "tired and bored" with the lessons about birds, sharks, and the coral reef? What do you think was going on? How do you think the children might become more engaged with the content? What do you think about the way Sofia integrates literacy instruction in her classroom? What do you think may have been Sofia's experiences with content area learning?

Remembering

What do you remember about how you learned content area material? What was considered important in your content area class—the content or communication about the content? Do you remember the use of textbooks and worksheets? How were you presented information in the content areas? How was your content area knowledge assessed? What made learning the content enjoyable for you? What made learning the content not so enjoyable for you?

Kristiina began her "teacher" years in Ontario, Canada, where she was trained to teach students French as a second language (differentiated from French as a foreign language because in Canada French and English are the two official languages). She not only had to teach the language, but also certain aspects of the cultures and histories of the Francophone world. The textbooks she was given to use in the classroom were categorically divided up into neat lessons. There was one lesson on each of the various language arts–reading, writing, speaking, and listening–and there were sections interspersed throughout entitled "Culture." Kristiina realized the strong connection between the languages and the cultures, along with the politics of language teaching. Teaching French in a predominantly Anglophone region of Ontario carried with it many political frustrations.

The content in the "Culture" sections of the textbooks privileged the French-speaking worlds primarily of the west, for example, Québec, France, Belgium, and Switzerland. Kristiina began to question why the textbooks didn't address other politically dominant Francophone countries, such as Haïti or Sénégal. She can't help but think how learning about the cultures and histories of Francophone countries would have enriched the students' language learning experience had she integrated other texts into her lessons. She could have used nonfiction texts in the form of trade books, newspaper articles, magazine articles, photographs, or Internet sources. The students could have learned not only about other countries in which French is an official language, but they would have learned vocabulary, sentence structures, grammar, and conversation—all of the elements dictated by the curriculum. Perhaps the students may have looked beyond many of the negative political messages they ingested from their social surroundings and found a genuine interest in learning about the beauty of the languages and cultures of the Francophone world.

What Is Integrated Literacy Instruction and How Is It Done?

In order to better understand the "how" it is important to develop an understanding of the "what" and the "why." This chapter examines what integrated literacy instruction is and why it is practically and philosophically important for students and teachers today. This chapter complements Chapters 9 and 10 because it completes the discussion of the planning–assessment–instruction circle. In fact, when we decided upon the order of the chapters for this book, we debated for long hours as to which chapter should appear first because they all speak to the entire package, but to borrow the words of Nobel Prize Literate José Saramago, "writing is extremely difficult, it is an enormous responsibility, you need only think of the exhausting work involved in setting out events in chronological order, first this one, then that, . . . or the present as a continuous process with neither beginning nor end, but, however, hard writers might try, there is one feat they cannot achieve, and that is to put into writing, in the same tense, two events that have occurred simultaneously" (Saramago, 1995). In this sense, Chapters 9, 10, and 11 could be read and reread in any order.

What Is Integrated Literacy Instruction?

To dwell on the term "integrated literacy instruction" is not as important as considering and understanding the actions needed to carry forward the meaning behind these words. Consider for a moment the fact that we do not interact with the world in isolated compartments. For example, our family life impacts and influences our work life, just as our philosophical meanderings permeate the way in which we form friendships and to the ways in which we read this world of ours. When considering the interaction between what happens within the four walls of the classroom, so to speak, it is essential to consider the individual and collective experiences each student brings to the classroom from the outside world, just as it is as important to validate what teachers contribute to classroom interactions from the outside world. To simply consider the notion of integrated literacy instruction as that which happens in the classroom limits its power (Gavelek, Raphael, Biondo, & Wang, 2000). We need to be aware that it includes integrating the language arts into the content areas, as well as engaging in curriculum integration, and community integration (Pearson & Johnson, 1994). Integrating literacy instruction needs to be everywhere.

As teachers, we create a harmony between what is considered the outside world and the classroom world. We blend, synthesize, unify, coordinate, and orchestrate understandings through the events, lessons, activities, and learning opportunities to which we expose our students. This said, would it not be absurd to consider that the world of science neither influences nor impacts the world of philosophy or the world of language and literature? Is it not absurd to think that the traditional ways of knowing—reading, writing, speaking, and listening—be considered in isolation, away from content area teaching? And now as the definition of literacy is expanding, shouldn't viewing, movement, touch, and smell, for example, also be considered when teaching content area material? All things considered, is it not inconceivable to imagine teaching math, for example, without teaching elements of the art of language? In the classroom, how can we create a harmony of understanding between and among the various content areas categorized by the curriculum?

Reflecting

Think about a classroom learning experience where you learned about static electricity, Mary Cassat–a famous U.S. American impressionist painter–another great historical figure. Do you remember how the content was presented to you in class? What was more important, remembering the facts and figures or understanding how the content related to your life? Now think about a learning experience when you visited a science center, an art museum, or visited an historical monument. Think about how the learning was the same and how it was different. Did one learning experience inform the other?

Do you recall what Jeanne, Donna, and Kristiina remembered about learning content area material when they were in elementary school, presented in Chapter 9? Each of us learned content as isolated, compartmentalized, and solitary units. To discuss the relationship between content and language arts was not often, if at all, done. In a sense, the secondary, college, and university models of education have encouraged this type of scheduling and teaching; it is a model dictated by a specialized curriculum and content area teachers. It is possible to teach students the art of talking about science, writing about math, listening about social studies, and reading about geography, for example, while studying the material of the content area. Keep this thought in mind as you read about Tien Tien later on in this chapter, a kindergartener who shared with us her literacy learning experiences with technology; and as you read about Isabelle, a preservice teacher's first attempt to get students to use multiple ways to think and learn about small machines as she taught students science. In fact, we believe that by integrating literacy instruction in the content areas, beginning in the elementary school, we contribute to the efficiency and effectiveness of what it means to teach and learn multiliteracies.

The Report of the National Reading Panel (2000) concluded that readers need to be engaged in activities that encourage active thinking and problem solving. Elementary school teachers are responsible for fostering a strong foundation for inquiry, expression, and understanding within each student in their classes. The responsibility to start forming the connections across all aspects of life is first and foremost begun in the home, but is certainly encouraged and fostered in the first days and subsequent years in the classroom. If elementary school teachers don't take responsibility for this, who will? It is as Paolo Freire (1983) once wrote, before learning to read the word, one learns to read the world. The teacher can therefore help the students read the word as well as the world. How exciting!

Gavelek et al. (2000) believe that too little time is spent on integrating literacy instruction into content areas. Hence, we ask the question: "What is so critical about teaching our students in a manner to show intrasubject as well as intersubject connections while providing them the tools with which to understand these connections?" To begin to answer this question, we look to the future. Doing so, we refer to five literacy scholars who wrote about the demands of literacy in the workplace in the next millennium. M. Cecil Smith argued that many of the fast-growing occupations (e.g., retail sales, truck drivers, health care aides) require minimal training, mostly found on the job, and the expectation is that they will be prepared for the rigors of the workplace by services provided to them in the public education system. In contrast, high-level jobs require much more than the mere mechanical ability to read and write; such jobs require the ability to think critically, creatively, effectively, and efficiently—described as "high literacy" by Janice Dole. In the same vein, Larry Mikulecky noted that workplaces now require employees to have knowledge of specialized vocabularies and con-

cepts in order to be considered functionally literate (and ultimately employable). In addition, Michael Kibby noted that in order to do a job well, "most future workplaces . . . will require accessing numerous knowledge bases (e.g., texts, manuals, tables, tapes, videos, graphics); reading, viewing, and listening to information (e.g., facts, viewpoints, analyses, critiques, demonstrations); understanding, analyzing, synthesizing, and evaluating this information and then distributing or applying it" (p. 380). In other words, multiliteracies will be increasingly expected in the years to come. Additionally, Mariam Jean Dreher believed that the workplace will involve the ability to negotiate meaning across diverse literacy dimensions (Smith, Mikulecky, Kibby, Dreher, & Dole, 2000). All of these arguments point in the direction and create a strong case for the need to integrate literacy into all areas of the curriculum. Why? For the future.

Gavelek et al. (2000) were surprised to find few research or data-driven articles about integrating literacy into content area instruction when compared to the large number of practitioner articles available. There were so few research articles that these researchers began to wonder if encouraging literacy integration into the content areas

may be premature or based in ill-founded assumptions at this time. On further consideration they concluded that albeit small, the empirical research on integrated literacy instruction offered some interesting ways of rethinking school curriculum.

For instance, Bristor (as cited in Gavelek et al., 2000) found that children receiving instruction in content areas with a strong emphasis on reading, writing, listening, and speaking had greater achievement gains in reading and in the content area. As well,

they exhibited more positive attitudes toward the subject area and greater self-confidence than those who received content area instruction without such a strong emphasis on literacy. Further, in a classroom where literacy was integrated throughout the curriculum, Morrow (as cited in Gavelek et al., 2000) noted that children experienced greater success when asked to engage in story retellings, comprehended story content at higher levels, and constructed stories of original content, all without negatively impacting their performance on standardized tests.

Additional evidence for the power of integrated instruction was reported by Winograd and Higgins (as cited in Gavelek et al., 2000). These researchers found that a focus on integrating language arts instruction into content areas facilitated children's

ability to solve problems; they moved beyond a superficial knowledge of content material to a deeper one. Finally, Timothy Shanahan (1997) believed that young children are simply not given enough practice gathering information from sources nor sufficient time to use what they have learned. From this evidence, we conclude that children need to be furnished with sufficient time, resources, and support in order to make connections and integrate new knowledge with what they already know, as discussed in Chapter 2.

ELA Standards

Multiple English Language Arts Standards encourage children to read a wide range of print and nonprint texts (Standard 1), to read a wide range of literature spanning time and genres (Standard 2), and to conduct research on issues and interests through inquiry (Standard 7), as addressed in Chapter 12.

One way you can facilitate the construction of deeper knowledge is to encourage students to gather information from a variety of sources. Teachers can use trade books as a vehicle to study content areas, thus giving students opportunities to pose more sophisticated questions about the content being studied as well as the human condition (Monson, Hove, & Greenlee as cited in Gavelek et al., 2000) and allow for a profound analysis of the topic. In fact, Morrow (as cited in Gavelek et al., 2000) found that children preferred the integration of literature into science instruction as opposed to a traditional method of science instruction. Integrating literacy instruction in the content areas would certainly give children more "time to practice," as Shanahan (1997) noted.

Web Link: www.ncte.org/positions/interdisciplinary_learning.shtml

This link leads you to the position statement issued by the National Council of Teachers of English regarding interdisciplinary learning, pre-K to grade 4. Guidelines are provided for characteristics of a quality interdisciplinary/integrated literacy instruction curriculum. The guidelines include such notions as the integrity of the disciplines, leading children to inquire—to ask questions, foster a community of learning, develop democratic classrooms, provide learning opportunities among diverse learners, respect diversity of thought and culture, encourage the use of multiple information sources (not just printed text), represent knowledge in myriad ways, and use a variety of assessments to evaluate student learning. The position statement is endorsed by other teaching organizations, such as the International Reading Association (www.reading.org), the National Council for the Social Studies and Teachers of Mathematics, Speech Communication Association, and the Council for Elementary Science International.

What Does It Mean to "Do" Integrated Literacy Instruction?

To integrate literacy into content areas is to "bring into close relationship such elements as concepts, skills, and values, so that they are mutually reinforcing" (Goodlad

& Su as cited in Gavelek et al., 2000, p. 594). The reinforcement of skills and knowledge can be metaphorically spoken of as the breaking of twigs. Imagine you hold one single twig in your hand. Try to break that twig. Can you imagine it easily being twisted or simply snapped to break in two? Now imagine you have several twigs in a bundle. Try to break them. It cannot be done easily, at least not with bare hands. The same is true when we integrate literacy into the content areas. Because learning literacy is multifaceted, learning skills in isolation, in the absence of authentic learning situations, is like walking around collecting one twig at a time, putting it down, and picking up another, putting it down and picking up another, and so forth. However, if all of these twigs are collected and bound together, the strength within is evident.

Oftentimes in the elementary classroom, literacy is promoted using narrative fiction. Logically, the writing that occurs tends to be a narrative and fictional type of writing, the kind that begins, for example, with "Once upon a time . . . ," a familiar story structure we mentioned in Chapter 5. Keep in mind that many daily literacy practices lean toward the informational, nonfiction side, such as interacting with research reports, directions, and reading images in the environment. Children in the elementary grades need to "practice" negotiating meaning with informational text. Christine Pappas (1991) believes the expository gap, one where children experience difficulty making meaning with informational text, will persist if children do not transact with quality informational books. As children work with expository text they will become more familiar with its various text structures, also discussed in Chapter 5. Typically, expository text is introduced to students in middle school. Graves (1989) argues that starting to work with expository text in fifth or sixth grade is too late because, as with many things, learning to work with expository text takes time, scaffolding, modeling, interest, and motivation. Perhaps these constructs can be thought of as the twigs to be gathered in a bundle. As children write and work with nonfiction text, they are also organizing their learning and ideas. In so doing, they begin to learn that writing is also a form of analysis.

Many teachers plan instruction around themes in order to attempt to create a cross-disciplinary curriculum in which various questions can be addressed through inquiry by taking advantage of a child's natural curiosity. Barton and Smith (2000) believe that a thematic unit fails when it is not organized by an overarching theme or question (the need to gather many twigs in order to strengthen learning), rather the binding elements of the thematic unit are loosely fitted commonalities (one twig picked up, one twig put down). They offer the example of the frequently used apple theme in instruction: "Children split apples into fractional parts [pick one twig up, put it down], look at apple trees [pick one twig up, put it down], read about Johnny Appleseed [pick one twig up, put it down], and write about how they would feel if they were apples [pick one twig up, put it down]" (p.55). Regie Routman (1991) refers to these as "themes of convenience." Even though the individual activities may be interactive, engaging, and pedagogically sound, the apple theme in this example is not substantive enough for students to make deeper connections to their life and the world around them, therefore perpetuating a superficial treatment of content.

Reflecting

There are many great activities, without a doubt, a teacher could do with apples. What problems do you see with creating a learning theme around apples? What is the motivating question or questions students could ask about apples? What purpose is there in studying apples? In the example just given, math is taught by splitting apples into fractional parts, but would the mathematical learning objectives be met any differently if the students split a pie, a pumpkin, or a bag of jelly beans into fractional parts? What does doing math with apples have to do with Johnny Appleseed, an important figure in U.S. history?

To integrate literacy into instruction it is important to keep the notion of teaching and learning across subject areas, life domains, and across cultures as a guiding light. Barton and Smith (2000) believe that many activities are skill driven, meaning that oftentimes activities are chosen to teach a particular skill as opposed to having "intrinsic meaning or application" (p. 56). We are not discouraging the use of apples in your instruction; what we are asking you to do is think carefully about how and when you use your activities involving apples. To continue with the metaphor of gathering twigs, make sure that your students need to bundle together the twigs in order to make meaning. If students need to bundle twigs together then they will continue to collect them, without putting the strong one back on the ground. For example, a popular theme in pre-K and kindergarten is "all about me." Children learn to understand elements about themselves throughout the school day, week, month, and year. The overarching question for the year could be something like "Who am I now and how do I know I am growing and learning?" Throughout the year, units can be built around this question and as children work within the content areas, they can come to a better understanding of who they are and how they are growing and learning through the content material. For example, as children learn about themselves they may see themselves growing taller and gaining weight—aspects related to their health. In this situation, you may want to talk about "eating an apple a day, to keep the doctor away" as children learn about nutrition, exercise, and health. You could also talk about how the apple seed grows and develops first into a flower and then into the fruit as you explore health with your students.

Typically, literacy integration into content areas focuses on printed text. However, as your definition of literacy continues to expand to include reading multiple sources of text, including visual and media literacy, perhaps the activities you create to answer the overarching question or questions will incorporate the use of printed text, fiction and nonfiction, photographs, art, and multimedia. Here you could talk about how sped up motion picture photography can demonstrate apple tree growth cycles. In art, you could refer to Picasso's and Cezanne's "apples." You could even talk about "reading" apple seeds under a microscope.

Using Technology to Integrate Literacy into Content Areas

Technology, literacy, and the content areas can be happily married together. Labbo, Eakle, and Montero (2002) demonstrate how this is possible by making use of digital photographs and KidPix Studio Deluxe from Broederbund, a kid-friendly photo soft-ware program, to enhance the traditional language experience approach (LEA) (Stauf-fer, 1970). They found that adding digital photography to LEA (D-LEA) created unique literacy learning opportunities for the children involving language, experience, visual images, and technology. The researchers worked with three children in kinder-garten, all exhibiting varying degrees of literacy abilities.

ELA Standards

The English Language Arts Standard #8 encourages that children "use a variety of techno-logical and information resources to gather and synthesize information and to create and communicate knowledge. Do you see how even in kindergarten, Tien Tien's learning met this eighth ELA standard?

Kristiina worked with Tien Tien, a five-year-old high-literacy ability kinder-gartener. As part of the D-LEA activity, Kristiina created an informal activity that she could share with Tien Tien: a walk in the schoolyard. With a digital camera and tape recorder in hand, the two engaged in casual conversation about things they observed during the walk. Tien Tien talked about the plants and insects and connected these to learning science in her classroom as well as incorporated out-of-school learning expe-riences as she made sense of what she observed. Consulting Tien Tien, Kristiina took photographs of different scenes around the school, for example, the class garden, the pumpkin patch, the bee mobile, fifth graders playing on the field, the trees, and other plant life. As the walk progressed, Tien Tien became so enthusiastic about photogra-phy that she asked Kristiina to help her take a picture on her own; she engaged in gath-ering her own visual information, knowing that she was going to create a multimedia slide show for her friends.

Earlier in the school year, before this D-LEA activity, Ms. Maggie, Tien-Tien's teacher, had introduced the children to plants and the growth cycle through literature, fiction and nonfiction, and experiments. One of the many books Ms. Maggie read to the children during her science lessons was *I'm a Seed* by Jean Marzollo discussing the growth cycle of plants, from seed to flower. (If you are working with older children, you might consider using Gail Gibbons' *The Pumpkin Book*, which also details the growth cycle of plants.) Ms. Maggie brought in pumpkins (the fruit of the vine) and the children carved orange pumpkins for Halloween, an American and Canadian festival, and toasted and ate the pumpkin seeds.

Kristiina took a picture of Tien Tien (see Figure 11.1) pointing to a growing pumpkin patch in the spring of that same school year. The following transcript reflects the conversation that occurred around the photographic experience. Read the tran-script and see how the social interaction influenced what Tien Tien dictated to Kristi-ina in the caption for the photograph.

FIGURE 11.1 Tien Tien examining the growing pumpkin patch in the schoolyard.

This is a pumpkin leaf and it is growing outside of our school and it will be a pumpkin and it will be orange. If you cook the pumpkin seed it will be good. I like it. I tried it.

(*Source:* Photograph taken by M. Kristiina Montero. Permission to use granted by Tien Tien and her parents).

> **TIEN TIEN:** Here's a pumpkin. These are the pumpkins that's growing. Those are the pumpkins that are growing.
>
> **KRISTIINA:** They're growing?
>
> **TIEN TIEN:** Yep, you can have a pumpkin patch.
>
> **KRISTIINA:** That's kind of exciting. What color are the pumpkins?
>
> **TIEN TIEN:** Green.
>
> **KRISTIINA:** And what do you use pumpkins for?
>
> **TIEN TIEN:** Hallowe'en stuff. But you, but you can eat the pumpkin seeds if they're cooked.
>
> **KRISTIINA:** Hmm hmm. Yeah pumpkins seeds are good if they're cooked aren't they?
>
> **TIEN TIEN:** I like 'em.

When the time came for Tien Tien to describe the photos, she either typed her thoughts underneath the digital photo (with some of Kristiina's help) or dictated sentences while Kristiina typed them underneath. Tien Tien's sentences were documentary style; she related the photo to information learned in the classroom, connected to the constructed experience between herself and Kristiina, and used technology to communicate her thoughts. After practicing reading the written captions under the photographs, Tien Tien read some of the sentences into the audio recording feature of the KidPix Studio Deluxe software so when the photograph flashed on the screen, the audience could hear Tien Tien's voice. Tien Tien created a multimedia presentation about nature and her school environment with digital photography and language.

Reflecting

Can you recreate in your mind's eye some of the literacy experiences that may have occurred in Ms. Maggie's classroom? Can you see how this information may be connected to the books Tien Tien had read? How can you use information from the previous example to assess Tien Tien's literacy abilities? How would you use this information to help you plan your instruction for Tien Tien and for other students who need to be challenged? According to a social constructionist framework, learning occurs in each person's social surroundings. Can you see how Tien Tien's interactions with Kristiina and with her world inside and outside the classroom were represented in her dictated text?

Integrating Literacy Instruction into a Science Lesson: A Preservice Teacher's First Attempt

As has been suggested throughout this chapter, integrating literacy instruction is not easy. It takes time reflecting, planning, organizing, and assessing, but once you understand both the philosophy behind what you are doing and the logistics of effectively integrating literacy into the content areas, both you and your students will reap great rewards.

We would like to introduce you to Isabelle, a preservice teacher, and present to you her first attempt of integrating literacy instruction into a science lesson. We invite you to take a look at Isabelle's efforts to integrate literacy into her lesson about small machines, keeping in mind that the example recounts the efforts of a preservice teacher who is just learning about the intricate details of the teaching craft as well as managing classroom instruction. The following scenario was recreated from Kristiina's field notes when she observed Isabelle teach.

> Two pieces of chart paper were taped to the blackboard with the students' tasks clearly outlined. On one piece of chart paper the names of the students and the groups to which they belonged were written; on the other were each group's expectations for the time spent in each learning center. This helped with the organization of the centers, as the students knew exactly where to go and what to do. They were aware of their responsibilities.
>
> The students were seated at their desks and Isabelle was reviewing the terms inclined planes, screws, pulleys, wheels, and levers by referring to the K-W-W-L chart she has created with the students in a previous lesson. She was reviewing what the students had said they knew about these small machines and what they said they wanted to

know. Isabelle then organizes the students into the learning centers she had created: reading, art, computer, and writing.

ISABELLE: Who can tell me what they are going to do in the reading center?

Isabelle tells the children to come to the beanbags at the front of the classroom. She tells the students that there are books of varying abilities about small machines from which to choose. She reminds them about the five-finger rule (as described in Chapter 10) for choosing a book to match their reading ability. She tells them to write down two things they learned about small machines in order to help complete the K-W-W-L chart.

ISABELLE: What will you do in the art center?
STUDENT: Draw a picture of the topic.

Isabelle set up the art center with various books containing illustrations or photographs of small machines. She instructs students to choose a small machine, then draw and label the details of the machine.

ISABELLE: What will you do at the computer center?
STUDENT: [the student gave an inaudible answer]
ISABELLE: Did everyone hear Daneedra?
STUDENTS: No.
ISABELLE: We need to listen carefully because Daneedra said something very important. She said that we would work with the Internet and CD-ROM. So, I should not see someone from the "pulley" group working at the computer center.

Isabelle instructed the students in the computer center how to find information about their chosen small machine from preselected websites and recorded two pieces of information that each learned to add to the K-W-W-L chart.

ISABELLE: What will you do in the writing center?
STUDENT: We are going to write about what we learned in class and the video.
ISABELLE: So in the writing center, which is right here, you will stay seated.

Isabelle tells the students in the writing center to discuss with each other about what each student had learned about small machines and to "write what you learned from the video about your simple machine." She tells the group that they can consult with each other about the work, but each must produce his or her own paragraph.

Isabelle provided the students with very clear instructions for the students to go into the centers.

ISABELLE: Before I tell you which group you are in, I want to talk about "ICB". Before we talked about "IVB." [The letters were written on the board in big letters.]
STUDENT: Center behavior.

ISABELLE: And what does the "I" stand for?

STUDENT: Inappropriate.

ISABELLE: Right. Inappropriate Center Behavior. What is an example of an ICB?

STUDENT: Not doing anything.

ISABELLE: What is another one? Cynthia can you tell me another one?

STUDENT: Not looking around.

ISABELLE: If you are looking around, you are not doing appropriate center behavior. Hopefully we will not call ICB, but you know that if I call your name and ICB twice you will get a "clip." [If a student received a clip, they had to stay behind at recess time to talk with the teacher about appropriate behavior.]

Isabelle called each group to move to their respective centers. After Isabelle directed all the children to their centers, she went over to the computer center to make sure the students were on their way to working on the assigned activity.

Isabelle then went over to the reading group. All children were seated on big comfortable beanbag pillows and reading some books about the topic at hand. The art group was working diligently. At this point, a few students at the computer center raised their hands. Isabelle went to answer their questions. It looked like they were having difficulty finding a website on the Internet. Isabelle helped them find it. A question was called out from the writing center, and before Isabelle finished figuring out the Internet problem she answered the writing center's query. The students asked if they had to write the same answer on the same paper. Isabelle told them that they had to write their own answers, but they could help each other and talk about the video together to get ideas.

All of the centers were functioning well. All students were on task. They were helping each other with spelling, reading to each other, listening to each other read, sharing art work with each other, and helping each other on the computer. *All* students were engaged. Isabelle moved around from group to group to check on the students' progress. Then one of the computers starts to play loud music. Isabelle responded immediately and gave the students headphones to listen to the music being produced on the website. She reacted calmly.

Isabelle then spends some time at the writing center. The students had some questions about one of the topics. She tried to get the students to explain as much as they could and then she offered enriching and explanative information. After she worked with the three students working together, she went over to the student who was reading on her own and talked to her about what she was reading.

ISABELLE: Tell me what you learned from the books?

Isabelle listened to two boys talk about the contents of the book. A girl joined the conversation. They referred back to the books as they talked. One of the students in the reading group continued to read silently while the rest talked about the content of the book.

Isabelle moved away from the reading group and suddenly turned around. She called an ICB on a student in the reading group. The student started to talk about the topic in the book again.

ISABELLE: I need everyone to stop. Thank you for following directions. If you have something in your hands or if you are looking at someone other than me, you are not following directions.

Isabelle gives the children directions to clean up. She tells the students where the beanbags need to go and how the desks need to be replaced. Isabelle told the children that they needed to clean up the centers so that they could get ready to go to another activity. All children came back and sat at their desks.

ISABELLE: Who was in the computer center? Raise your hand if you were in the computer center. Tell me one thing you learned from your work in the computer center.

One of the students offered her thoughts. Isabelle then asked one member from each group to talk about what they learned today. Isabelle then tells the students that on Friday they will be sharing their learning in more detail. Isabelle looks at her watch, it is time for the children to go to music class.

ISABELLE: If you are getting in line then you are following directions.

The students line up at the door and get ready to go out for their recess break.

Reflecting

This was Isabelle's first time trying to integrate literacy instruction into a science lesson. What are some of the things you think she did well? What are some of the things you think she may need to work on in order to improve student learning? How could she assess the students' knowledge of small machines? What information may be useful for her to improve instruction? What might she have done differently the "next time?" What other literacy strategies might she have employed other than the K-W-W-L? How are the concepts, skills, and values in this example mutually reinforcing? How might the instruction be improved? What questions might Isabelle ask of herself and of her students?

An Indirect Approach to Integrating Literacy in the Content Area Instruction

Many researchers have expressed the importance of tapping into community resources to help students read the printed word, thus helping them read the world in a critical and creative manner. Luis Moll (1992) stressed the importance of valuing literacy practices occurring in the home across ethnic, linguistic, and socioeconomic cultures. Moll's work focused on the literacy practices of Mexican and other Spanish-speaking families living in the United States and found that students had higher achievement when a bridge existed between the literacy learning culture in the classroom and that of the home.

Tchudi and Lafer (as cited in Gavelek et al., 2000) believe that one of the stumbling blocks to integrating the various literacy practices found in the home community into the classroom is that the teachers themselves do not have first-hand experience with the literacy practices of other cultures. Allen and Labbo (2001) tried to bridge this gap by the use of photography with their preservice teacher education students. In this project, a disposable camera was sent home with each child with instructions to the parent and child to take pictures of their interactions at home. The photographs were then developed, and the student teacher and child looked at the pictures and created a book where the child dictated the text to describe the photos. Allen and Labbo found that many of the teachers' preconceived, stereotypical notions about the child's culture had been dispelled, giving them a richer notion of the child's life. By using a multimodal approach to learning, a stronger home–school connection was initiated.

Try It!

Send a disposable camera home with a few of your students and ask them to take pictures of "life at home." Develop the photos and sit down with the student and ask them to dictate what they see occurring in the photos. Even if you are not able to buy and send home disposable cameras with all of your students, you may be pleasantly surprised at what you learn with only a few home photographic experiences. This will be a learning experience for you and your students.

Connecting with the community is not as difficult as some may make it seem, but it is crucial to student learning. While doing some volunteer work at an elementary school with a high Spanish-speaking student population, of which approximately 50 percent of students were labeled as having limited proficiency in English (LEP) and received pullout English language support services, Kristiina observed how many of the students were disenfranchised from their right to equal literacy education. Kristiina helped some of the classroom teachers with translations (Spanish–English) during parent–teacher conferences. One parent–teacher conference stands out in particular. The interview was between a second-grade teacher and the mother of one of her most struggling students. The teacher wanted to communicate to the parent that she suspected her child had a learning disability and wanted to recommend her to be formally assessed. The parent was shocked, saying she was aware her child was having difficulties with reading, writing, and math, but had no idea that there could have been a more serious problem. During the three years the child had been at the school, nobody communicated to the parent of the suspected problem even though the suspicion had been documented in her permanent record. The mother shared that her child's previous teachers told her that her child was simply doing "fine."

The following year, the school district hired a Spanish-speaking home–school liaison coordinator to help bridge this language gap. The home–school liaison coordinator translated letters going home, made phone calls home on behalf of many teachers, invited parents to visit the school, and organized other welcoming activities. Communication lines between parents, teachers, and staff became easier. As a result, the school has seen more Spanish-speaking parents attend parent–teacher conferences, more notes (written in Spanish) arriving to school from parents, more parent volunteers in the school, and more Spanish-speaking families taking their children to the public library. The literacy community was growing at this school. Parents were beginning to understand the school's literacy culture and teachers were beginning to understand the home literacy culture. Remember, creating a home–school connection is important for all students, not just for those whose home language is different from the mainstream.

Imagine the possibilities and implication for content area learning. If a student had difficulty understanding a certain concept, this could be communicated to the parents. Perhaps the parents might be able to help their child make meaning of a difficult concept if they could use their own language to explain or consult texts written in their own language. Naturally, it is important to establish a home–school connection for all children.

Web Link: On-Line Translators, www.worldlingo.com

Follow the link for "machine translation." You may not have the luxury of having a home–school liaison coordinator in your school, but you can still try to communicate with parents who may not speak or read English by writing a note in the home language, using the help of an on-line translator. It is important to remember that these on-line translators do not provide perfect translations; however, they may help you get a message across. In addition, if the parent sends you a note written in his or her native tongue, you can type the message into the "machine translator" and it can give you a rough translation. Keep in mind that the machine translator will provide a translation of the most common denotation of the word. Do not use figurative language. Use short sentences and simple language for the "machine" to understand.

Reconsidering

Teaching roles are forever in flux as teachers are challenged to change the traditional focus on curriculum, subjects, skills, concepts, knowledge, and the application of information. Teaching can be political. If teachers prepare students, no matter what age, for the rigors of the outside world, the focus will be shifted to provide learning opportunities for students at all seconds, minutes, and hours of the day. Now that you have read some of our thoughts about integrating literacy into content area instruction, what are some of your thoughts? What relevance do you see in integrating literacy into the content areas? Can you see this philosophy as part of the "lifelong learner" philosophy? Are you a lifelong learner? What makes you a lifelong learner? How can you foster lifelong, inquiry learning in the classroom for all students?

CHAPTER

12 Supporting Student Questioning or Inquiry

We believe student questioning—student inquiry—is an important perspective from which to view content area teaching and learning. In this final chapter, we take you on a journey to "catch" a glimpse of the future. Our focus? *Inquiry as curriculum*. Although there are many perspectives from which to view inquiry, we frame our discussion with Short, Harste, and Burke's (1996) view of inquiry as curriculum. We take you through the inquiry cycle and answer frequently asked questions (FAQ) we've heard (and asked). Finally, we provide two classroom examples to illustrate how a first-grade and a fourth-grade teacher interpret inquiry as curriculum.

"Inquiring minds want to know" is a familiar slogan used by the *National Enquirer* to entice readers who want to know the latest scoop on the rich and famous. This magazine has done well and others have followed its lead. Why have these publications done so well? For one reason, people are curious; they want to know about things unfamiliar to them. Elementary school students are also among the "inquiring minds" who want to know. Listen to what Chris Boyd (1993) said about her kindergarten students in the premier issue of *Primary Voices K–6*:

> Five year olds don't consciously try to "come up with" questions. Question asking for these children is wanting to know—it's a part of daily living, listening, learning, and figuring out. Their questions come from the very source of their beings and their senses of wonderment. (p. 22)

Boyd's students are not unique. Before children start school they are virtually a wellspring of questions. And their questions are not easy to answer. "Why?" seems to lurk around every corner: "Why is the grass green?" and "Why is the sky blue?" And then there's the old standard: "Where do babies come from?" Young children are naturally curious and have a passion for learning—learning about anything and everything. And then, they stop asking questions. What happens to their curiosity and their need to know?

Remembering

What do you remember about asking questions in elementary school? Were you encouraged to pursue your own questions or did you do all the interesting "stuff" at home or with your friends? Perhaps you remember K-W-L charts (Ogle, 1986) on which the teacher recorded questions you "Wanted to Know" (see K-W-W-L in teaching toolbox). But we suspect that in school you rarely examined topics you were truly passionate about.

What Jeanne, Donna, and Kristiina remember about asking questions in elementary school is that we really didn't, except for procedural-type questions to ensure we completed assignments correctly. However, teachers always asked many questions and our job as students was to answer the teacher's (and the textbook's) questions, but did these questions encourage learning?

This chapter begins by describing a curriculum in which inquiry is the focus rather than the disciplines (or content areas). Considering that this book is about content area literacy, you might wonder why we dedicate an entire chapter to inquiry. We believe student questioning—student inquiry—is an important perspective from which to view content area teaching and learning.

Although there are many perspectives from which to view inquiry, we frame our discussion with Short, Harste, et al.'s (1996) view of inquiry as curriculum. We define curriculum, knowledge sources for inquiry, and then examine an inquiry cycle as a framework for learning and instruction. In the section Frequently Asked Questions, we try to address the questions we've heard (and asked). Finally, we provide two classroom examples to illustrate how a primary grade and an intermediate grade teacher interpret inquiry as curriculum.

Linking ELA Standards with Inquiry

An inquiry curriculum is consistent with ELA Standards 1, 3, 4, 5, 7, 8, and 12, which state that students engage in personal inquiries, comprehend, interpret, evaluate, and synthesize data from a variety of sources, including technological and other informational resources, and communicate their discoveries in writing and other ways, depending on their purposes and audience.

Inquiry also supports Standards 2 and 9, which relate to understanding different aspects of human experiences and understanding and appreciating differences in the classroom community. (www.ncte.org/standards/standards.shtml)

Curriculum as Inquiry: Content Area Literacy for the Future?

In a themed issue of *The Reading Teacher* focusing on literacy in the content areas, Monson and Monson (1994) interviewed Jerome Harste about his view of content area literacy for the future. He suggested that, when considering curricular issues, we should think about what children will need for the future. Continuing, he proposed that all we know about children's future needs is that they will need to know how to solve problems in collaboration with others. Therefore, his view of content area literacy focused on curriculum as inquiry.

An inquiry curriculum draws from three sources of knowledge: the disciplines, sign systems, and personal and social knowledge. Traditionally, curriculum has focused on the disciplines in isolation: history, mathematics, science, reading, and writing. In fact, national and state standards are still organized in this way; at the same time, inquiry is a theme that runs through the English language arts, science, and social studies standards across the grade levels. Harste proposed, however, that when considering curriculum as inquiry, the disciplines (or knowledge systems) are viewed as lenses or ways of thinking about a topic, theme, or problem. The "topics" come from a variety of sources, such as a compelling context (such as a current event), from teacher and student interests, or state standards, just like topics in a traditional curriculum. However, the difference lies in the role of the disciplines in relation to a topic; they provide *perspectives* from which students can approach their inquiries. "The goal of inquiry is unpacking the complexity of the topic to find issues to pursue and trying out new perspectives on the topic *to see what can be learned* [*italics* added]" (Short, Harste, et al. 1996, p. 341).

To illustrate this view, Harste (1993) used the topic of "war" and rotated it through the disciplines by considering questions such as the following: How would a sociologist view war? What generalizations, conclusions, and facts would she or he want us to consider? What can we learn about war from artists? What can we learn from scientists? Figure 12.1 offers examples of children's literature that provide varying perspectives on war.

FIGURE 12.1   Children's Literature

Many trade books written for children and young adolescents can provide different perspectives on war. For example, *Parallel Journeys* (Ayer, Waterford, & Heck, 2000) tells the stories of two young people, a Holocaust survivor and a Nazi youth, who experienced World War II very differently. Likewise, *Passage to Freedom: The Sugihara Story* (Mochizuki, 1997) provides yet another view of WWII. This book is written from the perspective of a five-year-old Japanese boy whose father saved the lives of thousands of Jews in Lithuania because he was willing to disobey his government. And then there's *Baseball Saved Us*, also by Ken Mochizuki (1995), which tells the story of a Japanese–American family's struggles after they were moved to an internment camp during WWII. These books provide students with a human perspective on war but from different vantage points. After reading these books, it is hoped that students will begin to reflect upon war in terms of the people involved rather than only the facts, figures, causes, and effects.

The second source of knowledge is sign systems. Short, Kauffman, and Kahn (2000) define sign systems as "potential tools for thinking and exploring new ideas" (p. 169). There are many ways of communicating and making ideas public. Typically, we think of reading, writing, and speaking as *the* communication tools. These particular tools are privileged in schools (Fueyo, 1991), but people also communicate their thoughts through art, music, drama, dance, and even mathematics. Figure 12.2 illustrates how a second grader communicated through art what she knew about how seeds travel. Different sign systems provide opportunities for students to actually construct new, unique meanings. By extending the opportunity to use sign systems other than written language, students whose talents or preferences lean toward other forms of expression will be furnished with opportunities to inquire and learn in other ways. Think about the contributions of individuals such as Albert Einstein, Leonardo da Vinci, and Danny Glover who had difficulty expressing their creativity with written language, but excelled in other areas.

Web Activity: Famous Dyslexics

Go to www.google.com and search for "famous dyslexics." You'll find several websites with quotes from individuals who had difficulty in school. Compare your list with a partner and discuss how you think these individuals became successful when others have not.

Reflecting

Can you think of ways to provide your students with differing perspectives on topics they may have studied repeatedly? Take the ocean, for example. Have you ever thought about viewing the ocean through the eyes of an artist, an economist, a musician or an environmentalist? How would your thinking about the ocean change when viewed from these vantage points?

FIGURE 12.2   How Birds Sow Seeds

The third source of knowledge is personal and social knowing (Short, Harste, et al. 1996) and is at the heart of inquiry. Students' personal knowledge comes from their personal experiences and the cultural and social groups in which they are a part. What students wonder about—what they want to know—is the starting point for inquiry. Kohn (as cited in Wackerly & Young, 2002) posits, "the irrefutable fact is that students always have a choice about whether they will learn. We may be able to force them to complete an assignment, but we can't compel them to learn effectively or to care about what they are doing" (p. 17). Inquiry can compel students to care.

We turn to Short and Burke (as cited in Short, Harste, et al. 1996) to define curriculum. They write that curriculum is not a set of unchanging mandates that are imposed onto classrooms, but our best predictions about how people learn, what people should be learning, and the contexts that support that learning. It is an organizational device that we use as teachers to think about our classrooms (p. 27).

Inquiry Cycle

To put this theoretical view of curriculum into practice, Short, Harste, and Burke (1996) describe a framework that supports teachers in their day-to-day decisions about learning engagements (invitations). The inquiry cycle framework was drawn from their work with the authoring cycle and their observations of what young children do when they engage in learning about their world. Like the authoring cycle, the inquiry cycle represents a dynamic, nonlinear process such that there is no clearly defined beginning, middle, or end. Short, Schroeder, et al. (1996) describe the inquiry cycle as "recursive in nature: students continuously move back and forth across it. The cycle is actually a spiral of experiences that build on one another rather than circle back to start again at the same point" (p. 156).

The entry point of the inquiry cycle is what learners know, their interests, and their passions. The teacher designs "invitations"—engagements—related to a topic of study. These engagements provide opportunities for students to explore (wander), observe, and wonder. These invitations are grounded in a teacher's knowledge of her students, their interests, experiences, and knowledge. Invitations come in a variety of forms. For example, invitations may provide students with opportunities to engage in hands-on explorations, view a video, explore websites, view artwork, or browse through books and charts while simultaneously interacting with other learners, sharing intriguing ideas, and posing questions that will advance their inquiry and learning.

Moving to the next point in the cycle, "finding" questions (wondering), students explore a variety of print and nonprint resources, individually and with others, in order to learn more about a topic that intrigues them. This aspect of inquiry differs from a carte blanche question: "What do you want to know about . . . ?" Good questioning is founded in knowing. It is important to allow students time to wander through a wide range of resources so that they can ask questions relevant to them. Short, Harste, et al. (1996) recommend students be given time to be immersed in the world around them and be given "time to read, write, observe, talk, listen, paint, sing, and dance as they explore their worlds" (p. 55).

The teacher plays an important facilitative role as students explore their questions. She might suggest that students brainstorm about various sources of information that could help them answer their questions. Figure 12.3 shows a circle map, completed by a second grader, as the class brainstormed about possible resources for learning about rain forest fauna. (Notice how the term in the center represents new vocabulary and one aspect of interest, the next circle includes examples of fauna, and the frame includes the resources.)

As students are immersed in question finding, they are encouraged to examine questions from varying perspectives, another aspect of the inquiry cycle. Gaining these

FIGURE 12.3   Circle Map

varying perspectives helps students take their inquiry beyond learning a list of facts to in-depth learning that leads toward conceptual understandings. For example, a teacher might introduce the Sketch to Stretch strategy to help students tap into meaning making visually rather than with written language. (See Chapter 6 for details about Sketch to Stretch.) This engagement shifts the vantage point from which students view their questions, thus opening up new ways to think about their questions, and perhaps provide new insights. Teachers can facilitate the examination of content through different perspectives by varying their selection of texts for read alouds or literature discussion groups, of artifacts and primary source materials, and of invited speakers.

The inquiry cycle continues as students confront and attempt to resolve discontinuities that arise as they pursue their questions. These contradictory or inconsistent ideas may reflect differences that stem from students' background knowledge, disciplinary perspectives, and conflicting resources. Sometimes it is difficult for students to come to terms with the fact that answering a question is not as clear-cut as they might have expected. Discussion is one vehicle for introducing and considering discontinuities. The Discussion Web (Alvermann, 1991) is a tool that helps students organize their thoughts when considering an issue from multiple perspectives (see Figure 12.4). Students struggle together to come to a resolution (or perhaps develop additional questions!).

Another way to help students reflect on discontinuities is through a response log or reflective journal. As students deal with difficult issues that differ from what they expect, students often need time to reflect independently about these issues. A double

FIGURE 12.4   A Discussion Web: *The Great Fire* by Jim Murphy

entry journal can be used to organize students' ideas and help them reflect back to both the information they found and their feelings about that particular information.

Try It! Use a Double-Entry Journal

As you continue reading this chapter, record your responses in a double entry journal. Fold your paper lengthwise. Label the left side "the text" and the right side "my response." Choose ideas from the text that you find particularly troubling, exciting, worth remembering, and wonder about. Enter them on the left side. On the right side, write your response—what's troubling or exciting about it, why is it worth remembering, what do you wonder about it?

Discuss your entries with a friend you trust. Did she or he have some of the same responses as you did? What did you learn from your discussion?

At different points in the cycle, learners "go public" with (share) what they have learned. To do this, they draw from a variety of sign systems and transform what they have learned into a presentation designed for a particular audience. Sometimes they informally share what they have learned in a class meeting or they may present their learning as a formal presentation, sketch, song, piece of art work, dance, or multimedia presentation—the possibilities are endless. A written report is an option for sharing but is *not* a requirement.

English Language Arts Standard

Planning and presenting information in a variety of ways is consistent with ELA Standard 6, which reads "students apply knowledge of language structure, language conventions, media techniques, figurative language, and other genre to create . . . and discuss print and nonprint texts" (www.reading.org/advocacy/elastandards/standards.html).

Finally, students take the information they have learned and extend it to broader issues or related inquiries. To do this, students may plan new inquiries and decide how they wish to "reposition" themselves based on what they have learned. Perhaps their inquiry will lead them to question the very assumptions that led them to their initial inquiry. On the other hand, they may see a need to act upon their newfound understandings. Whatever the results, the inquiry cycle goes on; students continue exploring, questioning, investigating, conversing, struggling, revising, transforming, presenting, reflecting, and repositioning. Students become lifelong learners.

A Metaphor to Describe Inquiry-Based Curriculum

Rather than trying to further describe an inquiry-based curriculum, we use a metaphor to illustrate the inquiry cycle. Imagine you want to go on a road trip. You've decided upon a leisurely, loosely planned trip in which you can enjoy the entire journey, not just the destination. During the road trip you would like to engage in some sort of activity. What would be fun for you? Perhaps shopping for antiques, camping out, flea market scavenging, or visiting historical sites appeals to you. Once you have your *focus*, you're ready to starting planning your trip.

Next, you begin your *wanderings* and *wonderings*. What is the best route to travel so you can engage in your favorite (*focus*) activities? You peruse AAA guidebooks, surf the Web, and ask your like-minded friends for recommendations. Finally, you have a tentative idea about the direction you might drive and the sights you could see along the way.

Now it's time to share your plan with your traveling companion and *gain her perspective*. Unbeknowst to you, she has also done a bit of *wandering* and *wondering* on her own, also anticipating the upcoming trip. When you share your plans with one another, you discover that your antique enthusiast's perspective and her "communing with wildlife" perspective are not compatible. Perhaps you won't vacation together this year!

On second thought, rather than traveling solo, you decide to *attend to your differences* and explore alternatives. Keeping your friend's and your focus in mind, you do more research, sharing your findings periodically. Then after much research, collaboration, some frustration, and compromise, you agree on a general travel plan.

Now it's vacation time! You have your travel route planned, maps in hand, and time to explore. As you drive, you watch for signposts that could lead to unforeseen places of interest. Sometimes you take a detour, are delighted with the unexpected and other times, well. . . . After some time exploring, you return to the planned route and continue your investigations and outings as you travel. You proceed on your journey, visit the places you planned, take another detour or two, and reach your destination.

You spend a few days at your destination, *sharing* your "great finds" and photographs with new-found friends. When it's time to go back home, you *reflect* on your journey thus far and begin planning your return trip (your new inquiry). You get out the maps and travel brochures you gathered along the way, and make tentative plans.

You pack up your belongings and get back on the road again. And your journey continues. . . .

Conditions That Support Student Inquiry

Much has been written about the conditions necessary for supporting student questioning and inquiry. A safe, caring classroom environment in which community members trust one another is essential; the teacher and students recognize and respect one another's strengths, areas of need, unique expertise, and contributions to the community (Wackerly & Young, 2002). Because they know each other well, class members come to care about one another (Shamlin, 2001). The classroom community provides students with a supportive, risk-free environment in which they can live, work, and question together.

Collaboration is another necessary condition for inquiry. In a collaborative community, members trust, respect, and care about one another, and they work together on tasks of interest. Time and "space" (Fischer, 2002) to collaborate are important to promote questioning, meaningful discussion, wondering and wandering, and sharing what they learn. To support students in their collaborative efforts, it follows that students need well-developed interpersonal skills to work together effectively (Möller, 2002). Although collaboration is of utmost importance, individual inquiries are also supported. Nevertheless, students continue to share resources, their queries, and assist one another in other ways.

Intricately related to the communal and collaborative aspects of inquiry is student choice. Understanding students' interests and their areas of individual expertise provides teachers with insight to plan an inquiry-based curriculum. When students have an opportunity to choose what they study, "to bring the[ir] world into the classroom" (Fischer, 2002, p. 11) and to choose with whom they study, engagement is almost insured. Students have their own purposes—their own questions—to pursue. Thus, student ownership in their investigations is established. Furthermore, choosing how to learn and how to share their learning allows students to be more successful because a variety of sign systems and ways of knowing are available to them. Paddy Lynch (2001), a third-grade teacher, found that student choice provides the emotional, or affective, "hook" students need to become intellectually engaged in learning. This is especially key for readers who struggle academically. Not only does choice "hook" students into the content of the curriculum, it also helps build their confidence (Lynch, 2001). When students have choices about what they read and write, they have a personal need to read and write; their own real reasons spur them on (Fischer, 2002).

Inquiry Supports English Language Learners!

Premlata Mansukhani (2002) described how she used inquiry to support third- and fourth-grade students' content and English language learning. Within an Explorer's Club context, in which students determined and pursued their own questions, and employed multiple sign systems, she found her students learned both English and content as they investigated their own questions, which spanned the curriculum. Students decided how to investigate their questions and made decisions about how to present their inquiries ranging from traditional research reports to posters to writing a play. To evaluate their learning, she used multiple methods: her observation of student involvement and interest, the quality of students' products, and peer, parental, and self-evaluation. What she learned was that her students learned content to which they would not otherwise have had access. The students had the opportunity to use, with support, complex thinking and language processes. This allowed students to learn at their own pace, use and improve their English language skills, and use their mother tongue to aid their learning (see ELA Standard 10). She noted that students were enthusiastic and engaged in their learning as they pursued their inquiries. [See Copenhaver (1993) for more information about the Explorer Club.]

Access to substantive content is a necessary condition of an inquiry-based curriculum. In fact, when the substance of the curriculum "emerges from the lives and curiosity of kids" (Boyd, 1993), it may be much more sophisticated than what is sometimes mandated by state standards or included in textbooks. For example, second–grade students wanted to know: "If all the trees in rain forests were cut down, would we all die?" Others asked, "Why do grasshoppers have such a long body and tall legs?" (Schmidt, Gillen, Zollo, & Stone, 2002, p. 542). What about the question all young dinosaur experts want to know: "How do scientists know what bones go with what dinosaur and how to put them together when they can't find all the bones?" What about the young animal rights activist who wants to know why wild animals are put in zoos? These types of questions go far beyond the "community helpers" curriculum traditionally relegated to the primary grades and the facts and figures students are expected to memorize in the intermediate grades.

Try It! Your State's Content Standards

Go to your state department of education website. Find the standards for science, social studies, and mathematics—remembering that they reflect the minimum standards. Are there content requirements you are surprised by—are they too complex, too simple? Why do you think so?

Reflecting

Do your past experiences as a student reflect conditions that foster an inquiry curriculum? If you are currently teaching, how do you help establish a caring classroom community, support collaboration, build on student interests and choices, and choose content? Do you believe these conditions are important elements in an elementary school classroom? What could you do to make your own classroom more supportive of student inquiry?

Frequently Asked Questions about an Inquiry Curriculum

This section draws from our own and others' inquiries about an inquiry curriculum. Although this is by no means an exhaustive list of questions, if they peak your interest, perhaps you'll engage in further inquiry to learn more.

1. *How is an inquiry-based curriculum different from an integrated or thematic unit?* There are both theoretical and practical differences in instruction guided by a theme determined by the teacher and an inquiry focus that arises from students. To explain, we use an example from the book *Learning Through Inquiry Together* (Short, Schroeder, et al., 1996). Kathy Short provides a description of her own first-grade classroom discussion *before* she began investigating inquiry. She chose the ocean as a unit of study because she knew first graders typically are interested in the topic and she had many resources available to her. After she determined the other units they would study for the year, she scheduled the ocean unit. When the unit began, she read aloud picture books, provided theme sets of books for student browsing, and planned many student activities, including science experiments and art activities. She brought in her shell collection and other ocean artifacts, and even made blank fish-shaped books for children to write in. Finally, she asked each child to choose a sea creature to research and create an illustrated informational book. When the thematic unit on the ocean was finished, Kathy stored the materials for another time and moved to the next unit.

Now, consider Kathleen Crawford's multiage first/second-grade class in Tucson, Arizona. Initially she taught in the same manner as just described. This year, however, was different. Kathleen chose to study the ocean when several children came back from spring break talking excitedly about their visit to the ocean. Their discussions led to many questions and intrigued others in the class; after all, they lived in the desert! The students' questions led to their study of the ocean. Like Kathy, Kathleen gathered books and seashells, but also brought photographs, artwork, and music to school in hopes of inviting students to investigate the ocean using different resources and varying perspectives. The children added to these learning materials from their personal collections of books and artifacts. They engaged in story telling, materials browsing, and sharing of personal experiences. The students' questions, organized in a web, helped them decide what they wanted to learn more about. The students and teacher worked together to organize sets of resources that would be helpful. As they researched, they developed ways to record their findings and keep track of observations. Finally, the students presented what they learned in a variety of ways. The presentations did not represent the end of their inquiry. Their inquiry journey had only just begun. During their study of the ocean, students became intrigued by environmental issues, which developed into their next class inquiry.

Many of the materials, books, and activities were similar in the two classrooms. However, the study of the ocean came from different "places," one from Kathy's knowledge of student interests and availability of materials and Kathleen's from students' experiences and their subsequent questions. Kathleen's students had more time to explore and determine what they wanted to investigate than Kathy's students, who engaged in activities she planned. Kathleen invited students to experience the ocean from varying perspectives through photos, music, and artwork, along with the more traditional books and ocean artifacts.

We are not evaluating instruction in either of the two classrooms. Rather, we use these classroom examples to illustrate the philosophical and practical differences in thematic units and classroom inquiry.

2. *What does planning look like when inquiry is the focus of the curriculum?* The starting point of planning an inquiry-based curriculum is determining a focus. The focus for inquiry involves a negotiation among the school curriculum, including standards; teachers' interests and experiences; and students' interests and experiences. How can all these elements be interwoven? Standards are typically broad and leave room for approaching content from varying perspectives. A teacher can initiate an inquiry focus based on what she knows about students: their strengths, needs, and so forth and on her own interests and experiences. And then there are students' interests and experiences—the often overlooked but essential ingredients. Short et al. (1996) write that the most *crucial* aspect of planning is that the focus is determined through *negotiation with students.*

3. *How do you teach the mandated curriculum and meet minimum standards?* Most times mandated curriculum and standards are general enough that taking an inquiry approach provides opportunities for more in-depth learning than is considered the minimum. For example, state social studies curricula requires students to learn about their state in fourth grade. Rather than taking a state bird, flower, tree, and flag approach, using an inquiry approach would allow students to focus on issues, problems, or unique opportunities in a state. Instead of studying about the War Between the States from a chronological, battle-by-battle approach, an inquiry focus on issues related to slavery from differing perspectives could be examined. When there are topics that do not fit or relate to an inquiry focus, some teachers set aside a time several times a week for short-term class studies on mandated topics (Short, Schroeder, et al., 1996).

4. *Do students pass standardized tests?* Some school personnel (usually not classroom teachers) have come to believe that the best way for students to score well on standardized tests is to provide students with worksheet after worksheet so they can practice penciling in circles and get accustomed to the way questions are asked on the tests. Much attention is being given to test scores, but little attention is paid to how students use what they learn in school to survive and live productive lives outside the proverbial four walls of the school. In reality, children who learn and use these skills in context usually score higher on standardized tests than students who "learn" skills in a decontextualized fashion. A case in point is the success of students who attend the Center for Inquiry in urban Indianapolis, Indiana. The principal, Christine Collier (2002) wrote: [On the state ISTEP exam,] "87% of our sixth graders passed the reading standards compared to 36% district wide. . . . Our students continue to fare quite well compared to others in the district, scoring highest in reading comprehension and demonstrations of writing process at grades 3, 6, and 8" (p. 6).

5. *How can we find time to add inquiry to the school day?* Inquiry is not something to add to the curriculum, rather it can be woven throughout. Students' inquiries provide opportunities to examine topics from different perspectives and through varying sign systems. Inquiry is a lens through which content is viewed, not an add on. Science, social studies, mathematics, and English language arts standards mandate that inquiry is part of the curriculum. Even textbooks include ideas for using inquiry to learn content.

6. *How is student work evaluated when the curriculum is based in inquiry?* While it's true that evaluation most consistent with an inquiry curriculum looks different than the traditional A, B, and C grades, assessment is an integral component of an inquiry-based curriculum. Ideally, students would play a more central role in evaluating their own learning, reflecting on what they did well during the inquiry process and deciding what they need to work on. Checklists related to standards can be developed and used during observation. Student portfolios with artifacts that reflect what they've learned can be part of the evaluation, and narrative report cards, correlated to standards, can describe student learning. Rubrics can be developed collaboratively by teachers and students to evaluate most student products and the processes they use. If a school requires that traditional grades be given, rubrics can be quantified.

7. *How can an inquiry-based curriculum be used when a school is departmentalized?* We address this question because many elementary schools are shifting to a departmentalized organization, especially in grades 4 through 6. Although we do not necessarily support this change, we recognize that it does exist. Departmentalizing contradicts one of the basic tenets of an inquiry-based curriculum, that is, taking the emphasis off of the disciplines. But teachers can "make do" until they can make a change.

Teachers who work together in teams can approach their subject matter from an inquiry perspective. Teams of teachers and students determine a broad theme or topic that can be explored through the lens of each content area. A science teacher, for example, would be well suited to help students explore a theme or topic from a scientist's perspective. Rather than focusing on content as specified for each subject area, inquiry is the focus. If each teacher understands the inquiry philosophy and approaches the theme or topic from disciplinary perspectives, allows for student choice and collaboration, honors a variety of sign systems, and focuses on inquiry, a school can move toward an inquiry-based curriculum.

8. *How is inquiry different from the research students are required to do?* One difference is the way research is pursued. Remember the conditions for inquiry: community, collaboration, choice, and content. Although we know that some teachers approach research in much the same way as we describe, traditional "research" assignments do not reflect these conditions. Rather, the teacher assigns a topic; working independently, students look up information in the encyclopedia and copy the entry practically verbatim. Inquiry is not a research project but a way of approaching and exploring the world. Rather than ending with a "report," one inquiry typically leads to another.

9. *Help! I don't understand the whole "wandering" and "wondering" idea and the inquiry cycle.* Probably the most effective way to understand the inquiry cycle is to engage in the inquiry process yourself. Think about your passions, keep track of your questions in a "Wonder Book," and "inquire away!"

10. *What are the disadvantages of an inquiry-based curriculum?* An inquiry-based curriculum is not about a series of activities but is "a philosophical position on what both teachers and children do in the name of learning" (Short, Harste, et al. 1996, p. 49). Focusing on inquiry as the core of the curriculum and disciplines as the lenses through which curriculum is viewed may challenge your ways of thinking about what curriculum is and how to teach science, social studies, math, and English language arts. However, we don't believe that this challenge is a bad thing. Rather, it's important that we (educators, parents, politicians, concerned citizens) question our beliefs about "what counts" and consider what children need for today and the future.

11. *Can I gradually move into developing an inquiry-based curriculum or do I have to abandon everything else and jump in?* We do not suggest that you jump in without first getting your feet wet on a small scale. Although an inquiry-based curriculum reflects a philosophical stance toward teaching and learning rather than an approach or method, we believe that when you begin thinking and acting differently, you may need to wade a bit before you totally submerge yourself. Short and Armstrong (1993) suggest, based on their early experiences with inquiry, that teachers begin by "providing students with experiences that give them time to explore, connect, and find a focus for inquiry." (p. 197) In the classroom examples that follow, we illustrate how some teachers have approached the shift in different ways.

Web Activity: Support for Inquiry-Based Literacy Development

Check out www.readingonline.org. Click on Index icon. Then do a title search for the article, "Using the Web to support inquiry-based literacy development" (Bruce & Bishop, 2002). Link to the Inquiry page. Browse through the document. What ideas help you the most to understand inquiry? Discuss the ideas with a partner.

Classroom Examples

Moving from a Teacher-Designated Theme to Student Inquiry

Annyce Kuykendall, a first-grade teacher Jeanne worked with in west Texas, engaged in an inquiry journey with her first graders quite by accident—at least in the beginning. Before school started, she planned a year-long thematic study, focusing on habitats and ecosystems, that would link social studies and science instruction and provide a meaningful context within which students could use their developing reading and writing skills. Her plan was that they would study the desert, polar regions, prairie, wetlands, and other areas. She chose this particular theme for several reasons. She believed students could learn more substantive content than the traditional "community helpers"; they would be interested in this theme; and she had access to plenty of resources that she and her students could use.

The classroom environment was very inviting and print-rich. In fact, it often resembled the bookstore described in Chapter 9. Students were always actively engaged in reading, writing, discussing, drawing, and problem solving throughout the day. A sense of community was obvious as the students and teacher supported one another.

Things were going as Annyce had planned, until February, when they began a study of the polar regions. As always, Annyce read aloud portions of informational books to provide an overview of the region and help build students' background knowledge. Then, it happened. She read one sentence that intrigued the first graders and kept their attention for the next several months. What was the sentence about? Perhaps you guessed it: the iceberg that sank the *Titanic*! (It's important to note that this study took place *before* the movie was even advertised, and students knew little about the *Titanic*). Students started asking questions. Annyce answered them and then continued reading, or at least tried to continue reading. Although she had not planned a study of the *Titanic*, her students persisted, asking question after question. Reflecting on what she knew about inquiry, she decided to follow her students' lead—to take advantage of their curiosity, questions, and interest in the topic.

The first thing they did was visit the school library to find out what resources were available. The librarian taught a minilesson on how to search for books about the *Titanic* using the school's on-line catalog and how to use call numbers to locate materials. In addition to finding several books, they found a video published by the National Geographic Society. Annyce checked out all the resources and took the stack back to their room. The students wanted to start learning about the *Titanic* immediately, so Annyce decided to begin by viewing the video. She wanted to take advantage of that medium with which the students were so familiar. They discussed information from the video, and students began perusing the library books. This is how their inquiry began. Along the way, students chose topics they were most interested in pursuing. Sometimes they worked with other students with similar interests and other times they worked individually, but they always shared what they learned during large group time and shared resources when they found information they thought others might need.

Families got involved too. Students went home talking about the *Titanic* and asking their parents to help them find information about the *Titanic*. Some students brought in resources, such as information downloaded from the Internet and books not available in the classroom. One day a child went home and asked her mother what she thought about having a "watery grave." The mother, Annyce's close friend, knew where the question "came from" but was still surprised that such a "big" and serious question came from a six year old.

Students approached their study from a variety of perspectives. One child focused on Robert Ballard and viewed the *Titanic* from the perspective of an explorer. At one point the class examined the *Titanic* disaster from a mathematical perspective.

They cut out two-inch squares of paper, each one representing ten people who died when the *Titanic* sank. They used different colored squares to designate on which deck the causalities had rooms. Then they made a bar graph to compare the number of people who died by social class.

Although graphing was specified in the state standards for first grade, constructing and using the bar graph flowed from their inquiries, not from the curriculum guide. As they discussed what information other people could learn from reading their graph, students began asking questions from a sociologist's perspective. One question they discussed at length was: "Why did so many more poor people die than rich people?" Getting into the social issues of that time went far beyond the curriculum designated by the state, but this is what students were concerned about. They also wanted to know why people sometimes saved their dogs and let people drown—big questions, indeed.

During the first week of study, the class decided to write a big book together about the *Titanic*. When they had gathered and shared enough information to write an interesting book, small groups of students authored different chapters. They went through the drafting, sharing, responding, revising, and editing phases of the authoring cycle, completing the big book. Finally, they shared it with their parents, other first-grade classes, and kindergarteners.

Although Annyce was just beginning to learn about the potential for using multiple sign systems in her classroom, she provided opportunities for her students to learn about the *Titanic* in a number of ways: listening to read alouds, reading books on their own, viewing videos, searching the Web, viewing photographs and illustrations, discussing, writing, and drawing. She also encouraged the first-graders to represent what they learned in multiple ways. A few students made posters at home representing various aspects of the disaster. Several girls, who were quite fluent readers and writers, wrote a script for a play using writing workshop. (They were familiar with scripts because they had written one during interactive writing in kindergarten.) Other students made models of the *Titanic*. No one model was alike and all represented individual's interpretations of what they learned about the *Titanic*. A little girl who rarely did any homework and received little support from her family with schoolwork created a model. It was obviously her own creation, not one older siblings or parents undertook. She used an old milk crate to represent the ocean. Some dirty blue scraps of cloth covered the bottom of the crate; broken glass represented broken plates found on the bottom of the ocean. A paper doll she had obviously drawn also lay on the bottom of the crate. She brought her model to school two weeks after everyone else brought theirs. In fact, the class was not studying about the *Titanic* any more; they had moved on to the prairie. She was obviously intrigued by the *Titanic* and wanted to share her model with her classmates. Her school learning spilled over to her home because she was intrigued by the content, had choices about how she represented what she learned, and had the freedom to continue her individual inquiry after the class study moved on.

The themed study Annyce planned at the beginning of the year was teacher directed until the students became intrigued and began asking questions. Two-thirds of the way through the year, student inquiry became the driving force behind the curriculum.

Beginning with an Attic Find

Phyllis Whitin tells the story of how the "inquiry at the window" came about in her fourth-grade classroom (Whitin & Whitin, 1996). It all began when Phyllis found an old bird feeder in her attic and decided to hang it outside her classroom window. Her purpose was to provide an invitation for students to engage in scientific writing. She placed a blank "bird journal" (p. 82) beside the window and different students volunteered to record and share their observations each day. Students were encouraged to tell the recorder what they liked about the journal entries and to ask questions, which ultimately resulted in more precise journal entries. Still later, students began asking the recorders why they drew certain conclusions about the birds' activities. This questioning attitude reflected students' developing ability to become critical consumers of information.

After students had the opportunity to observe the birds for several weeks, record their observations, and respond to and revise their entries, Phyllis brought books about birds into the class. She taught students how to take notes during minilessons.

Students continued their "inquiry at the window," using many of the strategies scientists do—observing, questioning, wondering, and hypothesizing. When they ran into problems such as writing fast enough to record everything the birds were doing at the window, the class brainstormed and later implemented several suggested solutions to the problem.

Their observations led to more questions and more hypotheses. When Kevin noticed that the birds rarely ate certain seeds, that observation began an investigation that led to a feed store where students asked an expert. They continued observing, reading, hypothesizing, and testing their hypotheses, experiencing what it was like to think and act like a scientist. The problems were not designed by the teacher, rather the students' inquiries led them to identify their own problems.

This classroom example provides a different entry point to inquiry. This time a concrete invitation—a bird feeder and observation log—encouraged students to engage in scientific inquiry. Although the teacher had a particular purpose for hanging the bird feeder outside the window, she followed the students' inquiries, which went beyond her original purposes, and she supported their inquiries by providing instruction they needed to successfully solve the problems they identified.

Inquiry: Beneficial for All Students

An inquiry-based curriculum can be particularly intriguing for struggling readers. When teachers choose a broad theme or topic through negotiating with students and making links to their interests and knowledge, struggling readers are more likely to accept classroom invitations. Schmidt and her colleagues (2002) write that when struggling readers have the opportunity to demonstrate their knowledge about a topic, they gain recognition and respect from other students. This respect provides students with confidence they need to learn even more.

An inquiry-based curriculum can be "just what the doctor ordered" for some gifted students and quite a challenge for others. It can be especially disconcerting to students who are accustomed to knowing the answers to questions and do not feel comfortable "not knowing." Nevertheless, when a safe classroom environment is provided in which the value of questioning is demonstrated, gifted students can be encouraged to become empowered inquirers (Schillereff, 2001).

Reconsidering

Now that you've read this chapter, what do you think about curriculum as inquiry? What advantages do you see? What disadvantages? Perhaps you agree philosophically with the notion that students' inquiries should guide the curriculum. If so, how can you begin to organize student knowledge and interests, your knowledge and interests, and curriculum standards to make learning in your classroom more inquiry based? What questions do you have? To support your future inquiries, we recommend you read Short, Harste, and Burke's (1996) book *Creating Classrooms for Authors and Inquirers*. There's so much more to explore, ponder, and reflect upon. Your journey has just begun.

PART FIVE

Toolbox of Teaching and Learning Strategies

BIOPOEM

Purpose

The BioPoem, a formula poem, offers students a creative and inviting way to write about, analyze, and understand details about a person's life, whether real or imaginary, by asking them to answer certain biographical questions. The activity asks students to synthesize their knowledge about an individual. Oftentimes, when writing about the lives of individuals, students may get caught up in the details of the surrounding events; the BioPoem asks the students to focus on the details of the person being studied. This strategy can be used with students of all ages, across all content areas, as an individual, small or large group activity. The BioPoem can be adapted to serve your curricular, instructional, and assessment needs by simply getting creative and playing around with the poem structure.

Step-by-Step Procedure

1. Identify a character to be studied. Students may self-select the character or you may choose to give them a character to write about, depending on your instructional goal.
2. Provide the students with the BioPoem structure, create your own structure, or have the students create or modify the presented structure.
3. Ask students to create!

BioPoem Structure

Line 1: First name~
Line 2: Four adjectives to describe the person's character traits
Line 3: Relative of (list three people)
Line 4: Lover of (list three different things or people)
Line 5: Who feels (list three different feelings)
Line 6: Who needs (list three different things)
Line 7: Who gives (list three different things)
Line 8: Who fears (list three different things)
Line 9: Who would like to see (list three different things or people)
Line 10: Who lives (brief description)
Line 11: ~Last name

Adapted from Richardson, J. S., & Morgan, R. F. (2000). *Reading to learn in the content areas* (4th ed.). Belmont, CA: Wadsworth.

DISCUSSION WEB

Purpose

To engage students in a meaningful text-based discussion by encouraging them to use supporting evidence in their arguments. Frequently, we ask students to explain *why* some event occurred in an expository selection. More often than not they seem to fall into the "narrative trap"—that is, they describe *what* happened without attempting to analyze *why* it happened. The Discussion Web is designed to stimulate a small group's critical thinking.

Step-by-Step Procedure

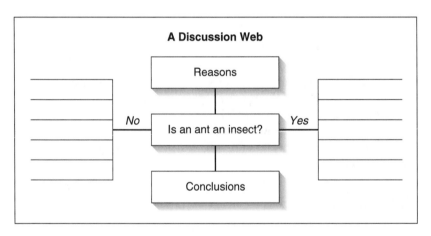

FIGURE 13.1   A Discussion Web

Adapted from Duthie, J. (1986). *The History and Social Science Teacher*, 21, 232–236

1. After reading a selection (silently or orally to a partner), form groups of two students each.
2. Together with your partner, discuss the question in terms of the evidence that can be found to support the yes/no columns. Remember to jot down only key words or phrases in the yes/no columns. You do *not* have to fill every space.
3. After time is called, join anoither group of two students. In your new group of four, try to come to consensus by stating your conclusion and reason(s) for your conclusion. It is perfectly acceptable to have a dissenting view, but the discussion process will be more effective if you try to reach consensus.

4. Finally, after time is called again, appoint a person from your group to read the conclusion and reason(s) for that conclusion. Be sure to include the minority viewpoint if consensus was not reached.
5. As a follow-up activity to the discussion, write your own answer to the question. You may include your group's ideas as well as the ideas expressed by other groups.

Adaptations of the Discussion Web that make it particularly suited to different content areas follow.

Math. When students are asked to solve mathematical word problems, the words *relevant information* and *irrelevant information* could be substituted for the *yes* and *no* classification scheme.

Science. In science, students are often asked to make predictions about what they think the outcome will be for a particular experiment. In this case, the question in the center of the Discussion Web could be changed to: "What do you think will happen in the experiment?" Students could then generate hypotheses. Two hypotheses could be chosen from class comments and used as the classification scheme (instead of the *yes* and *no* scheme). Students could then write information in each of the Web's two columns that support their predictions.

Social studies. In social studies, famous people are often the topic of study. Thus, a Discussion Web could focus on two historical figures and their beliefs. The classification scheme could be the names of each person. A controversial topic (e.g., women's right to vote) could be written in the center of the Web. In each column of the Web, students could provide support for how they believe each historical figure would respond to the controversial topic.

Literature. After reading a short story, such as "The Tell-Tale Heart" by Edgar A. Poe, the discussion could focus on the story's narrator. The question in the center of the Web might be "Is the narrator of the story sane or insane?" In this example, the classification scheme would be *sane* and *insane*. Students could use information from the story to support their stances.

DOUBLE-ENTRY JOURNAL

Purpose

Reading and writing are explicitly connected with the Double-Entry Journal strategy. This strategy can be used with students of all ages with varying degrees of scaffolding and teacher support. The strategy provides opportunities for students to choose parts of a text they wish to connect more profoundly in writing. This activity has many possibilities and can be used before, during, or after reading. It can be used to encourage and facilitate small group or large group discussion and can be a forum in which other students can respond to ideas. The possibilities of this strategy are virtually endless. The Double-Entry Journal can be used to respond to expository as well as narrative text.

Step-by-Step Procedure

1. Divide a sheet of paper in half to create two columns. In the left-hand column, students will write an idea found in the text–a quote, a word, or a concept from the text. In the right-hand column, students reflect or react to the text or make a connection. This open format encourages students to make text-to-text, text-to-self, and text-to-world connections.
2. When students reflect, react, and/or connect to the text, encourage and support them to describe their thoughts in detail and to move beyond literal level connections to make inferences about the text and evaluate it.
3. This activity is ideal for activating prior or background knowledge and integrating all five of the language arts: reading, writing, listening, speaking, and viewing.

Adapted from Nugent, S.M., & Nugent, H.E. (1987). Theory into practice: Learning through writing: The double-entry journal in literature classes. *English Quarterly*, 20, 325–330.

EMBEDDED QUESTIONS

Purpose

To help struggling readers internalize the dialogue associated with monitoring their comprehension of content area texts. Embedded questions help the passive reader engage more actively in the reading process. They also show readers the value in knowing something about themselves as readers, about the task and its demands, and about recovering meaning once it is lost. In short, embedded questions enable the struggling reader to think about what it is they *should* be doing *during* reading and, ultimately, to self-assess whether or not they *are* doing it.

Step-by-Step Procedure

1. Choose a passage from the students' content area text that has proven difficult for students to comprehend in the past (see example below).
2. Insert sticky notes at appropriate places that will reinforce the need for students to answer questions about themselves as readers, about the demands of the task, and about their ability to recognize when they no longer are comprehending.
3. The sticky notes should also provide quick "fix-up" clues (see example below).
4. After students have worked through the passage and attended to the sticky notes, hold a full-class discussion over the value of embedded questions.

Excerpt from "The Lost Colony" by Dan Lacy (1995). In *Just imagine* (pp. 86–91). Lexington, MA: D.C. Heath.

Roanoke Island is small, flat, and sandy—about twelve miles long and three miles wide. It lies between Pamlico and Albemarle sounds, hidden from the Atlantic Ocean by a long chain of narrow islands, really little more than sand dunes, known as the Outer Banks of North Carolina.

> What can you do as a reader to picture this island?

Even today only very small ships can reach the sounds by threading their way through narrow inlets in the Outer Banks, inlets that may change with every storm.

> Could a sound be something other than a noise? If sounds let ships pass through, what might they be?

Adapted for younger children; adapted from Weir, C. (1998). Using embedded questions to jump-start metacognition in middle school remedial readers. *Journal of Adolescent and Adult Literacy, 41*, 458–467.

GUIDED IMAGERY

Purpose

Guided imagery is a strategy used to get the mind's movie camera playing, to elicit background knowledge, and to make connections with the outside world. Guided imagery takes time and practice to do well. Harp (1988) suggests that before using this strategy with books, ask students to practice visualizing and describing objects, scenes, people, or experiences with which they are familiar.

Step-by-Step Procedure

Option 1—Guided Imagery for the entire class

1. Choose a scenario you would like the students to visualize. For example, if you are going to read a book on the rain forest, you may choose to walk the students through a rain forest, using a verbal description.
2. Invite students to get into a comfortable position somewhere in the classroom.
3. Ask them to close their eyes, breathe, and try to relax. You may even want to turn off the lights and slightly close the curtains in the classroom to create a relaxed atmosphere.
4. Using descriptive words, describe the sights, sounds, odors, bouquets, tastes, feelings, motions, and so on, of the rain forest. Try to create a free-flowing scenario—one that does not constrain the student to see what you are describing, but allows the student's imagination to go wherever it wants to go.
5. Once this portion of the activity is finished, preview the book(s) with the students and ask them to connect what they saw in their mind's eye to what they are reading in the book.

Option 2—Individual Guided Imagery

1. Ask students to choose a book they have not yet read and browse through the book, looking at the illustrations, charts, tables, or any other graphic.
2. Invite students to get into a comfortable position and get into a relaxed state somewhere in the classroom.
3. Invite the students to let their minds wander and think deeply about the topic of the book. Have them create their own scenarios for the book in their minds.

Adapted from Harp, Bill (1988). When the principal asks: "Why are you doing guided imagery during reading time?" *Reading Teacher*, 41, 588–590.

4. You may want to guide this process by giving the students general instructions, for example: Think about the subject of the book. What do you see? What does it look like, feel like, smell like, taste like? What is the subject of the book doing? How does it move? With what does it interact?
5. When the students have finished visualizing about the book, have them share and discuss their mental pictures with a partner.

K-W-W-L: QUESTIONING THE KNOWN

Purpose

To extend the K-W-L instructional activity (What I Know, What I Want to Learn, What I Learned), which Donna Ogle (1986) developed. The adaptation helps young learners generate questions based on their knowledge and experiences. With its additional fourth column—the "where" column—K-W-W-L helps young learners know where to go to find answers to the questions they generate.

Step-by-Step Procedure

1. Begin with a simple brainstorming session in which you ask the class to name as many things as they can about a particular concept. For example, Jan Bryan asked the 9 year olds she was working with in a Midwestern rural school district in the United States to brainstorm what they knew about oceans. The class brainstormed the following:

   - oceans are salty
   - salt water burns your eyes
   - hurricanes begin over oceans, and so on . . .

2. Next, building on their knowledge but going further to create a certain disequilibrium, Jan tried to facilitate their need to know more about what they already volunteered as information. She scaffolded questions that helped students query what they already knew and felt comfortable knowing. For example, she posed this question: "Why are oceans salty while most lakes and rivers are not?" She followed up with "How much salt is in the water?" and "Do all oceans contain the same amount of salt?"

3. As the students caught on, they began to question the known. For example, one child asked, "If our tears are salty, then why does ocean salt irritate?" Other questions followed until one child chimed in with "This could go on forever!"

4. Satisfied that a measure of disequlibrium had been created, Jan moved to the next step: brainstorming with the students about where they might look for answers to their questions. They listed the following ideas: encyclopedia, scientist, marine biologist (why are oceans salty), optometrist (why does salt water

Adapted from Bryan, J. (1998). K-W-W-L: Questioning the known. *The Reading Teacher, 51,* 618–620.

burn the eyes), weather person (what causes waves), music teacher (what are some surf songs), etc.

5. In the last step, What I Learned, students made connections between the K-W-W-L session and an earlier science experiment with tuning forks, which when placed in bowls of water produced sound waves.

L I S T – G R O U P – L A B E L

Purpose

To encourage students to brainstorm concepts or words that are known to them as a way of making connections to a new concept or topic. List–Group–Label also encourages students to categorize words and label the categories as an aid to remembering.

Step-by-Step Procedure

1. Begin by selecting a concept or topic that you want to serve as the stimulus for a brainstorming session, either with a small group or the whole class (e.g., *transportation*). Write the word on an overhead transparency, whiteboard, or chart paper.

2. Invite students to think of words that come to mind when they see or hear the word *transportation*. As they call out the words, *list* them under the stimulus word. A sample list of words follows:

   car, bike, space capsule, garage, plane, airport, boat, ski lift, subway, camel, donkey, cart, hangar, train, air balloon, skateboard, horse, elephant

3. Next ask the students to *group* the words that have something in common with each other. Keeping the original list to 20 words or less will ensure that enough words have been generated to group. From the sample list just given, students might group the words in this way:

car	airport	boat	elephant
bike	garage	air balloon	donkey
train	hangar	space capsule	horse
cart		ski lift	camel
skateboard		plane	

4. Finally, ask students to think of a *label* for each group. For example, they might decide on *wheeled vehicles*, *buildings*, *nonwheeled vehicles*, and *animals*, respectively, for the groups just named. Engage students in a short discussion of how the labels all tell something about (or relate to) the stimulus word *transportation*.

5. Note: If some students bring up the point that planes have wheels, accept that response and then ask if the wheels are the chief means of movement. Some may say "Yes, when the plane is on the ground." Again, accept legitimate responses.

Adapted from Taba, H. (1967). *Teacher's handbook for elementary social studies*. Reading, MA: Addison-Wesley.

QUESTION-ANSWER RELATIONSHIPS (QAR)

Purpose

The QAR strategy helps promote reading comprehension by explicitly showing students where meaning can be made with a text and how the reader can interact with the text. This strategy encourages students to monitor their reading, ask questions as they read, and make connections to the text making use of their prior and background knowledge. It also encourages the student to become more involved with the text, thus creating opportunities to understand and make connections with the text in a profound way. This is important when working with content area texts because it allows the student to question the oftentimes presumed authority of printed text.

Step-by-Step Procedure

1. Explain to your students that there are two ways a reader can transact with text: (1) with information within the text itself and (2) with information from the reader.
   a. For information found within the text, explain to students that information can be found "*right there*"—that the authors have explicitly provided information in the words of the text—or "*think and search*"—that the reader will need to think about the question asked and search within the ideas presented in various parts of the text in order to find meaning.
   b. For information using the resources of the reader, explain to students that they will have to capitalize on their personal knowledge in order to make meaning. The information will either be "*on my own*"—meaning that the answer comes from the students' thinking about the content, using what they already know about the content to make meaning with the text—or "*author and you*"—meaning that understanding of the text will arrive from thinking about what the reader knows along with what the author infers in the text. This last place where meaning is made can be thought of as detective work, making different pieces fit together in order to make sense of something.
2. When you introduce this strategy to students, begin using short passages where the elements of the QAR are evident and then move on to more complex passages until you feel students could use this strategy "on their own."

Adapted from Taffy Raphael's (1986) discussion of question–answer relationship in *The Reading Teacher*, 39, 516–522 entitled Teaching Children Question-Answer Relationships, Revisited.

READERS' THEATRE

Purpose

Readers' Theatre takes advantage of the joy of performing and multivocal reading to allow children to improve reading fluency, comprehension, and to have fun! The strategy emphasizes dialogue, not action. Children are encouraged to practice enunciation, pronunciation, and to play around with reading speed and voice for effect. Because less emphasis is placed on movement and action, the audience will have to listen to the words and form visual images as the scene is being acted out. Children practice reading aloud a scripted version prepared from a piece of literature. Because children are "practicing" for the performance, they are engaging in repeated reading, which improves fluency, comprehending subtleties of the text when they add voices, intonation, and expression to the reading, and are given a purpose to read. Readers' Theatre is like radio theatre, popular before the television era.

Step-by-Step Procedure

1. Choose a piece of literature the children have read or you would like them to read where there is a good amount of dialogue and character interaction. You may adapt the piece of literature to be more conversational or choose a ready-made Readers' Theatre script. Many scripts are available on the internet. Go to www.google.com and search for "reader's theater scripts" to find many examples.
2. Tell children that they will perform a reading of a text. If the children have not read the text prior to this activity, be sure to engage the students in activities that will lead them to greater comprehension of the text.
3. It is important to remind the students that they need not memorize the text; they will read from the script. The important thing is to engage the audience with voice and reading performance.
4. You may even choose to have the students present their reading performance to a younger grade, giving them an even greater purpose for rehearsing and performing the text.

Adapted from Sloyer, S. (1982). *Readers theatre: Story dramatization in the classroom.* Urbana, IL: National Council of Teachers of English.

RECIPROCAL TEACHING

Purpose

This strategy teaches students that meaning does not lie solely in the text, but shows them how a reader can form text-to-text, text-to-self, and text-to-world (Keene and Zimmerman, 1997) connections. Reciprocal teaching highlights the social and interactive nature of the reading and meaning making processes. This strategy requires students to elicit prior and background knowledge, as well as have textual knowledge as they form questions about the text.

Reciprocal Teaching involves four strategies that should take place continuously when reading and making meaning with text: asking questions about the text, predicting what might occur, summarizing salient points of the text, and clarifying vocabulary and concepts important to the comprehension of the text. These reading strategies need not be followed as they are written here. As the title of the strategy suggests, reciprocal teaching puts both students and teachers into the "teacher" role.

Step-by-Step Instructions

1. Introduce or remind students of the importance of the four reading strategies noted earlier: questions, prediction, summarizing, and clarifying.
2. Using a reading passage appropriate for instruction and complex enough to challenge students to think through the text, model the use of these strategies. This may be an opportune time to use the "Think Aloud" strategy also found in the Toolbox of Teaching and Learning Strategies.
3. As you work through the text, show students how they will need to ask questions of the text or "wonder" about the text. For example, using the sentence: *Claudia's tendency to suffer from triskaidekaphobia prevented her from ever staying on the thirteenth floor of a hotel*, you may ask, "What does triskaidekaphobia mean in this sentence?" (clarifying vocabulary); "Why does Claudia not want to stay on the thirteenth floor of the hotel?" (questioning the text); "I think Claudia will or will not stay on the thirteenth floor of the hotel the next time she goes on vacation because...." (prediction); "Triskaideskaphobia is the fear of the number 13. This is why Claudia will most likely not stay on the thirteenth floor of any hotel" (summarizing).
4. As students become more comfortable asking questions about a text, allow them to use this strategy with a reading buddy or small group.
5. Encourage students to use this strategy to monitor their reading and comprehension of any text. The goal is to get students to internalize these reading strategies.

Note: Taken from Palincsar, A. S., & Brown, A. L. (1984). Reciprocal teaching of comprehension-fostering and monitoring activities. *Cognition and Instruction, 1*, 117–175.

THINK ALOUDS

Purpose

To help students become aware of the internal dialogue that occurs when an individual tries to make meaning with a text. Think alouds work well before, during, or after reading as it is a strategy to show students how to monitor their own reading. It works well with both narrative and expository texts. Think alouds model different reading strategies to students (e.g., making predictions—i.e., what you think will happen next in the text; monitoring reading comprehension—when comprehension breaks down, show students how you deal with the problem; eliciting background and prior knowledge—show students how you form connections with the text) and demonstrate not only how to use them but when to use them. Think Alouds will also show the students that not all reading strategies are appropriate for every reading situation.

Step-by-Step Procedure

1. Choose a passage from a content area text that may prove to be difficult for students to comprehend.
2. Optional: Copy the passage onto an overhead transparency so you may write out the reading strategies you employ as you work your way through the text with the students.
3. Tell the students this is the first time you are reading this passage and that you will share your thinking as you read the text aloud to them.
4. As you read the passage to the students, be sure to think through the reading process aloud, demonstrating the reading strategies mentioned earlier, e.g., if you miscue a word, be sure to recognize the fact that a word was miscued. You could tell the students, "The word that I just pronounced doesn't make sense with the rest of sentence. Let me go back and see if I can figure the word out. I can sound it out, try to see if I can figure it out through context, see if there are any pictures that may help me, or if nothing else works, ask someone."
5. After demonstrating this technique with the students, ask them to "Try it!" with a classmate.

Adapted from Davey, B. (1983). Think-aloud—modeling the cognitive processes of reading comprehension. *Journal of Reading*, 4, 44–47.

APPENDIX A

Leveled Informational Books

Appendix A lists informational books that can be used for teaching reading and content. The list is certainly not exhaustive but provides a glimpse at what is available. We include books from five publishers with which we are most familiar. There are certainly many more companies that are publishing simple informational books, written especially for early reading instruction. For additional sources, surf the Net using "leveled books" as your search term.

The books are organized by (1) content area and (2) guided reading levels provided by the publishing companies using Fountas and Pinnell's (1999) leveling system. The organization by content area is unique to this list. We hope it will help teachers think about more ways to relate reading and content instruction.

We include emergent and beginning books (levels A: kindergarten–J: beginning second grade) because fewer informational texts are published at these early levels than higher ones. Each list is organized by content area, beginning with health/physical fitness and general science. Next, we include animals in a separate list because of the substantial numbers of books related to the topic. Then we proceed to math, social studies and geography, how-to, and art/music. All categories are not listed for each level because books at particular levels were not always available in our sources.

Book Titles	Level	Series	Publisher
Level A			
Health Physical Fitness			
Basketball	A	Wonder World	Wright Group
Bath Time	A	Wonder World	Wright Group
Bike	A	TWiG Books	Wright Group
Getting Fit	A	Wonder World	Wright Group
I Am Running!	A	Rigby PM Plus	Rigby
Play Ball!	A	TWiG Books	Wright Group
Playground	A	TWiG Books	Wright Group
Playing	A	AlphaKids Guided Readers	Sundance
Science			
Big and Green	A	Wonder World	Wright Group
Flower Box	A	TWiG Books	Wright Group
In the Garden	A	Rigby PM Plus	Rigby
Pond	A	Discovery Links Science	Newbridge

Book Titles	Level	Series	Publisher
Push and Pull	A	Discovery Links Science	Newbridge
Seed	A	Wonder World	Wright Group
Up in the Sky	A	Rigby PM Plus	Rigby
What Season Is This?	A	Wonder World	Wright Group
Science: Animals			
Bats	A	TWiG Books	Wright Group
Big Mammals	A	Little Red Readers	Sundance
A Cat's Day	A	TWiG Books	Wright Group
Nests	A	Wonder World	Wright Group
Science: Senses			
Can You See Me?	A	AlphaKids Guided Readers	Sundance
Glasses	A	AlphaKids Guided Readers	Sundance
I Hear!	A	Emergent Nonfiction	Benchmark
Noise!	A	Little Green Readers	Sundance
Things That Go (colors)	A	Little Reader Twin Texts	Sundance
Math			
Big and Little	A	Little Reader Twin Texts	Sundance
Big and Small	A	AlphaKids Guided Readers	Sundance
Guess How Many I Have	A	Emergent Nonfiction	Benchmark
It's Time!	A	Emergent Nonfiction	Benchmark
What's Round?	A	Discovery Links Science	Newbridge
Social Studies			
Baby	A	Rigby PM Plus	Rigby
Chinese Kites	A	TWiG Books	Wright Group
Circus	A	TWiG Books	Wright Group
Circus	A	AlphaKids Guided Readers	Sundance
Circus Train	A	Little Red Readers	Sundance
Clown Face	A	TWiG Books	Wright Group
In our Classroom	A	Rigby PM Plus	Rigby
Life on a Farm	A	Emergent Nonfiction	Benchmark
People Use Tools	A	Emergent Nonfiction	Benchmark
Things I Like Doing	A	Emergent Nonfiction	Benchmark
Geography			
Going on Vacation	A	Rigby PM Plus	Rigby
Helicopter Over Hawaii	A	TWiG Books	Wright Group
In the Mountains	A	TWiG Books	Wright Group
How To			
Face Painting	A	AlphaKids Guided Readers	Sundance
Magnet Fishing Game	A	Emergent Nonfiction	Benchmark

Book Titles	Level	Series	Publisher
Level B			
Health/Physical Fitness			
My Dinner	B	AlphaKids Guided Readers	Sundance
Play Ball!	B	AlphaKids Guided Readers	Sundance
Team Sports	B	TWiG Books	Wright Group
Teeth	B	Wonder World	Wright Group
Science			
Beautiful Flowers	B	Wonder World	Wright Group
Closer and Closer	B	TWiG Books	Wright Group
Fall	B	Discovery Links Science	Newbridge
In the Sky	B	Little Red Readers	Sundance
In the Spring	B	Discovery Links Science	Newbridge
Life in a Tree	B	Little Green Readers	Sundance
Living and Nonliving	B	AlphaKids Guided Readers	Sundance
Night Sky	B	TWiG Books	Wright Group
Rain	B	Little Reader Twin Texts	Sundance
Seasons	B	Discovery World	Rigby
Snow	B	Discovery Links Science	Newbridge
Snowball Fight	B	Wonder World	Wright Group
Trees	B	TWiG Books	Wright Group
What Do I See?	B	TWiG Books	Wright Group
Science: Animals			
Animal Homes	B	Emergent Nonfiction	Benchmark
Animals I Like to Feed	B	Little Red Readers	Sundance
Animal Legs	B	Discovery World	Rigby
Ants	B	Discovery Links Science	Newbridge
At the Wild Animal Park	B	Little Red Readers	Sundance
Baby Chimp	B	TWiG Books	Wright Group
Big Sea Animals	B	Rigby PM Plus	Rigby
Bug-Watching	B	TWiG Books	Wright Group
Fishbowl	B	AlphaKids Guided Readers	Sundance
Frogs	B	TWiG Books	Wright Group
Legs, Legs, Legs	B	Wonder World	Wright Group
My Little Cat	B	Rigby PM Plus	Rigby
What Can Fly?	B	Discovery Links Science	Newbridge
Zoo	B	Wonder World	Wright Group
Math			
Big and Little	B	Emergent Nonfiction	Benchmark
Counting One to Five	B	Emergent Nonfiction	Benchmark
Shapes	B	Discovery World	Rigby
Stripes	B	TWiG Books	Wright Group
What Time Is It?	B	Little Blue Readers	Sundance

Book Titles	Level	Series	Publisher
Social Studies			
At the Library	B	Little Blue Readers	Sundance
Getting There	B	Wonder World	Wright Group
Growing Up	B	Discovery Links Social Studies	Newbridge
Hats	B	TWiG Books	Wright Group
Homes for People	B	Emergent Nonfiction	Benchmark
Jobs Up High	B	Emergent Nonfiction	Benchmark
My Baby Sister	B	AlphaKids Guided Readers	Sundance
My Clothes	B	Rigby PM Plus	Rigby
Old and New	B	Emergent Nonfiction	Benchmark
Party Hats	B	Rigby PM Plus	Rigby
Sending Messages	B	Wonder World	Wright Group
Things I Can Do	B	Little Red Readers	Sundance
Things I Do for Fun	B	Little Red Readers	Sundance
Toy Box	B	Rigby PM Plus	Rigby
Trucks	B	TWiG Books	Wright Group
We Dress Up	B	Rigby PM Plus	Rigby
Geography			
Desert Day	B	TWiG Books	Wright Group
In the Mountains	B	TWiG Books	Wright Group
Ocean Waves	B	TWiG Books	Wright Group
World Around Us	B	Little Red Readers	Sundance
How To			
Making a Bird	B	Rigby PM Plus	Rigby
Making a Dinosaur	B	Rigby PM Plus	Rigby
Making a Mask	B	Little Blue Readers	Sundance
Making a Rabbit	B	Rigby PM Plus	Rigby
Art/Music			
Making Music	B	AlphaKids Guided Readers	Sundance
Painting	B	AlphaKids Guided Readers	Sundance
Level C			
Health/Physical Fitness			
Playing Outside	C	Rigby PM Plus	Rigby
Science			
Animal Habitats	C	Little Red Readers	Sundance
Animal Noises	C	Little Red Readers	Sundance
At the Water Hole	C	Little Red Readers	Sundance
Divers	C	Wonder World	Wright Group
Everyone Eats	C	Discovery Links Science	Newbridge
Eyes	C	Wonder World	Wright Group
In Space	C	Little Blue Readers	Sundance
In the Ocean	C	AlphaKids Guided Readers	Sundance

Book Titles	Level	Series	Publisher
Light	C	TWiG Books	Wright Group
Machines That Travel	C	Little Blue Readers	Sundance
My Body	C	Discovery World	Rigby
Sniff	C	AlphaKids Guided Readers	Sundance
Sunflower	C	Exploring Science 1	Rigby
Things on Wheels	C	Little Red Readers	Sundance
Tools We Use	C	Little Red Readers	Sundance
Wetlands	C	Little Green Readers	Sundance
We Use Water	C	Emergent Nonfiction	Benchmark
What Floats?	C	TWiG Books	Wright Group
Wheels	C	Discovery Links Science	Newbridge

Science: Animals

Animal Tracks	C	Wonder World	Wright Group
Butterfly	C	AlphaKids Guided Readers	Sundance
Dinosaur Time	C	AlphaKids Guided Readers	Sundance
Porcupine	C	Wonder World	Wright Group
Tails	C	Wonder World	Wright Group
Under Water	C	TWiG Books	Wright Group
What Kind of Dog am I?	C	TWiG Books	Wright Group
Who Lives in This Hole?	C	TWiG Books	Wright Group

Math

Add the Animals	C	Emergent Nonfiction	Benchmark
Big and Little	C	Rigby PM Plus	Rigby
Counting Seeds	C	Emergent Nonfiction	Benchmark
Looking for Numbers	C	Emergent Nonfiction	Benchmark
Patterns	C	Discovery Links Science	Newbridge
Patterns All Around	C	Emergent Nonfiction	Benchmark
Rainy Day Counting	C	TWiG Books	Wright Group
Sizes	C	Discovery World	Rigby
Using Numbers at Work	C	Emergent Nonfiction	Benchmark

Social Studies

At Work	C	Discovery Links Social Studies	Newbridge
Bus	C	TWiG Books	Wright Group
City Signs	C	Discovery Links Social Studies	Newbridge
Families	C	Discovery Links Social Studies	Newbridge
Helping in the Yard	C	AlphaKids Guided Readers	Sundance
People Who Help	C	Little Reader Twin Set	Sundance
Places	C	Little Red Readers	Sundance
Today and Long Ago	C	Little Reader Twin Set	Sundance
We Are Special	C	Discovery Links Social Studies	Newbridge
Working at Home	C	Little Red Readers	Sundance
Working Together	C	Emergent Nonfiction	Benchmark
Zookeepers	C	Little Green Readers	Sundance

Book Titles	Level	Series	Publisher
Geography			
In a Cold, Cold Place	C	AlphaKids Guided Readers	Sundance
Where Is Water?	C	TWiG Books	Wright Group
How To			
Making a Pizza	C	AlphaKids Guided Readers	Sundance
Making Pancakes	C	Little Blue Readers	Sundance
Art/Music			
Just Add Water	C	Discovery World	Rigby
Painters	C	TWiG Books	Wright Group
Level D			
Health/Physical Fitness			
Playground Fun	D	Emergent Nonfiction	Benchmark
Where Is It Safe to Play?	D	Rigby PM Plus	Rigby
Science			
Amazing Magnets	D	TWiG Books	Wright Group
Balancing	D	TWiG Books	Wright Group
Behind the Rocks	D	Wonder World	Wright Group
Fish	D	Wonder World	Wright Group
Litterbug	D	Little Green Readers	Sundance
Looking at Flowers	D	AlphaKids	Sundance
Look into Space	D	Discovery World	Rigby
Machines	D	TWiG Books	Wright Group
My Skin	D	Wonder World	Wright Group
Old to New	D	Little Green Readers	Sundance
On the Computer	D	TWiG Books	Wright Group
Our Earth	D	Discovery Links Science	Newbridge
Plants	D	AlphaKids	Sundance
Pond	D	AlphaKids	Sundance
Rain and the Sun	D	Wonder World	Wright Group
Skin, Skin	D	Wonder World	Wright Group
Summertime	D	Exploring Science I	Rigby
Water Changes	D	Discovery Links Science	Newbridge
What Did I Use?	D	Discovery World	Rigby
What Do Scientists Do?	D	TWiG Books	Wright Group
Where Are the Seeds	D	Wonder World	Wright Group
Science: Animals			
Animals and Their Babies	D	Emergent Nonfiction	Benchmark
Animals Hide and Seek	D	TWiG Books	Wright Group
Baby Animals	D	Discovery Links Science	Newbridge
My Hamster	D	Exploring Science I	Rigby
Tadpoles and Frogs	D	AlphaKids	Sundance
What's Alive?	D	Discovery Links Science	Newbridge
Where's the Frog?	D	Discovery Links Science	Newbridge

Book Titles	Level	Series	Publisher
Math			
Bigger Than? Smaller Than?	D	Emergent Nonfiction	Benchmark
Counting Money	D	Emergent Nonfiction	Benchmark
Everyday Math	D	Emergent Nonfiction	Benchmark
How Many?	D	Little Reader Twin Sets	Sundance
Shapes Everywhere	D	Emergent Nonfiction	Benchmark
What Comes in Twos?	D	Emergent Nonfiction	Benchmark
Social Studies			
Feelings	D	Little Reader Twin Sets	Sundance
Fourth of July	D	Discovery Links Social Studies	Newbridge
Here I Am	D	Discovery Links Social Studies	Newbridge
Houses	D	Little Reader Twin Sets	Sundance
Long Ago	D	Emergent Nonfiction	Benchmark
My Neighborhood	D	Discovery Links Social Studies	Newbridge
No One Else Like Me	D	Emergent Nonfiction	Benchmark
Park Rangers	D	Little Green Readers	Sundance
People Everywhere	D	Discovery Links Social Studies	Newbridge
People Who Keep You Safe	D	Emergent Nonfiction	Benchmark
Rules	D	Discovery Links Social Studies	Newbridge
Together	D	Discovery Links Social Studies	Newbridge
Transportation Over the Years	D	Discovery Links Social Studies	Newbridge
What People Do	D	Emergent Nonfiction	Benchmark
Where We Live	D	Discovery Links Social Studies	Newbridge
How To			
Make a Plan of Your Classroom	D	Emergent Nonfiction	Benchmark
Make a Safety Puppet	D	Emergent Nonfiction	Benchmark
Making a Cat and Mouse	D	Rigby PM Plus	Rigby
Level E			
Health/Physical Fitness			
Gymnastics	E	AlphaKids Guided Readers	Sundance
Science			
Apple Tree Year	E	Discovery Links Social Studies	Newbridge
Big Machines	E	Little Blue Readers	Sundance
Big Rocks, Little Rocks	E	Emergent Nonfiction	Benchmark
Day and Night	E	TWiG Books	Wright Group
Earthquake!	E	Wonder World	Rigby
Fast, Faster, Fastest	E	TWiG Books	Wright Group
Growing Tomatoes	E	AlphaKids Guided Reader	Sundance
Grow, Seed, Grow	E	Discovery Links Science	Newbridge
Hiding in the Sea	E	AlphaKids Guided Reader	Sundance
In the Rain Forest	E	TWiG Books	Wright Group
Machines in the Home	E	Little Blue Readers	Sundance
Magnets	E	Discovery Links Science	Newbridge

Book Titles	Level	Series	Publisher
Plants We Eat	E	Little Reader Twin Sets	Sundance
Recycling	E	Little Reader Twin Sets	Sundance
Sun	E	Discovery Links Science	Newbridge
Tools at Home	E	Little Blue Readers	Sundance
Tracks	E	TWiG Books	Wright Group
Using Machines	E	Little Blue Readers	Sundance
We Need Water	E	Discovery Links Social Studies	Newbridge
Wind	E	Discovery Links Science	Newbridge
Winter	E	Discovery Links Science	Newbridge
Science: Animals			
Animals at Risk	E	Little Green Readers	Sundance
Animal Coverings	E	Emergent Nonfiction	Benchmark
Animal Skeletons	E	AlphaKids Guided Reader	Sundance
Baby Animals at Home	E	TWiG Books	Wright Group
Cats	E	Wonder World	Rigby
Cranes	E	Exploring Science I	Rigby
Mammals	E	AlphaKids Guided Reader	Sundance
My Five Senses	E	Emergent Nonfiction	Benchmark
Spider Legs	E	TWiG Books	Wright Group
Spiders	E	Discovery Links Science	Newbridge
Tails	E	Discovery Links Science	Newbridge
Math			
Adding Animals	E	Number Concepts	Newbridge
How Many?	E	Number Concepts	Newbridge
How Many?	E	Emergent Nonfiction	Benchmark
Measuring Time	E	Emergent Nonfiction	Benchmark
More or Less?	E	Number Concepts	Newbridge
Numbers Are Everywhere	E	Emergent Nonfiction	Benchmark
Parts of a Whole	E	Emergent Nonfiction	Benchmark
Reading a Graph	E	Emergent Nonfiction	Benchmark
Who Is the Tallest?	E	AlphaKids Guided Reader	Sundance
Social Studies			
Communities	E	Wonder World	Rigby
Homes Around the World	E	Emergent Nonfiction	Benchmark
Long Ago	E	Discovery Links Social Studies	Newbridge
My Flag	E	Discovery Links Social Studies	Newbridge
Needs	E	Discovery Links Social Studies	Newbridge
Our Heroes	E	Discovery Links Social Studies	Newbridge
People Dance	E	Wonder World	Rigby
Rules	E	Little Reader Twin Sets	Sundance
School Then and Now	E	Discovery Links Social Studies	Newbridge
Sharing News	E	Discovery Links Social Studies	Newbridge
This Is America	E	Discovery Links Social Studies	Newbridge
Wonderful Wheat	E	Discovery Links Social Studies	Newbridge

Book Titles	Level	Series	Publisher
Geography			
Desert Life	E	Little Green Readers	Sundance
How To			
You Can Make a Timer	E	How-To Series	Benchmark
Art/Music			
From the Air	E	Wonder World	Rigby
Shadow Puppets	E	AlphaKids Guided Reader	Sundance
Level F			
Health/Physical Fitness			
Children at Play	F	Little Red Readers	Sundance
From Peanuts to Peanut Butter	F	Food and Nutrition	Newbridge
Processed Food	F	Wonder World	Wright Group
Science			
Changing Weather	F	Early Nonfiction	Benchmark
Clean Air	F	Little Green Readers	Sundance
Clean Beaches	F	Early Nonfiction	Benchmark
Don't Throw It Away!	F	Wonder World	Wright Group
Growing Pumpkins	F	Plants	Newbridge
Hot Sunny Days	F	Rigby PM Plus	Rigby
It Is Raining	F	Rigby PM Plus	Rigby
I Wonder Why?	F	Wonder World	Wright Group
Kids for the Earth	F	Systems	Newbridge
Light	F	Early Nonfiction	Benchmark
Listen	F	Exploring Science I	Rigby
My Body Works	F	TWiG Books	Wright Group
Old Teeth, New Teeth	F	Wonder World	Wright Group
Our Senses	F	Discovery Links Science	Newbridge
Push and Pull	F	Physical World	Newbridge
Rainforest Plants	F	AlphaKids Guided Readers	Sundance
Rain Is Water	F	Rigby PM Plus	Rigby
Space Shuttle	F	Planet Earth/Space	Rigby
Sun, the Wind, and the Rain	F	Rigby PM Plus	Rigby
What Floats? What Sinks?	F	Early Nonfiction	Benchmark
What Pushes? What Pulls?	F	Early Nonfiction	Benchmark
Where Are the Eggs?	F	Discovery Links Science	Newbridge
Where Did All the Water Go?	F	Rigby PM Plus	Rigby
Worker's Tools	F	Discovery World	Rigby
Science: Animals			
Animal Babies	F	TWiG Books	Wright Group
Endangered Animals	F	Early Nonfiction	Benchmark
Fly Butterfly	F	Discovery Links Science	Newbridge
Fuzz, Feathers, Fur	F	TWiG Books	Wright Group

Book Titles	Level	Series	Publisher
How Animals Hide	F	Wonder World	Wright Group
Our Pets	F	Exploring Science I	Rigby
Reptiles	F	AlphaKids Guided Readers	Sundance
Spiders	F	AlphaKids Guided Readers	Sundance
Whales	F	AlphaKids Guided Readers	Sundance
Math			
Counting Stars	F	Early Nonfiction	Benchmark
Keeping Time	F	Early Nonfiction	Benchmark
Numbers Are Everywhere	F	TWiG Books	Wright Group
Seven	F	Early Nonfiction	Benchmark
Shapes	F	Little Reader Twin Texts	Sundance
Time for the Party	F	Discovery World	Rigby
What Comes Next?	F	Early Nonfiction	Benchmark
Social Studies			
Houses Around the World	F	Discovery Links Social Studies	Newbridge
Over the Oregon Trail	F	TWiG Books	Wright Group
Plane Ride	F	Little Red Readers	Sundance
Sarah and Will	F	AlphaKids Guided Readers	Sundance
Then and Now	F	Early Nonfiction	Benchmark
Trains	F	Little Blue Readers	Sundance
What I'd Like to Be	F	Little Red Readers	Sundance
Who Helps?	F	Discovery Links Social Studies	Newbridge
How To			
How to Make an Earthworm Farm	F	Little Green Readers	Sundance
Make an Animal Mobile	F	How-To Series	Benchmark
Make a Paper Airplane	F	How-To Series	Benchmark
Making a Caterpillar	F	Rigby PM Plus	Rigby
Making Concrete	F	AlphaKids Guided Readers	Sundance
Making Spaghetti	F	AlphaKids Guided Readers	Sundance
Art/Music			
Music Everywhere	F	TWiG Books	Wright Group
Level G			
Health/Physical Fitness			
Best Thing about Food	G	TWiG Books	Wright Group
Science			
Bubbles, Bubbles Everywhere	G	Physical World	Newbridge
Clouds	G	TWiG Books	Wright Group
Flying Machines	G	Little Blue Readers	Sundance
Growing a Plant: A Journal	G	Discovery World	Rigby
Habitat Is Where We Live	G	TWiG Books	Wright Group

Book Titles	Level	Series	Publisher
Machines that Fly	G	AlphaKids Guided Readers	Sundance
My Computer (technology)	G	Wonder World	Wright Group
Recycle it!	G	Discovery Links Science	Newbridge
Technology Today	G	Early Nonfiction	Benchmark
Tidal Pools	G	Little Green Readers	Sundance
Up Close	G	Discovery Links Science	Newbridge
Watching the Weather	G	Discovery Links Science	Newbridge
What Can Change?	G	Discovery Links Science	Newbridge
What Happens to Trash?	G	Little Green Readers	Sundance
When the Sun Goes Down	G	Wonder World	Wright Group
Where Does All the Garbage Go?	G	Earth and Beyond	Newbridge
Wood and Other Materials	G	Discovery World	Rigby
Your Amazing Body	G	AlphaKids Guided Readers	Sundance
Your Body	G	Early Nonfiction	Benchmark

Science: Animals

Animals and Their Babies	G	Physical World	Newbridge
Animals from Long Ago	G	Discovery Links Science	Newbridge
Animal Homes	G	Rigby PM Plus	Rigby
Beaks and Feet	G	AlphaKids Guided Readers	Sundance
Butterfly Is Born	G	Physical World	Newbridge
Gorillas	G	AlphaKids Guided Readers	Sundance
How Animals Move	G	Discovery Links Science	Newbridge
Salmon Story	G	TWiG Books	Wright Group
Sea Turtles	G	Little Green Readers	Sundance
Spinning a Web	G	Systems	Newbridge
Tarantula	G	AlphaKids Guided Readers	Sundance
Where Do the Animals Live?	G	World of Animals	Newbridge
Who Lays Eggs?	G	TWiG Books	Wright Group

Math

It's Time!	G	Math in Our World	Newbridge
Money Book	G	Patterns and Shapes	Newbridge
My Time Box	G	Early Nonfiction	Benchmark
Patterns Everywhere	G	Classification Skills	Newbridge
Short, Tall, Big or Small?	G	Classification Skills	Newbridge
Sorting My Money	G	Early Nonfiction	Benchmark
Sort It Out	G	Classification Skills	Newbridge
Up, Down, All Around	G	Classification Skills	Newbridge
What Can You Measure with a Lollipop?	G	Early Nonfiction	Benchmark
What Comes Next?	G	Math in Our World	Newbridge
Who Wears Shoes?	G	Number Concepts	Newbridge

Social Studies

Building the Railroad	G	TWiG Books	Wright Group
Celebrations Around the World	G	Early Nonfiction	Benchmark

Book Titles	Level	Series	Publisher
City Buildings	G	Discovery Links Science	Newbridge
Families	G	TWiG Books	Wright Group
Jacques Cousteau	G	Early Nonfiction	Benchmark
March for Freedom	G	TWiG Books	Wright Group
Matthew Henson	G	Early Nonfiction	Benchmark
Newspaper	G	TWiG Books	Wright Group
Our Class Survey	G	Early Nonfiction	Benchmark
Our House Is A Safe House	G	Rigby PM Plus	Rigby
Our New House	G	Rigby PM Plus	Rigby
Sally Ride: Astronaut	G	Little Reader Twin Sets	Sundance
Soccer Coach	G	Little Reader Twin Sets	Sundance
Stamps	G	Wonder World	Wright Group
What Families Do	G	Discovery Links Social Studies	Newbridge
What Kids Say	G	Little Reader Twin Sets	Sundance
When Do You Feel . . .	G	TWiG Books	Wright Group
When Lincoln Was a Boy	G	TWiG Books	Wright Group
Wildlife Helpers	G	TWiG Books	Wright Group

Geography

African Grasslands	G	Little Green Readers	Sundance
Mountains and Oceans	G	Little Reader Twin Sets	Sundance
Rainforests	G	Little Green Readers	Sundance

How To

Making an Ooze Monster	G	Little Blue Readers	Sundance
Making a Plane	G	Little Blue Readers	Sundance
Making a Toy House	G	Rigby PM Plus	Rigby
Making Ice Cream	G	Early Nonfiction	Benchmark
Making Paper	G	Little Green Readers	Sundance
You Can Make a Scrapbook	G	Early Nonfiction	Benchmark

Art/Music

Art	G	AlphaKids Guided Readers	Sundance
Going to the Symphony	G	TWiG Books	Wright Group

Level H
Health/Physical Fitness

Food Is Fun	H	Rigby PM Plus	Rigby
Germs	H	TWiG Books	Wright Group
Getting Glasses	H	Wonder World	Wright Group
Healthy Food	H	Rigby PM Plus	Rigby
Pasta, Please!	H	Food and Nutrition	Newbridge
Super Snack Recipes	H	Little Reader Twin Texts	Sundance

Science

Amazing Water	H	Physical Science	Newbridge
An Apple a Day	H	Plants	Newbridge

Book Titles	Level	Series	Publisher
At the Science Center	H	Discovery Links Science	Newbridge
Computers (technology)	H	Little Blue Readers	Sundance
Coral Reef	H	Discovery Links Science	Newbridge
Corn: From Farm to Table	H	Discovery Links Science	Newbridge
Electric Motors	H	Little Blue Readers	Sundance
Four Seasons	H	Earth and Beyond	Newbridge
Gifts From the Earth	H	Discovery Links Social Studies	Newbridge
Golden Leaf	H	Exploring Science 2	Rigby
Hospital	H	Little Blue Readers	Sundance
How We Use Electricity	H	Physical World	Newbridge
Life in a Pond	H	Systems	Newbridge
Light	H	Physical Science	Newbridge
Make an Island	H	Early Nonfiction	Benchmark
Moon	H	TWiG Books	Wright Group
Mystery of Magnets	H	Physical Science	Newbridge
Seeds Get Around	H	Plants	Newbridge
Sound	H	Physical World	Newbridge
Stars	H	Discovery Links Science	Newbridge
Trash-Free Lunch Day	H	Little Green Readers	Sundance
Vegetable Garden	H	Plants	Newbridge
What Do Scientists Do?	H	Discovery Links Science	Newbridge
Where Does Breakfast Come From?	H	Discovery World	Rigby
Where Does Water Go?	H	Discovery Links Science	Newbridge
Who Cares about the Weather?	H	Earth and Beyond	Newbridge

Science: Animals

Book Titles	Level	Series	Publisher
American Buffalo	H	Little Green Readers	Sundance
Animals Build	H	Discovery Links Science	Newbridge
Animals in Hiding	H	World of Animals	Newbridge
Big and Little Dinosaurs	H	Planet Earth	Rigby
Chameleons	H	TWiG Books	Wright Group
Fur, Feathers, Scales, Skin	H	Discovery Links Science	Newbridge
How Do Animals Stay Alive?	H	Early Nonfiction	Benchmark
Insects	H	AlphaKids Guided Readers	Sundance
Leaping Frog	H	Life Cycles	Newbridge
Life in the Sea	H	World of Animals	Newbridge
Squirrels All Year Round	H	Life Cycles	Newbridge
What Dinosaurs Ate	H	Planet Earth	Rigby

Math

Book Titles	Level	Series	Publisher
Every Shape and Size	H	Wonder World	Wright Group
Guessing Jar	H	Early Nonfiction	Benchmark
Lines	H	AlphaKids Guided Readers	Sundance
Math Stories	H	Everyday Applications	Newbridge
Measuring Up	H	Math in Our World	Newbridge
Money	H	TWiG Books	Wright Group

Book Titles	Level	Series	Publisher
Numbers Every Day	H	Number Concepts	Newbridge
Parts of a Whole	H	Math in Our World	Newbridge
Shapes in the City	H	TWiG Books	Wright Group
Units of Measure	H	Everyday Applications	Newbridge
Social Studies			
American Indian Weaving	H	Discovery Links Social Studies	Newbridge
Hiking With Dad	H	Wonder World	Wright Group
John James Audubon	H	Early Nonfiction	Benchmark
New Citizens	H	TWiG Books	Wright Group
Sports Around the World	H	Early Nonfiction	Benchmark
Taking a Trip	H	Discovery Links Social Studies	Newbridge
What Do Historians Do?	H	Discovery Links Social Studies	Newbridge
What Is a Park?	H	Discovery World	Rigby
Wright Brothers	H	Early Nonfiction	Benchmark
Geography			
Around My Classroom	H	Exploring Geography	Rigby
Around My Home	H	Exploring Geography	Rigby
Around My School	H	Exploring Geography	Rigby
How To			
Making Lemonade	H	Little Blue Readers	Sundance
Making Party Food	H	Rigby PM Plus	Rigby
Art/Music			
Meet the Orchestra	H	Little Reader Twin Texts	Sundance
Level I			
Health/Physical Fitness			
Our Bodies	I	Rigby Plus PM	Rigby
Taking Care of Ourselves	I	Rigby Plus PM	Rigby
You Are What You Eat	I	Food & Nutrition	Newbridge
Science			
Building Strong Bridges	I	TWiG Books	Wright Group
Erosion	I	Early Nonfiction	Benchmark
Growing Older	I	Early Nonfiction	Benchmark
Jane Goodall and the Chimps	I	TWiG Books	Wright Group
Machines in the School	I	Little Blue Readers	Sundance
Machines on the Farm	I	Little Blue Readers	Sundance
Making Electricity	I	Little Blue Readers	Sundance
My Body	I	Early Nonfiction	Benchmark
Power from the Sun	I	Little Green Readers	Sundance
Space Travel	I	AlphaKids Guided Readers	Sundance
Things We Throw Away	I	Little Green Readers	Sundance

Book Titles	Level	Series	Publisher
Storm!	I	Wonder World	Wright Group
Unusual Machines	I	Little Red Readers	Sundance
Water	I	Wonder World	Wright Group
Water for You	I	Little Blue Readers	Sundance
Water: Liquid, Solid, Gas	I	TWiG Books	Wright Group
Water Power	I	Little Green Readers	Sundance
Weather Watching	I	AlphaKids Guided Readers	Sundance
Where Does All the Garbage Go?	I	TWiG Books	Wright Group

Animals

Animal Builders	I	AlphaKids Guided Readers	Sundance
Animal Groups	I	Early Nonfiction	Benchmark
Animal Messengers	I	Discovery Links Science	Newbridge
Animals Grow	I	Wonder World	Wright Group
Animals in Danger	I	Little Red Readers	Sundance
City Animals	I	Little Green Readers	Sundance
Fireflies	I	TWiG Books	Wright Group
Katydid's Life	I	TWiG Books	Wright Group
Looking After Chicks	I	AlphaKids Guided Readers	Sundance
Lost Dinosaur	I	Planet Earth	Rigby
Sea Animals	I	Little Red Readers	Sundance
Starfish	I	AlphaKids Guided Readers	Sundance
Where Is My Caterpillar?	I	Wonder World	Wright Group

Astronomy

Our Moon	I	Early Nonfiction	Benchmark
Our Sun	I	Early Nonfiction	Benchmark

Math

Graph It!	I	Patterns and Shapes	Newbridge
How Long Is a Foot?	I	TWiG Books	Wright Group
How Many Are Left?	I	Early Nonfiction	Benchmark
Measuring Tools	I	Early Nonfiction	Benchmark
Money: Then and Now	I	Little Reader Twin Texts	Sundance
Parts Make Up a Whole	I	Early Nonfiction	Benchmark
Skip-Counting	I	Patterns and Shapes	Newbridge
Solve it!	I	Math in Our World	Newbridge
Travel Money, U.S.A.	I	Early Nonfiction	Benchmark
What Is Place Value?	I	Everyday Applications	Newbridge

Social Studies

Busy Harvest	I	Discovery Links Social Studies	Newbridge
Community Jobs	I	Early Nonfiction	Benchmark
Father Fights Back: FDR and Polio	I	TWiG Books	Wright Group
Flags Flying	I	Discovery Links Social Studies	Newbridge

Book Titles	Level	Series	Publisher
Food Around the World	I	Early Nonfiction	Benchmark
Friends	I	Early Nonfiction	Benchmark
George Washington Carver	I	Early Nonfiction	Benchmark
Helping Others	I	Little Reader Twin Texts	Sundance
How Did This City Grow?	I	Early Nonfiction	Benchmark
Lady Liberty	I	TWiG Books	Wright Group
Living with Others	I	Rigby Plus PM	Rigby
Making Mount Rushmore	I	TWiG Books	Wright Group
Meet the Astronauts	I	Discovery Links Social Studies	Newbridge
Mexico City Is Muy Grande	I	TWiG Books	Wright Group
Old and New Trains	I	Little Blue Readers	Sundance
River Road	I	Discovery Links Social Studies	Newbridge
Totem Poles	I	Little Reader Twin Texts	Sundance
Underground Railroad	I	TWiG Books	Wright Group
Who Makes the Rules?	I	Early Nonfiction	Benchmark
Why People Move	I	Discovery Links Social Studies	Newbridge

Geography
Deserts	I	Early Nonfiction	Benchmark

How To
Fun Things to Make and Do	I	Discovery World	Rigby
How to Draw a Dinosaur	I	AlphaKids Guided Readers	Sundance

Art/Music
Backstage	I	TWiG Books	Wright Group
Making a Tape	I	Little Blue Readers	Sundance

Level J

Science
All From an Oak Tree	J	Discovery Links Science	Newbridge
Balance and Motion	J	Systems	Newbridge
Discovery Teams	J	Discovery Links Social Studies	Newbridge
Everyone Needs Tools	J	Discovery Links Social Studies	Newbridge
First on the Moon	J	Planet Earth: Space	Rigby
Fossils	J	Early Nonfiction	Benchmark
Natural Disasters	J	AlphaKids Guided Readers	Sundance
Oil from the Sea	J	Planet Earth: Technology	Rigby
Our Amazing Bones	J	Little Reader Twin Texts	Sundance
Rain, Hail, and Snow	J	Discovery World	Rigby
Science Fair	J	Discovery Links Science	Newbridge
Skylab	J	Planet Earth: Space	Rigby
Sounds	J	Early Nonfiction	Benchmark
Under the Sea	J	AlphaKids Guided Readers	Sundance
What Is Matter?	J	Early Nonfiction	Benchmark

Book Titles	Level	Series	Publisher
Science: Animals			
Amazing Eggs	J	Discovery World	Rigby
Ants	J	Wonder World	Wright Group
Bird Beaks	J	Wonder World	Wright Group
Whales on the World Wide Web	J	AlphaKids Guided Readers	Sundance
World of Dinosaurs	J	World of Animals	Newbridge
Math			
Keeping Score	J	Early Nonfiction	Benchmark
Looking for Patterns	J	Early Nonfiction	Benchmark
Measuring Up	J	Little Reader Twin Texts	Sundance
Nature's Patterns	J	Discovery Links Science	Newbridge
Our Money	J	Early Nonfiction	Benchmark
Penny Candy	J	Early Nonfiction	Benchmark
Social Studies			
Astronauts	J	Wonder World	Rigby
Colonial Williamsburg	J	Discovery Links Social Studies	Newbridge
Cotton Plant to Cotton Shirt	J	Early Nonfiction	Benchmark
Emergency Vehicles	J	Rigby PM Plus	Rigby
Grandma Moses	J	Early Nonfiction	Benchmark
Life in the City	J	Early Nonfiction	Benchmark
Maybe I Could	J	Discovery Links Social Studies	Newbridge
Remember George Washington	J	Discovery Links Social Studies	Newbridge
Running for the Gold	J	Little Reader Twin Texts	Sundance
Sacajawea	J	Early Nonfiction	Benchmark
Ships at Sea	J	Rigby PM Plus	Rigby
Then and Now	J	Discovery World	Rigby
Trains on the Rails	J	Rigby PM Plus	Rigby
Trucks on the Road	J	Rigby PM Plus	Rigby
Vehicles for Fun and Sports	J	Rigby PM Plus	Rigby
Vehicles in the Air	J	Rigby PM Plus	Rigby
Vote for Me!	J	AlphaKids Guided Readers	Sundance
Voting	J	Little Reader Twin Texts	Sundance
Where People Live	J	Early Nonfiction	Benchmark
Geography			
Fantastic Landmarks	J	Little Reader Twin Texts	Sundance
Florida and Colorado	J	Little Reader Twin Texts	Sundance
Following Directions	J	Exploring Geography	Rigby
Islands of the World	J	Little Reader Twin Texts	Sundance
Living Here	J	Exploring Geography	Rigby
Looking at Maps	J	Exploring Geography	Rigby
Mountains	J	Early Nonfiction	Benchmark

Book Titles	Level	Series	Publisher
How To			
Making a Terrarium	J	Early Nonfiction	Benchmark
Art/Music			
Art Around the World	J	Early Nonfiction	Benchmark
Origami	J	Early Nonfiction	Benchmark

Informational Texts and Children's Literature for Teaching Content

Appendix B lists some of our favorite trade books for teaching content. The list is organized by content area beginning with social studies, biography (includes stories of people who have contributed to science, history, fine arts, and so forth), science, and mathematics. In the annotations, we include what we consider to be the high points of the books, and structural features are listed for most books. We hope that this list, along with the trade books cited in the children's book references, will provide many hours of reading and learning pleasure for teachers and elementary school students.

Social Studies

Aliki. (1999). *William Shakespeare and the Globe*. NY: HarperCollins. Written in five acts and multiple scenes. Four acts reflect Shakespeare's life and work at the Globe Theater. The last act is about Sam Wanamaker, who spearheaded the reconstruction of the Globe Theater in the twentieth century. Features: table of contents, list of Shakespeare's works, chronology of his life, words and expressions used today that originated with Shakespeare, list of sites to visit in England.

Allen, T.B. (2001). *Remember Pearl Harbor*. Washington DC: National Geographic Society. WWII, Japanese and American survivors' stories. Features: photos, maps, websites, index.

Bradby, M. (1995). *More than anything else*. NY: Orchard Books. Partial biography of Booker T. Washington. More than anything else he wants to learn to read. Setting: 1865 in West Virginia. Historical fiction. Illustrations by Soentpiet are breathtaking. Good model for demonstrating the power of word choices. Strategy: Imagery.

Bunting, E. (1991). *Fly away home*. NY: Clarion Books. Realistic look at homelessness. Realistic fiction.

Durbin, W. (1999). *The journal of Sean Sullivan: A transcontinental railroad worker*. NY: Scholastic. "My Name is America" series. Diary of a young boy. Features: photographs, drawings, historical note, table of contents. Historical fiction. Note: "My Name is America" series about young men in the United States follows similar themes as the "Dear America" series about young women (see McKissack reference).

Fleischman, P. (1997). *Seedfolks*. NY: Joanna Cotler Books. Each chapter tells the story of a person from a different cultural and ethnic background. They live in the same urban neighborhood but do not know one another. Seeds, planted by a young girl, turn an empty lot into a garden that brings people together. Fiction.

Fritz, J. (1969). *George Washington's breakfast*. NY: Putnam Grosset. A boy's inquiry to find out what George Washington ate for breakfast. Good example of doing research using multiple sources. Inquiry-inspired.

Garza, C.L. (1996). *In my family En mi familia*. San Francisco: Children's Book Press. Tomas Rivera Mexican American Children's Book Award. Reflects the author/artist's memories of her Mexican American traditions and culture in Texas. Bilingual text (Spanish, English). Garza is a world-renowned artist. Questions/answers by Garza at end of book.

Gregory, K. (1999). *Cleopatra VII: Daughter of the Nile*. NY: Scholastic. "The Royal Diaries" series. Diary of a young Cleopatra. Features: Ptolemy family tree, historical note, table of contents. Historical fiction. Note: Series is similar in theme to "Dear America" and "My Name is America" series. (See McKissack and Durbin entries.)

Gibbons, G. (1999). *Behold the dragons!* NY: Morrow Junior Books. A historical look at the origin of dragon tales, labeled dragons from all over the world, short text in boxes. Information about more dragons in back of the book. Colorful illustrations communicate well. Note: The award-winning author has written many informational books for children.

Giblin, J.C. (1986). *Milk: The fight for purity*. NY: Thomas Y. Crowell. Giblin brings to life a taken-for-granted food source: milk. Traces the history of milk, complete with details of pre-pastuerization days. Text structure: chronology. Features: table of contents, photographs, index, bibliography. Note: This award-winning author has written many informational books about what seem to be commonplace things. He makes even the most mundane seem fascinating.

Harness, C. (2002). *Ghosts of the Civil War*. NY: Simon & Schuster. Abe Lincoln's son travels to the present and takes a young girl with him to the past. Time travel. Features: timeline, sidebars, glossary, maps, firsts in Civil War. Informational story.

Hartman, G. (1991). *As the crow flies: A first book of maps*. NY: Aladdin. Simple text and maps from varying perspectives: a crow, an eagle, a rabbit, etc. Shows a "big map" of the city and surrounding countryside to culminate the book.

Hest, A. (1997). *When Jessie came across the sea*. Cambridge, MA: Candlewick Press. A young girl journeys to America. Sews lace to earn money to bring her grandmother to America. Hardships of immigrants and leaving family members behind. Illustrations depict the feelings of characters and setting. Historical fiction.

Homan, L.M. (2002). *Tuskegee airmen story*. Gretna, LA: Pelican. WWII, desegregating Army Air Corp. Different perspective on desegregation.

Innocenti, R. (1985). *Rose Blanche*. NY: Stewart, Tabori and Chang. Holocaust story told from young girl's perspective. Inquiry-inspiring.

Johnson, S.A. (1999). *Mapping the world*. NY: Atheneum Books for Young Readers. Maps of the world, from ancient maps on clay tablets to the modern-day maps of the earth and beyond created with the assistance of technology. Demonstrates the social and cultural influences on cartographers throughout history. Text structure: chronology. Features: table of contents, chapter titles, illustrated with maps—old and new, list of books about maps.

Lawrence, J. (1993). *The great migration: An American story*. NY: Museum of Modern Art. An artist's perspective on the migration of African Americans from the South to the North after WWII. Illustrations, originally painted on sixty panels, tell the story along with simple, yet potent text.

Leacock, E., & Buckley, S. (2001). *Places in time: A new atlas of American history*. Boston: Houghton Mifflin. Journey to settlements across the United States from 1200 to 1953. Each two-page spread, with detailed illustrations, features a different town.

Lourie, P. (2001). *Lost treasure of the Inca*. Honesdale, PA: Boyds Mill Press. Book begins with background about the Inca treasure in the Llanganati Mountains in Ecuador. Travel with the author to look for the lost treasure. Features: chapter titles, maps, photographs, glossary, index, Valverde's guide to the treasure. Inquiry-inspired book. Note: Lourie has written many informational books about rivers. Text structure: chronology.

Maestro, B., & Maestro, G. (1986). *The story of the Statue of Liberty*. NY: Mulberry. Text structure: chronology. Features: table of dates, important people, story of building of statue.

McKissack, P.C. (2000). *Color me dark: The diary of Nellie Lee Love, the great migration north.* NY: Scholastic. (Dear America series). Diary of a young girl and her family's migration from Tennessee to Chicago after WWI in search of better jobs, education, and to escape the racism in the South. Historical fiction that reflects the story of many African Americans at this time in the United States. Features: table of contents, photographs, historical note.
Note: Each book in the Dear America series includes stories of young women in the United States. All reflect stories representing people who have made a difference in the world. Written by established authors. Diary format.

Paul, A.W. (1991). *Eight hands round: A patchwork alphabet.* NY: HarperCollins. In A-to-Z sequence, describes twenty-six old quilt patterns. Different perspective on history. Short introduction about historical significance of quilts.

Rappaport, D. (2002). *No more!* Cambridge, MA: Candlewick. Slave resistance in United States. Features: important dates, index, sources, selected resources.

Reneaux, J.J. (2001). *How animals saved the people: Animal tales from the south.* NY: HarperCollins. Especially good for listening to language and dialects of tales with southern roots. Introduction notes the importance of these stories to each culture represented. Glossary explains colloquialisms in book. Sources of stories noted. Traditional literature.

Rylant, C. (1991). *Appalachia: The voices of sleeping birds.* Orlando, FL: Harcourt Brace Jovanovich. Reflects Appalachian Mountain culture, the language of the people and the beauty of the land.

Siebert, D. (1989). *Heartland.* NY: HarperTrophy. Travel through the Midwest from the perspective of the "heartland." Book-length poem. Wendell Minor's amazing illustrations make you feel like you're there. Note: *Mojave* and *Sahara* are similar books by the author and illustrator.

Smucker, B. (1977). *Underground to Canada.* London: Penguin Group. Traces journey of two girls along the Underground Railroad and describes life after they safely reach their destination. Historical fiction.

Stanley, J. (1992). *Children of the dust bowl: The true story of the school at Weedpatch Camp.* NY: Crown. Hardships incurred by "Okies" who traveled to California during the Depression—the same people Steinbeck wrote about in *The Grapes of Wrath.* Many lived in federal labor camps set up by the government to provide housing for displaced individuals. The children were so despised that they could not attend public schools. Visionary, Leo Hart, decided to build a school for them. Students and teachers built the school from ground up. Depicts prejudice toward the poor, courage, and hope for a better future. Black and white photographs with captions. Features: table of contents, index, afterward, bibliographic information, acknowledgments.

Sweeny, J. (1996). *Me on the map.* NY: Crown. Young girl shows readers "me on the map" of her room, her room on a map of her house, zooming out to "me on the map" of the world. Then travel in reverse order back to her room, following maps. Geography. Picture book.

Tsuchiya, Y. (1990). *Faithful elephants: A true story of animals, people and war.* NY: A Trumpet Club Special Edition. A different perspective on the effects of World War II. Setting: a Tokyo zoo. Get ready for many questions from readers. Strategy: Discussion web. Recommended for older elementary children.

Watson, M. (1995). *Butterfly seeds.* NY: Tambourine Books. Story of a young boy who immigrates with his immediate family to the United States. Butterfly seeds (flower seeds), a gift from his grandfather, remind him of home. Picture book, fiction.

Wild, M. (1991). *Let the celebrations begin.* NY: Orchard Books. Watercolor images of life within a Nazi concentration camp during World War II.

Winter, J. (1988). *Follow the drinking gourd.* NY: Knopf. Slaves living in the Deep South escape to freedom. Historical fiction.

Woodson, J. (2001). *The other side.* NY: Putnam. Friendship between two girls—one Black and one White—who live on opposite sides of the proverbial fence. Focus: breaking down racial barriers. Picture book. Fiction.

Woodson, J. (2002). *Our Gracie Aunt*. NY: Hyperion Books for Children. Children neglected by their mother are put into foster care with "Gracie Aunt." Realistic fiction. Picture book.

Biography

Adler, D. (2000). *America's champion swimmer: Gertrude Ederle*. San Diego: Gulliver Books. Partial biography of the first woman to swim the English Channel. Her determination and courage challenged the adage of the day that women were the "weaker sex." She set many world records in swimming. Note: Adler has also written a series of "picture book biographies."

Ancona, G. (1994). *The piñata maker: El pinatero*. San Diego: Harcourt Brace. Bilingual text (Spanish & English), Latin American art (piñata). Features Don Ricardo: the piñata maker, step-by-step process of making a piñata.

Burleigh, R. (1991). *Flight: The journey of Charles Lindbergh*. NY: Philomel Books. Partial biography. Lindbergh's historic flight to Paris in 1927. Picture book. Illustrations bring the words to life.

Dingle, D.T. (1998). *First in the field: Baseball hero Jackie Robinson*. NY: Hyperion Books for Children. Chronicles Jackie Robinson's life and influence on desegregation of baseball. Features: chapters, photographs with captions, timeline of milestones in Black sports, selected bibliography. A different perspective on segregation and desegregation.

Earle, S.A. (2000). *Dive! My adventures in the deep frontier*. NY: Scholastic. Ocean exploration by Sylvia Earle. Perspective on the ocean and its creatures from a diver's and scientist's perspective. Author was in charge of first all woman aquanaut team to spend two weeks living in underwater lab. Features: note from the author, table of contents, glossary, time line of ocean exploration, resources, acknowledgments, index.

Freedman, R. (1993). *Eleanor Roosevelt: A life of discovery*. Boston: Houghton Mifflin. Newbery Honor Book. Traces her life from a young child to her young adulthood, her

marriage to FDR, her influence as First Lady, advocate for social justice, and a member of the United Nations Commission on Human Rights. Superbly written. Book received several awards for nonfiction. Features: table of contents, photo album, bibliography, acknowledgments and photo credits, index. Note: The award-winning author has written many other highly acclaimed biographies.

Fritz, J. (1995). *You want women to vote, Lizzie Stanton?* NY: G.P. Putnam's Sons. Fought for women's rights along with Susan B. Anthony and others in last quarter of nineteenth century. Features: notes, bibliography, index. Note: Award-winning author has written many biographies about famous historical figures. Good writing model for making people in biographies come alive.

Garland, S. (2000). *Voices of the Alamo*. NY: Scholastic. In chronological order, brief first-person accounts of people from different cultures, who lived in Texas from 1500 to today. Includes accounts from people such as a Payaya Indian woman, a Spanish Conquistador, a Texas farmer, a Mexican peasant, and concludes with a boy visiting the Alamo today. Features: historical note, glossary, selected bibliography, and suggestions for further reading.

Gold, A.L. (1997). *Memories of Anne Frank: Reflections of a childhood friend*. NY: Scholastic. Get to know Anne Frank from the memories of her childhood friend Hannah Pick-Goslar. Tells of their friendship before WWII and their meeting at a concentration camp. Author's note about her interviews with Hannah, note by Hannah, photographs. Different perspective.

Hurst, C.O. (2001). *Rocks in his head*. NY: Greenwillow Books. Tells the story of author's father, a passionate collector of rocks—people said he had "rocks in his head." His passion led to his eventual work in a museum as curator of mineralogy. Presents a view of the world from a "rock collector's" perspective.

Krull, K. (1996). *Wilma unlimited: How Wilma Rudolph became the world's fastest woman*. San Diego: Harcourt Brace. Themes: overcoming adversity, determination, African American women athletes, segregation. Picture book. Collage illustrations by David Diaz. Strategy: Sensory imagery.

Lasky, K. (2000). *Vision of beauty: The story of Sarah Breedlove Walker*. Cambridge, MA: Candlewick Press. Themes: overcoming adversity, determination, personal ingenuity. Started a company and created hair and beauty products for African American women. Entrepreneur. Text structure: chronology.

Lewis, J.P. (2000). *Freedom like sunlight: Praise-songs for Black Americans*. Mankato, MN: Creative Editions. Poems reflecting mini-biographies of thirteen courageous, modern African Americans, including Arthur Ashe and Billie Holliday. Features: table of contents, biographical notes, paintings.

Marston, H.I. (1995). *Isaac Johnson: From slave to stonecutter*. NY: Cobblehill. Chronicles life of Isaac Johnson, born into slavery. After escaping to freedom, he became a much sought-after stonecutter. Some of his buildings and bridges stand today. Based on a book Johnson wrote and interviews with his descendants. Features: table of contents, index, important dates, further reading, chapters, black and white drawings and photographs.

McGill, A. (1999). *Molly Bannaky*. NY: Houghton Mifflin. English dairymaid, who could read, was sent to America as an indentured servant when she was seventeen. An independent, courageous, determined woman. She staked a claim on a piece of land and later married a freed slave, a scandalous act for White women in the mid-1600s. Her grandson was Benjamin Bannaker, a scientist and mathematician. Illustrations by Chris K. Soentpiet communicate much of the story. Text structure: chronology. Historical fiction, based on life of Molly Walsh Bannaky.

Pinkney, A.D. (1995). *Alvin Ailey*. NY: Hyperion. Short, beautifully illustrated biography of the African American dancer who began one of the first integrated, world-renowned modern dance companies. Demonstrates results of determination, hard work, risk-taking, and great talent. Text structure: chronology.

Rappaport, D. (2000). *Freedom River*. NY: Jump at the Sun. John Parker's escape from slavery in pre-Civil War Ohio. Themes: determination, freedom, underground railroad. Features: map, historical note, additional resources.

Rappaport, D. (2001). *Martin's big words*. NY: Jump at the Sun. (Coretta Scott King Honor Book, Newbery Honor Book) Legacy of Martin Luther King. Simple text and extraordinary collage and watercolor illustrations take the reader through King's life and his words that live on. Civil Rights. Features: important dates, additional resources.

Science

Baker, J. (1991). *Window*. NY: Greenwillow Books. Wordless picture book depicts the changing environment from the view of a child's window. Text structure: chronology. Makes a powerful, yet subtle environmental statement through three-dimensional collages.

Barr, G. (1962). *Here's why: Science in sports*. NY: Scholastic Book Services. Good ideas for problem solving that are fun and great discussion starters.

Brooks, T. (2002). *First encyclopedia of our world*. London: Usborne. Includes a quick link for each topic at www.usborne-quicklinks.com.

Cherry, L. (1992). *A river ran wild*. San Diego: Gulliver Green Book. Traces the history of the Nash-a-way River from the days when Nashua Indians depended on it for life, to the days when "progress" polluted the river until it died, and then to its restoration. Features: time lines and maps on end pages, author's note, acknowledgments reflect her study, labeled borders around text reflects aspects of human "progress" at different periods in history. Brilliant illustrations reflect the devastation of pollution.

Dixon, D. (2000). *Amazing dinosaurs: The fiercest, the tallest, the toughest, the smallest*. Honesdale, PA: Boyds Mill Press. Organized in four sections by dinosaur types. Large and simple text, also short segments of text in smaller font, labeled diagrams, boldface key words, facts & figures box. Illustrations add to the printed text. Features: table of contents, dinosaur family tree, "Did You

Know?" section, glossary, index, resources to read.

Ehlert, L. (2001). *Waiting for wings*. San Diego: Harcourt. Simple text, life cycle of butterfly. Bright, collage illustrations with graduated-sized pages. Picture book. End of the book: Butterflies identified, information about butterflies, labeled diagram, flowers identified, how to make a butterfly garden. Note: Ehlert has many more books, most of which are informational.

Fleischman, P. (1999). *Weslandia*. Cambridge, MA: Candlewick Press. Young boy invents Weslandia, a civilization he created through his own ingenuity. Scientific inquiry at its finest! Picture book. "Must see" illustrations by Kevin Henkes. Fiction.

Florian, D. (2001). *Lizards, frogs, and polliwogs*. San Diego: Harcourt Brace. Hilarious poetry about reptiles and amphibians—a different perspective on creeping creatures. Features: table of contents and colorful, often humorous paintings. Note: Check out author's other books, written and illustrated in the same style.

George, J.C. (1990). *One day in the tropical rain forest*. NY: HarperCollins. Young native Indian boy searches for a rare insect that will halt the destruction of the Rain Forest of the Macaw. Informational story is told chronologically by time of day. Black and white drawings clearly illustrate the text. Features: index, bibliography. Note: Author writes many science-related books.

Hawkes, N. (1995). *The fantastic cutaway book of spacecraft*. Brookfield, CT: Copper Beech. Current enough to launch great discussions about life inside a spacecraft.

Jenkins, M. (1999). *Emperor's egg*. Cambridge, MA: Candlewick Press. Read and Wonder series. Outstanding science trade book. Boxes and sidebars lead reader in terms of directionality. Print is laid out differently from one page to another.

Lasky, K. (1995). *Pond year*. Cambridge, MA: Candlewick Press. Written from the perspective of two young girls—budding scientists—who examine pond life for a year. Text structure: chronology. Informational story. Picture book.

Lauber, P. (1986). *Volcano: The eruption and healing of Mount St. Helens*. NY: Bradbury Press. (Newbery Honor Book) Experience what scientists have learned about the

destruction and healing process of volcanoes. Features: table of contents, index, color photographs and captions, maps. Photographic essay. Text structure: chronology. Note: Award-winning author has many informational books.

Livingston, M. (1990). *Dog poems*. NY: Holiday House. All shapes, sizes, and breeds.

McDonald, M. (1995). *Insects are my life*. NY: Orchard Books. Story about a young girl who is passionate about insects. Great inspiration for inquiry. Picture book, fiction.

McMillan, B. (1995). *Nights of the pufflings*. Boston: Houghton Mifflin. Tells the story of the journey of puffins returning to their island home off the coast of Iceland each spring to lay their eggs. Children help rescue the pufflings that become disoriented by the city lights. Brilliant color photographs, pronunciation key for Icelandic words integrated into text. Additional information about puffins and pufflings, bibliography, information about how the photographs were taken. Text structure: chronology. Note: Look for more of the author's books related to math, science, beginning concepts.

Montgomery, S. (1999). *The snake scientist*. Boston: Houghton Mifflin. (Scientists in the Field series) Features Dr. Robert Mason, the "snake scientist" and his study of the red-sided garter snakes in Manitoba, Canada, at Narcisse Snake Dens. Visit the field, with the author, where Dr. Mason does his research. Theme: don't fear snakes, get to know them, respect them. Color photographs give a sense of "being there." Features: unsolved mysteries, website, further reading, acknowledgments reflect how information for book was collected, index.

Murawski, D.A. (2000). *Bug faces*. Washington, DC: National Geographic Society. View bugs' faces like you've never seen them before, up close and personal. Each two-page spread includes interestingly formatted descriptive text alongside photographs of bugs' faces. Definitely a different perspective on bugs!

Patent, D.H. (2001). *Horses*. NY: Lerner. Good glossary and index for intermediate age researchers.

Pfeffer, W. (1996). *What's it like to be a fish?* NY: Harper Collins. Let's-Read-and-Find-Out

Science series, Level 1. Text structure: description overall, compare/contrast for fish and human breathing, cold-blooded/warm-blooded. How to set up a fish bowl (sequence) at end.

Ryder, J. (2000). *Each living thing*. San Diego: Gulliver Books. Beautifully written verse depicts the importance of appreciating and caring for living things. Good model for writing descriptively. Picture book. Note: Author has many more informational books written from a scientist's perspective and using verse.

Sloan, C. (2000). *Feathered dinosaurs*. Washington, DC: National Geographic Society. Presents evidence that birds are descendents of dinosaurs. Features: table of contents, introduction by paleontologist, glossary, index, chapter titles, captions, cross-sections, maps, photographs, drawings.

Sobol, D. (1984). *Encyclopedia Brown's book of wacky sports*. NY: William Morrow & Company. Sports trivia to use in math word problems, science puzzlers, and the like.

Storod, C.J. (1999). *Don't call me pig!: A javelina story*. Tempe, AZ: Resort Gifts Unlimited. Describes javelinas in verse from the perspective of a javelina. Additional information in expository form at the end of the book.

Swinburne, S.R. (1998). *In good hands*. San Francisco: Sierra Club. Photo essay chronicles the rescue and release of a barred owl. Written from the perspective of a teen-aged girl who volunteers at the Vermont Raptor Center. Features: table of contents, index, chapter titles, boxed information about raptors, sidebars, photographs with captions, line drawings. Includes dialogue in chronological order.

Swinburne, S.R. (1999). *Unbeatable beaks*. NY: Henry Holt. Describes bird beaks of all kinds with an unbeatable rhythm. Features: includes a glossary, author's note, and labels identifying birds. Brilliantly colored collage illustrations.

Swinburne, S.R. (2002). *What color is nature?* Honesdale, PA: Boyds Mill Press. Concept book: colors. Gorgeous photographs.

Tanaka, S. (1998). *Graveyards of the dinosaurs: What it's like to discover prehistoric creatures*. NY: Hyperion. "I Was There" series. Follow the work of two paleontologists on a "dig" in the Gobi Desert—get a sense of "being there." Highlights inquiry as a driving force in scientists' work. Prologue features the 1922 Gobi Desert expedition of Roy Chapman Andrews whose children's book inspired many aspiring paleontologists. Features: table of contents, boxed information, photographs and drawings with captions, maps, epilogue, time line, glossary, recommended reading.

Webb, S. (2000). *My season with penguins: An Antarctic journal*. Boston: Houghton Mifflin. First-hand account by Sophie Webb, who spent two months studying penguins. Chronology in journal entries. Watercolor illustrations. Describes the personal challenges of camping and doing research in the Antarctic from a scientist's and artist's perspective.

Wright-Frierson, V. (1998). *An island scrapbook: Dawn to dusk on a barrier island*. NY: Simon & Schuster. An island from an artist's perspective. Handwritten notes and sketches on spiral note pad. Theme: ecology. Text structure: chronology.

Mathematics

Daniels, T. (2001). *Math man*. NY: Orchard Publishers. Group fun in mathematical problem solving.

Lesser, C. (1999). *Spots: Counting creatures from sky to sea*. NY: Scholastic. Count creatures from one to ten, beautiful descriptive language. Good model for introducing descriptive verse. Features less common animals like leopard ray. "More to Explore" section introduces different biomes.

Mora, P. (1996). *Uno, dos, tres; one, two, three*. NY: Clarion. Count from one to ten in Spanish and English within the context of shopping for mama's birthday. Rhyme, repetition.

Murphy, S.J. (2001). *Dinosaur deals*. NY: HarperCollins. Math Start series, Level 3. Equivalent values/comparative values. Extra: Facts about some dinosaurs. Children make deals trading dinosaur cards. Different cards have different values. Need to figure how many and which dinosaurs can be traded for more valuable cards.

Murphy, S.J. (2001). *Missing mittens*. NY: HarperCollins. Math Start series, Level 1. Odd and even numbers.

Murphy, S.J. (2001). *Shark swimathon*. NY: HarperCollins. Math Start series, Level 3. Two-digit subtraction.

Murphy, S.J. (2002). *Safari park*. NY: Harper-Collins. Math Start series, Level 3. Figure how many tickets children will need to ride each ride at the amusement park.

Pallotta, J. (2000). *Reese's pieces count by fives*. NY: Scholastic. Count Reese's pieces from one to ten and then by fives to 100. Ends with zero when someone eats all the candy. Extra information: different kinds of trucks haul Reese's pieces on each page.

Schwartz, D.M. (1998). *G is for google*. Berkeley, CA: Tricycle Press. Text structure: sequential. Math alphabet with math-related vocabulary for all twenty-six letters with an explanation and other math-related words. For example, L is for light year, O is for obtuse, X is for "x".

Schwartz, D.M. (1999). *If you hopped like a frog*. NY: Scholastic. Compare/contrast. "If you were as strong as an ant, you could lift a car. If you could scurry like a spider, you could run down a football field in two seconds."

Schwartz, D.M. (1999). *On beyond a million: An amazing math journey*. NY: Dragonfly. A professor helps children investigate really big numbers. Counting by powers of ten (e.g., 10^6), introduces concept of infinity. Features: speech bubbles, "Did you know?" sidebar with interesting number facts.

Sweeney, J. (2001). *Me and the measure of things*. NY: Dell Dragonfly. From teaspoons to a gallon, ounces to pounds to one ton, inches to feet to a mile, cups in a pint to quarts in a gallon, to quarts in a peck and pecks in a bushel.

Swinburne, S.R. (1998). *Lots and lots of zebra stripes: Patterns in nature*. Honesdale, PA: Boyds Mill Press. Beautiful color photographs introduce young children to patterns in nature. Concept book.

Swinburne, S.R. (2000). *What's a pair? What's a dozen?* Honesdale, PA: Boyd's Mill Press. Introduces number-related vocabulary (e.g., single, double, couple). Second half of the book is a math guessing game. Gorgeous photographs support concept development.

Tang, G. (2001). *Grapes of math*. NY: Scholastic. Solve mind-boggling math riddles using visual clues in brightly-colored illustrations. Answer key. A different perspective on problem-solving. Visual literacy.

Tang, G. (2002). *The best of times*. NY: Scholastic. Multiplication tables zero through ten, written in rhyme. Different ways to calculate doubling and tripling numbers. A different perspective on math facts.

Correlation Matrix of English Language Arts Standards and Reading Professional Standards with Chapter Content

Standards for the English Language Arts

Approved by the International Reading Association and the National Council of Teachers of English. Retrieved October 30, 2002 from: http://www.reading.org/advocacy/ elastandards/excerpt.html. Reprinted with permission of the International Reading Association.

	1	2	3	4	5	6	7	8	9	10	11	12
1. Students read a wide range of print and nonprint texts to build an understanding of texts, of themselves, and of the cultures of the United States and the world; to acquire new information; to respond to the needs and demands of society and the workplace; and for personal fulfillment. Among these texts are fiction and nonfiction, classic and contemporary works.	+	+	+		+	+	+				+	+
2. Students read a wide range of literature from many periods in many genres to build an understanding of the many dimensions (e.g., philosophical, ethical, aesthetic) of human experience.		+	+		+	+	+				+	+
3. Students apply a wide range of strategies to comprehend, interpret, evaluate, and appreciate texts. They draw on their prior experience, their interactions with other readers and writers, their knowledge of word meaning and of other texts, their word identification strategies, and their understanding of textual features (e.g., sound-letter correspondence, sentence structure, context, graphics).		+		+	+	+	+	+		+	+	
4. Students adjust their use of spoken, written, and visual language (e.g., conventions, style, vocabulary) to communicate effectively with a variety of audiences and for different purposes.	+	+		+	+		+	+	+			+

5. Students employ a wide range of strategies as they write and use different writing process elements appropriately to communicate with different audiences for a variety of purposes.

6. Students apply knowledge of language structure, language conventions (e.g., spelling and punctuation), media techniques, figurative language, and genre to create, critique, and discuss print and nonprint texts.

7. Students conduct research on issues and interests by generating ideas and questions, and by posing problems. They gather, evaluate, and synthesize data from a variety of sources (e.g., print and nonprint texts, artifacts, people) to communicate their discoveries in ways that suit their purpose and audience.

8. Students use a variety of technological and information resources (e.g., libraries, databases, computer networks, video) to gather and synthesize information and to create and communicate knowledge.

9. Students develop an understanding of and respect for diversity in language use, patterns, and dialects across cultures, ethnic groups, geographic regions, and social roles.

10. Students whose first language is not English make use of their first language to develop competency in the English language arts and to develop understanding of content across the curriculum.

11. Students participate as knowledgeable, reflective, creative, and critical members of a variety of literacy communities.

12. Students use spoken, written, and visual language to accomplish their own purposes (e.g., for learning, enjoyment, persuasion, and the exchange of information).

	1	2	3	4	5	6	7	8	9	10	11	12
5	+	+		+	+		+		+			+
6		+		+	+	+	+					+
7			+	+			+	+		+		+
8	+	+	+	+	+	+	+		+		+	+
9			+	+			+	+		+	+	+
10			+		+			+			+	+
11	+	+	+				+	+	+	+	+	+
12	+	+	+				+	+	+	+	+	+

International Reading Association Standards for Reading Professionals

http://www.reading.org/advocacy/standards/introduction.html. Reprinted with permission of the International Reading Association.

KNOWLEDGE AND BELIEFS ABOUT READING

1.0 THEORETICAL BASE
The reading professional will:

	1	2	3	4	5	6	7	8	9	10	11	12
1.1 recognize that reading should be taught as a process;	+	+	+		+	+		+		+	+	+
1.2 understand, respect, and value cultural, linguistic, and ethnic diversity;	+		+		+	+		+		+	+	+
1.3 recognize the importance of literacy for personal and social growth;	+					+	+	+			+	
1.4 recognize that literacy can be a means for transmitting moral and cultural values;	+		+			+	+		+	+	+	
1.5 perceive reading as the process of constructing meaning through the interaction of the reader's existing knowledge, the information suggested by the written language, and the context of the reading situation;	+	+	+			+	+	+	+	+	+	
1.6 understand the major theories of language development, cognition, and learning;	+	+					+	+				
1.7 understand the impact of physical, perceptual, emotional, social, cultural, environmental, and intellectual factors on learning, language development, and reading acquisition.	+			+		+	+	+	+	+	+	

2.0 KNOWLEDGE BASE
The reading professional will:

	1	2	3	4	5	6	7	8	9	10	11	12
2.1 understand that written language is a symbolic system;	+			+		+	+					+
2.2 understand the interrelation of language and literacy acquisition;	+						+					
2.3 understand principles of new language acquisition;	+			+			+					
2.4 understand the phonemic, morphemic, semantic, syntactic, and pragmatic systems of language and their relation to the reading and writing process;				+			+	+			+	+
2.5 understand the interrelation of reading and writing, and listening and speaking;	+	+		+			+		+	+	+	+

2.0 KNOWLEDGE BASE Continued
The reading professional will:

2.6 understand that students need opportunities to integrate their use of literacy through reading, writing, listening, speaking, viewing, and representing visually;

2.7 understand emergent literacy and the experiences that support it;

2.8 understand the role of metacognition in reading and writing, and listening and speaking;

2.9 understand how contextual factors in the school can influence student learning and reading (e.g., grouping procedures, school programs, and assessment);

2.10 know past and present literacy leaders and their contributions to the knowledge base;

2.11 know relevant reading research from general education and how it has influenced literacy education;

2.12 know classic and contemporary children's and young adults' literature, and easy-reading fiction and nonfiction for adults, at appropriate levels;**

2.13 recognize the importance of giving learners opportunities in all aspects of literacy (e.g., as readers, writers, thinkers, reactors, or responders);

2.14 understand that goals, instruction, and assessment should be aligned.

	1	2	3	4	5	6	7	8	9	10	11	12
2.6	+	+			+	+	+		+	+	+	
2.7	+		+				+				+	
2.8		+		+			+	+				
2.9							+	+	+	+	+	
2.10	+	+	+	+	+		+		+		+	+
2.11	+	+		+		+	+	+				
2.12			+			+	+			+		
2.13	+	+				+		+	+		+	+
2.14				+			+	+		+	+	+

3.0 INDIVIDUAL DIFFERENCES
The reading professional will:

3.1 recognize how differences among learners influence their literacy development;

3.2 understand, respect, and value cultural, linguistic, and ethnic diversity;

3.3 understand that spelling is developmental and is based on students' knowledge of the phonological system and of the letter names, their judgments of phonetic similarities and differences, and their ability to abstract phonetic information from letter names;

3.4 recognize the importance of creating programs to address the strengths and needs of individual learners;

3.5 know federal, state, and local programs designed to help students with reading and writing problems.

	1	2	3	4	5	6	7	8	9	10	11	12
3.1	+	+					+	+		+		
3.2	+		+				+	+		+	+	+
3.3	•	•	•	•	•	•	•	•	•	•	•	•
3.4	+						+	+	+		+	+
3.5	+						+			+		

4.0 READING DIFFICULTIES
The reading professional will:

	1	2	3	4	5	6	7	8	9	10	11	12
4.1 understand the nature and multiple causes of reading and writing difficulties;				+			+	+		+		
4.2 know principles for diagnosing reading difficulties;				+				+		+		
4.3 be well versed on individualized and group instructional interventions targeted toward those students in greatest need or at low proficiency levels;				+		+	+	+				
4.4 know the instructional implications of research in special education, psychology, and other fields that deal with the treatment of students with reading and learning difficulties.				+			+	+				

INSTRUCTION AND ASSESSMENT

5.0 CREATING A LITERATE ENVIRONMENT
The reading professional will be able to:

	1	2	3	4	5	6	7	8	9	10	11	12
5.1 create a literate environment that fosters interest and growth in all aspects of literacy;	+		+			+			+	+	+	+
5.2 use texts and trade books to stimulate interest, promote reading growth, foster appreciation for the written word, and increase the motivation of learners to read widely and independently for information, pleasure, and personal growth;	+	+	+	+	+	+			+	+	+	+
5.3 model and discuss reading and writing as valuable, lifelong activities;		+	+				+	+		+	+	+
5.4 provide opportunities for learners to select from a variety of written materials, to read extended texts, and to read for many authentic purposes;	+		+			+	+	+		+	+	+
5.5 provide opportunities for creative and personal responses to literature, including storytelling;			+				+			+	+	+
5.6 promote the integration of language arts in all content areas;	+	+	+	+	+	+	+		+	+	+	+
5.7 use instructional and information technologies to support literacy learning;	+			+		+	+				+	
5.8 implement effective strategies to include parents as partners in the literacy development of their children.							+	+			+	

6.0 WORD IDENTIFICATION, VOCABULARY, AND SPELLING

The reading professional will be able to:

6.1 teach students to monitor their own word identification through the use of syntactic, semantic, and grapho-phonemic relations;

6.2 use phonics to teach students to use their knowledge of letter/sound correspondence to identify sounds in the construction of meaning;

6.3 teach students to use context to identify and define unfamiliar words;

6.4 guide students to refine their spelling knowledge through reading and writing;

6.5 teach students to recognize and use various spelling patterns in the English language as an aid to word identification;

6.6 employ effective techniques and strategies for the ongoing development of independent vocabulary acquisition.

	1	2	3	4	5	6	7	8	9	10	11	12
6.1	+	+		+	+		+	+				
6.2	•	•	•	•	•	•	•	•	•	•	•	•
6.3	+	+		+	+		+	+				
6.4	•	•	•	•	•	•	•	•	•	•	•	•
6.5				+				+				
6.6		+	+	+	+		+	+		+		

7.0 COMPREHENSION

The reading professional will be able to:

7.1 provide direct instruction and model when and how to use multiple comprehension strategies, including retelling;

7.2 model questioning strategies;

7.3 teach students to connect prior knowledge with new information;

7.4 teach students strategies for monitoring their own comprehension;

7.5 ensure that students can use various aspects of text to gain comprehension, including conventions of written English, text structure and genres, figurative language, and intertextual links;

7.6 ensure that students gain understanding of the meaning and importance of the conventions of standard written English (e.g., punctuation or usage).

	1	2	3	4	5	6	7	8	9	10	11	12
7.1		+	+		+		+	+	+		+	+
7.2		+				+		+	+			+
7.3		+		+			+	+		+	+	
7.4		+	+	+			+	+				
7.5		+	+	+	+	+	+	+	+			+
7.6				+	+		+					

8.0 STUDY STRATEGIES
The reading professional will be able to:

8.1 provide opportunities to locate and use a variety of print, nonprint, and electronic reference sources;

8.2 teach students to vary reading rate according to the purpose(s) and difficulty of the material;

8.3 teach students effective time-management strategies;

8.4 teach students strategies to organize and remember information;

8.5 teach test-taking strategies.

1	2	3	4	5	6	7	8	9	10	11	12
+	+	+	+		+			+	+		+
	+						+		+		
					+						
	+		+	+	+						
•	•	•	•	•	•	•	•	•	•	•	•

9.0 WRITING
The reading professional will be able to:

9.1 teach students planning strategies most appropriate for particular kinds of writing;

9.2 teach students to draft, revise, and edit their writing;

9.3 teach students the conventions of standard written English needed to edit their compositions.

1	2	3	4	5	6	7	8	9	10	11	12
				+		+				+	
						+				+	
			+								

10.0 ASSESSMENT
The reading professional will be able to:

10.1 develop and conduct assessments that involve multiple indicators of learner progress;

10.2 administer and use information from norm-referenced tests, criterion-referenced tests, formal and informal inventories, constructed response measures, portfolio-based assessments, student self-evaluations, work/performance samples, observations, anecdotal records, journals, and other indicators of student progress to inform instruction and learning.

1	2	3	4	5	6	7	8	9	10	11	12
					+				+	+	
					+	+	+		+		

ORGANIZING AND ENHANCING A READING PROGRAM

11.0 COMMUNICATING INFORMATION ABOUT READING

The reading professional will be able to:

11.1 communicate with students about their strengths, areas for improvement, and ways to achieve improvement;

11.2 communicate with allied professionals and paraprofessionals in assessing student achievement and planning instruction;

11.3 involve parents in cooperative efforts and programs to support students' reading and writing development;

11.4 communicate information about literacy and data to administrators, staff members, school-board members, policymakers, the media, parents, and the community;

11.5 interpret research findings related to the improvement of instruction and communicate these to colleagues and the wider community.

1	2	3	4	5	6	7	8	9	10	11	12
	+					+	+		+		
									+	+	
					+	+				+	
									+		
									+		

12.0 CURRICULUM DEVELOPMENT

The reading professional will be able to:

12.1 initiate and participate in ongoing curriculum development and evaluation;

12.2 adapt instruction to meet the needs of different learners to accomplish different purposes;

12.3 supervise, coordinate, and support all services associated with literacy programs (e.g., needs assessment, program development, budgeting and evaluation, and grant and proposal writing);

12.4 select and evaluate instructional materials for literacy, including those that are technology based;

12.5 use multiple indicators to determine effectiveness of the literacy curriculum;

12.6 plan and implement programs designed to help students improve their reading and writing, including those supported by federal, state, and local funding;

12.7 help develop individual educational plans for students with severe learning problems related to literacy.

1	2	3	4	5	6	7	8	9	10	11	12
								+	+		+
		+	+	+	+	+	+	+	+	+	+
•	•	•	•	•	•	•	•	•	•	•	•
+		+	+	+	+	+			+		
										+	+
								+		+	+
								+			

13.0 PROFESSIONAL DEVELOPMENT
The reading professional will be able to:

	1	2	3	4	5	6	7	8	9	10	11	12
13.1 participate in professional-development programs;	•	•	•	•	•	•	•	•	•	•	•	•
13.2 initiate, implement, and evaluate professional-development programs;	•	•	•	•	•	•	•	•	•	•	•	•
13.3 provide professional-development experiences that help emphasize the dynamic interaction among prior knowledge, experience, and the school context as well as among other aspects of reading development;	•	•	•	•	•	•	•	•	•	•	•	•
13.4 provide professional-development experiences that are sensitive to school constraints (e.g., class size or limited resources);	•	•	•	•	•	•	•	•	•	•	•	•
13.5 use multiple indicators to judge professional growth;										+		
13.6 model ethical professional behavior.										+		

14.0 RESEARCH
The reading professional will be able to:

	1	2	3	4	5	6	7	8	9	10	11	12
14.1 apply research for improved literacy;	+			+		+	+	+				
14.2 conduct research with a range of methodologies (e.g., ethnographic, descriptive, experimental, or historical);	•	•	•	•	•	•	•	•	•	•	•	•
14.3 promote and facilitate teacher- and classroom-based research.	•	•	•	•	•	•	•	•	•	•	•	•

15.0 SUPERVISION OF PARAPROFESSIONALS
The reading professional will be able to:

	1	2	3	4	5	6	7	8	9	10	11	12
15.1 plan lessons for paraprofessionals;	•	•	•	•	•	•	•	•	•	•	•	•
15.2 observe and evaluate paraprofessionals interacting with children and provide feedback to them on their performance;	•	•	•	•	•	•	•	•	•	•	•	•
15.3 provide professional development and training for paraprofessionals;	•	•	•	•	•	•	•	•	•	•	•	•
15.4 provide emotional and academic support for paraprofessionals.	•	•	•	•	•	•	•	•	•	•	•	•

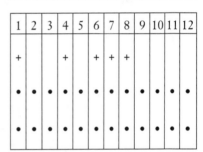
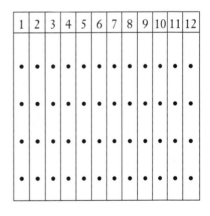

16.0 PROFESSIONALISM
The reading professional will be able to:

	1	2	3	4	5	6	7	8	9	10	11	12
16.1 pursue knowledge of literacy by reading professional journals and publications, and participating in conferences and other professional activities;	•	•	•	•	•	•	•	•	•	•	•	•
16.2 reflect on one's practice to improve instruction and other services to students;	+			+		+	+			+	+	
16.3 interact with and participate in decision making with teachers, teacher educators, theoreticians, and researchers;										+	+	
16.4 support and participate in efforts to improve the reading profession by being an advocate for licensing and certification;	•	•	•	•	•	•	•	•	•	•	•	•
16.5 participate in local, state, national, and international professional organizations whose mission is the improvement of literacy;	•	•	•	•	•	•	•	•	•	•	•	•
16.6 promote collegiality with other literacy professionals through regular conversations, discussions, and consultations about learners, literacy theory, and assessment and instruction;	•	•	•	•	•	•	•	•	•	•	•	•
16.7 write for publication;	•	•	•	•	•	•	•	•	•	•	•	•
16.8 make presentations at local, state, regional, and national meetings and conferences.	•	•	•	•	•	•	•	•	•	•	•	•

*While important, these standards are beyond the scope of this book.

**Appendices A and B address standard 2.12

REFERENCES

A word with you. (n.d.). Retrieved November 1, 2002, from http://www.wordwithyou.com.

Allen, J., & Labbo, L.D. (2001). Giving it a second thought: Making culturally engaged teaching culturally engaging. *Language Arts, 79,* 40–52.

Alvermann, D.E. (1991). The discussion web: A graphic aid for learning across the curriculum. *Reading Teacher, 45,* 92–99.

Alvermann, D.E. (2001). Reading adolescents' reading identities: Looking back to see ahead. *Journal of Adolescent and Adult Literacy, 44,* 676–690.

Alvermann, D.E. (Ed.) (2002). *Adolescents and literacies in a digital world.* New York: Peter Lang.

Alvermann, D.E., Moon, J.S., & Hagood, M.C. (1999). *Popular culture in the classroom: Teaching and researching critical media literacy.* Newark, DE: International Reading Association.

American Library Association. (2002). *ALSC: Awards and grants.* American Library Association. Retrieved November 2, 2002, from http://www.ala.org/alsc/awards.html.

Anders, P., & Bos, C. (1986). Semantic feature analysis: An interactive strategy for vocabulary development and text comprehension. *Journal of Reading, 29,* 610–616.

Appraisal: Science books for young people, (n.d.). Northeastern University. Retrieved November 1, 2002, from http://www.appraisal.neu.edu.

Atwell, N. (1998). *In the middle: New understandings about writing, reading, and learning* (2nd ed.). Portsmouth, NH: Boynton/Cook.

Baghban, M. (1984). *Our daughter learns to read and write: A case study from birth to three.* Newark, DE: International Reading Association.

Baker, M., & Swafford, J. (2000). Using authentic assessment for understanding emergent literacy development: A case study. In T. Shanahan & F.V. Rodriguez-Brown (Eds.), *National Reading Conference Yearbook* (Vol. 49, pp. 277–290). Chicago: National Reading Conference.

Bamford, R.A., & Kristo, J.V. (1998). *Making facts come alive: Choosing quality nonfiction literature K–8.* Norwood, MA: Christopher-Gordon Publishers.

Bamford, R.A., & Kristo, J.V. (2000). *Checking out nonfiction K–8: Good choices for best learning.* Norwood, MA: Christopher-Gordon.

Banks, J.A. (1993). Multicultural education: Characteristics and goals. In J.A. Banks & C.A.M. Banks (Eds.), *Multicultural education: Issues and perspectives* (2nd ed., pp. 3–28). Boston: Allyn & Bacon.

Banks, J.B., & Weiss, L. (1995). Where's the water? *Literacy's Images* (pp. 40–43). Lexington, MA: D.C. Heath.

Barksdale-Ladd, M.A., & Thomas, K.F. (2000). What's at stake in high-stakes testing: Teachers and parents speak out. *Journal of Teacher Education, 51,* 382–397.

Barton, D., & Hamilton, M. (2000). Literacy practices. In D. Barton, M. Hamilton, & R. Ivanic (Eds.), *Situated literacies: Reading and writing in context* (pp. 7–15). New York: Routledge.

Barton, D., Hamilton, M., & Ivanic, R. (2000). *Situated literacies: Reading and writing in context.* New York: Routledge.

Barton, K.C., & Smith, L.A. (2000). Themes or motifs? Aiming for coherence through interdisciplinary outlines. *Reading Teacher, 54,* 54–63.

Barton, P.E. (2001). *Facing the hard facts in education reform.* Princeton, NJ: Educational Testing Service.

Baumann, J.F., Kame'enui, E.J., & Ash, G.E. (2003). Research on vocabulary instruction: Voltaire redux. In J. Flood, J. Jensen, D. Flood, & J. Squire (Eds.), *Handbook of research on teaching the English language arts* (2nd ed., pp. 752–785). New York: Macmillan.

Bell, D. & Jarvis, D. (2002). Letting go of "letter of the week." *Primary Voices, 11*(2), 10–24.

Bernhardt, E. (2000). Second-language reading as a case study of reading scholarship in the 20th century. In M.J. Kamil, P.B. Mosenthal, P.D. Pearson, & R. Barr (Eds.), *Handbook of reading research* (Vol. 3, pp. 793–811). Mahwah, NJ: Erlbaum.

Bissex, G.L. (1980). *GNYS AT WRK: A child learns to write and read.* Cambridge, MA: Harvard University Press.

Blachowicz, C.L.Z. (1986). Making connections: Alternatives to the vocabulary notebook. *Journal of Reading, 29,* 643–649.

Blachowicz, C., & Fisher, P.J. (2000). Vocabulary instruction. In M.L. Kamil, P.B. Mosenthal, P.D. Pearson, & R. Barr (Eds.), *Handbook of reading research* (Vol. 3, pp. 503–523). Mahwah, NJ: Erlbaum.

Blachowicz, C., & Fisher, P.J. (2002). *Teaching vocabulary in all classrooms* (2nd ed.). Upper Saddle River, NJ: Merrill Prentice Hall.

Boyd, C. (1993). Creating curriculum from children's lives. *Primary Voices K–6, 1*(1), 22–27.

Brock, C.H. (1997). Exploring the use of book club with second-language learners in mainstream classrooms. In S.I. McMahon, T.E. Raphael, V.J. Goatley, & L.S. Pardo (Eds.), *The book club connection* (pp. 141–158). Newark, DE: International Reading Association.

Bromley, K. (2002). *Stretching students' vocabulary*. New York: Scholastic.

Brown, A.L., & Palincsar, A.S. (1989). Guided, cooperative learning, and individual knowledge acquisition. In L.B. Resnick (Ed.), *Knowing, learning, and instruction: Essays in honor of Robert Glaser* (pp. 393–451). Hillsdale, NJ: Erlbaum.

Brown, D.K. (1997). *The children's literature webguide: Children's book awards*. Doucette Library of Teaching Resources. Retrieved November 1, 2002, from http://www.acs.ucalgary.ca/~dkbrown/awards.html.

Brown, R., Pressley, M., Van Meter, P., & Schuder, T. (1996). A quasi-experimental validation of transactional strategies instruction with low-achieving second grade readers. *Journal of Educational Psychology, 88*, 18–37.

Bruce, B.C., & Bishop, A.P. (2002). Using the web to support inquiry-based literacy development. *Journal of Adolescent and Adult Literacy, 45*, 706–714. [Electronic version]

Bruchac, J. (n.d.). *Joseph Bruchac: Story teller and writer*. Retrieved October 30, 2002, from http://www.josephbruchac.com.

Bruner, J.S. (1986). *Actual minds, possible worlds*. Cambridge, MA: Harvard University Press.

Bryan, J. (1988). K-W-W-L: Questioning the known. *Reading Teacher, 51*(51), 618–620.

Buckingham, D. (1993). Just playing games. *The English & Media Magazine, Summer*, 21–25.

Buehl, D. (2001). *Classroom strategies for interactive learning* (2nd ed.). Newark, DE: International Reading Association.

Bustamante, D.M. (2002). Telling our stories, finding our voices: Nurturing a community of learners. *Primary Voices K–6, 11*(1), 2–6.

Cairney, T.H. (2000). Developing parent partnerships in secondary literacy learning. In D.W. Moore, D.E. Alvermann, & K.A. Hinchman (Eds.), *Struggling adolescent readers: A collection of teaching strategies* (pp. 58–65). Newark, DE: International Reading Association.

Calkins, L.M. (1994). *The art of teaching writing*. Portsmouth, NH: Heinemann.

Calkins, L.M. (2001). *The art of teaching reading*. New York: Addison-Wesley.

Canadian Teachers' Federation. (n.d.). *Standardized testing and high-stakes decisions*. Retrieved November 1, 2002, from http://www.ctf-fce.ca/E/WHAT/OTHER/ASSESSMENT/high-stakes.htm.

Caswell, L.J., & Duke, N.K. (1998). Non-narrative as a catalyst for literacy development. *Language Arts, 75*, 108–117.

Coady, J., Magoto, J., Hubbard, P., Graney, J., & Mokhtari, K. (1993). High frequency vocabulary and reading proficiency in ESL readers. In T. Huckin, M. Haynes, & J. Coady (Eds.), *Second language reading and vocabulary learning* (pp. 217–228). Norwood, NJ: Ablex.

Collier, C.F. (2002). A snapshot of the center for inquiry. *Primary Voices K–6, 10*(3), 2–7.

Connor, J. (2002). *General readability checklist*. Retrieved November 1, 2002, from http://www.indiana.edu/~l517/readability.htm.

A conversation with Lisa Delpit. (1991). *Language Arts, 68*, 541–547.

Cook, D., & Finlayson, H. (1999). *Interactive children, communicative teaching: ICT and classroom teaching*. Buckingham, UK: Open University Press.

Cooney, M.H. (1995). Readiness for school or for school culture? *Childhood Education, 71*(3), 164–166. [Electronic version]

Copenhaver, J. (1993). Instances of inquiry. *Primary Voices K–6, 1*(1), 6–12.

Cudd, E.T., & Roberts, L. (1989). Using writing to enhance content area learning in the primary grades. *Reading Teacher, 42*, 392–404.

Cunningham, P.M. (2000). *Phonics they use*. New York: Longman.

Davey, B. (1983). Think aloud-modeling the cognitive processes of reading comprehension. *Journal of Reading, 4*, 44–47.

Davis, F.B. (1944). Vocabulary learning and instruction. *Journal of Educational Psychology, 33*, 365–372.

de St. Exupéry, A. (2001). *El Principito* (R. Howard, Trans.). San Diego, CA: Harcourt. [Original work published 1943]

Delpit, L. (1995). *Other people's children: Cultural conflict in the classroom*. New York: New Press.

Dick, A. (1997). *Village science*. The Alaska Native Knowledge Network. Retrieved October 30, 2002, from http://www.ankn.uaf.edu/VS/index.html.

Dickson, S.V., Simmons, D.C., & Kameenui, E.J. (1995a). *Text organization and its relation to reading comprehension: A synthesis of the research.* Eugene, OR: National Center to Improve the Tools of Educators.

Dickson, S.V., Simmons, D.C., & Kameenui, E.J. (1995b). *Text organization: Curricular and instructional implications for diverse learners.* Eugene, OR: National Center to Improve the Tools of Educators.

Dole, J.A., Duffy, G.G., Roehler, L.R., & Pearson, P.D. (1991). Moving from the old to the new: Research on reading comprehension instruction. *Review of Educational Research, 61,* 239–264.

Donovan, C.A., & Smolkin, L.B. (2002). Considering genre, content, and visual features in the selection of trade books for science instruction. *Reading Teacher, 55,* 502–520.

Dowhower, S.L. (1991). Speaking of prosody: Fluency's unattended bedfellow. *Theory Into Practice, 30,* 165–175.

Duke, N.K. (2000). 3.6 minutes per day: The scarcity of informational texts in first grade. *Reading Research Quarterly, 35,* 202–224.

Duke, N.K., & Pearson, P.D. (2002). Effective practices for developing reading comprehension. In A.E. Farstrup & S.J. Samuels (Eds.), *What research has to say about reading instruction* (3rd ed., pp. 205–242). Newark, DE: International Reading Association.

Dunn, M.A. (2000). Closing the book on social studies: Four classroom teachers go beyond the text. *Social Studies, 91*(3), 132–136.

Durkin, D. (1978–1979). What classroom observations reveal about reading comprehension instruction. *Reading Research Quarterly, 14,* 481–533.

Duthie, J. (1986). The web: A powerful tool for the teaching and evaluation of the expository essay. *The History and Social Science Teacher, 21,* 232–236.

Dutro, E. (2001). "But that's girls' book!": Exploring gender boundaries in children's reading practices. *Reading Teacher, 55,* 376–384.

Dyson, A.H. (1997). *Writing superheroes: Contemporary childhood, popular culture, and classroom literacy.* New York: Teachers College Press.

Dyson, A.H. (2002). *Brothers and sisters learn to write: Popular literacies in childhood and school cultures.* New York: Teachers College Press.

Echevarria, J., Vogt, M.E., & Short, D.J. (2000). *Making content comprehensible for English language learners.* Boston: Allyn and Bacon.

Environmental Media. (2002). *Nature Works.* Retrieved October 27, 2002, from http://www.envmedia.com/catalog/products/natureworks/html.

Ethnomathematics on the Web. (n.d.). Retrieved October 30, 2002, from http://www.rpiedu/~eglash/isgem.dir/links.htm.

Fink, R.P. (1995/1996). Successful dyslexics: A constructivist study of passionate interesting reading. *Journal of Adolescent and Adult Literacy, 39,* 268–280.

Finn, P.J. (1999). *Literacy with an attitude: Educating working-class children in their own self-interest.* Albany: SUNY Press.

Fischer, P. (2002). Wow! Kindergarten/first-grade inquiry. *Primary Voices K–6, 10*(3), 15.

Flake, S.G. (1998). *The skin I'm in.* New York: Hyperion.

Fountas, I.C., & Pinnell, G.A. (1999). *Matching books to readers: Using leveled books in guided reading, K–3.* Portsmouth, NY: Heinemann.

Franquiz, M.E., & de la Luz Reyes, M. (2000). Examining the relationship among opportunity, inclusion, and choice. *Primary Voices K–6, 8*(4), 3–9.

Freebody, P., & Luke, A. (1990). "Literacies" programs: Debates and demands in cultural context. *Prospect: The Australian Journal of TESOL, 5*(5), 7–16.

Freire, P. (1983). The importance of the act of reading. *Journal of Education, 165,* 5–11.

Fueyo, F.A. (1991). Reading "Literate Sensibilities": Resisting a verbocentric writing classroom. *Language Arts, 68,* 641–648.

García, G.E. (2000). Bilingual children's reading. In M.J. Kamil, P.B. Mosenthal, P.D. Pearson, & R. Barr (Eds.), *Handbook of reading research* (Vol. 3, pp. 813–834). Mahwah, NJ: Erlbaum.

Gardner, S.A., Benham, H.H., & Newell, B.M. (1999). Oh, what a tangled web we've woven! Helping students evaluate sources. *English Journal, 89*(1), 39–44.

Gavelek, J., & Raphael, T.E. (1996). Changing talk about text: New roles for teachers and students. *Language Arts, 73,* 182–192.

Gavelek, J.R., Raphael, T.E., Biondo, S.M., & Wang, D. (2000). Integrated literacy instruction. In M.J. Kamil, P.B. Mosenthal, P.D. Pearson, & R. Barr (Eds.), *Handbook of reading research* (Vol. 3, pp. 587–607). Mahwah, NJ: Erlbaum.

Gee, J.P. (1996). *Social linguistics and literacies: Ideology in discourses* (2nd ed.). London: Taylor & Francis.

Gergen, K. (1999). *An invitation to social construction.* Thousand Oaks, CA: Sage.

Graves, D.H. (1989). *Investigate nonfiction.* Portsmouth, NH.: Heinemann.

Graves, M.F. (1986). Vocabulary learning and instruction. In E.Z. Rothkopf (Ed.), *Review of research in education* (Vol. 13, pp. 49–89). Washington, DC: American Educational Research Association.

Graves, M.F. (2002, May). *The place of English vocabulary instruction in multilingual classrooms.* Paper presented at the annual meeting of the International Reading Association, San Francisco.

Guillaume, A.M. (1998). Learning with text in the primary grades. *Reading Teacher, 51,* 476–486.

Guthrie, J.T., McGough, K., Bennett, L., & Rice, M.E. (1996). Concept-oriented reading instruction: An integrated curriculum to develop motivations and strategies. In L. Baker, P. Afflerbach, & D. Reinking (Eds.), *Developing engaged readers in school and home communities* (pp. 165–190). Hillsdale, NJ: Erlbaum.

Guthrie, J.T., & Wigfield, A. (2000). Engagement and motivation in reading. In M.J. Kamil, P.B. Mosenthal, P.D. Pearson, & R. Barr (Eds.), *Handbook of reading research* (Vol. 3, pp. 403–422). Mahwah, NJ: Erlbaum.

Guthrie, J.T., & Wigfield, A. (Eds.) (1997). *Reading engagement: Motivating readers through integrated instruction.* Newark, DE: International Reading Association.

Guzzetti, B.G., Kowalinski, B.J., & McGowan, T. (1992). Using a literature-based approach to teaching social studies. *Reading Teacher, 36,* 114–122.

Guzzetti, B.G., Snyder, T.E., Glass, G.V., & Gamas, W.S. (1993). Promoting conceptual change in science: A comparative meta-analysis of instructional interventions from reading education and science education. *Reading Research Quarterly, 28,* 116–159.

Harp, B. (1988). When the principal asks: "Why are you doing guided imagery during reading time?" *Reading Teacher, 41,* 588–590.

Harris, C.R. (1988). *Cultural conflict and patterns of achievement in gifted Asian-Pacific children.* Paper presented at the National Association for Asian and Pacific American Education.

Harris, T.L., & Hodges, R.E. (Eds.) (1995). *The literacy dictionary: The vocabulary of reading and writing.* Newark, DE: International Reading Association.

Harste, J.C. (1993). Inquiry-based instruction. *Primary Voices K–6, 1*(1), 2–5.

Harvey, S., & Goudvis, A. (2000). *Strategies that work.* Portland, ME: Stenhouse.

Heath, S.B. (1983). *Ways with words: Language, life, and work in communities and classrooms.* Cambridge, UK: Cambridge University Press.

Hobbs, R. (2001). *Classroom strategies for exploring realism and authenticity in media messages.* Reading Online, 4(9). Retrieved February 11, 2002, from http://www.readingonline.org/newliteracies/.

http://www.berylphotographs.com. *Beryls free photographs.* Retrieved October 28, 2002, from http://www.berylsphotographs.com.

Hull, G., & Schultz, K. (2001). Literacy and learning out of school: A review of theory and research. *Review of Educational Research, 71,* 575–611.

Images. (1995). The living desert. *Heath Literacy, 4*(1), pp. 20–29.

Ink, G., & Grabois, A. (2001). Book title output and average prices: 1999 final and 2000 preliminary figures. In D. Bogart (Ed.), *The Bowker annual library and book trade almanac* (46th ed., pp. 485–489). New York: Bowker.

International Reading Association. (1999). *Summary of a position statement of the International Reading Association: High stakes assessments in reading.* Retrieved November 1, 2002, from http://www.reading.org/positions/high_stakes.html.

International Study Group on Ethnomathematics. (n.d.). *Ethnomathematics on the web.* International Study Group on Ethnomathematics. Retrieved November 2, 2002, from http://www.rpi.edu/~eglash/isgem.dir/links.htm.

Jimenez, R. (1997). The strategic reading abilities and potential of five low-literacy Latina/o readers. *Reading Research Quarterly, 32,* 224–243.

Jimenez, R.T., Moll, L.C., Rodriguez-Brown, F.V., & Barrera, R.B. (1999). Conversations: Latina and Latino researchers interact on issues related to literacy learning. *Reading Research Quarterly, 34,* 217–230.

Johns, J.L., & Lenski, S.D. (2000). *Improving writing: Resources, strategies, assessments.* Dubuque, IA: Kendall-Hunt.

Joshua, M.B. (2002). Inside picture books: Where are the children of color? *Educational Horizons, 80,* 125–132.

Kameenui, E.J., Dixon, D.W., & Carnine, R.C. (1987). Issues in the design of vocabulary instruction. In M.G. McKeown & M.E. Curtis (Eds.), *The nature of vocabulary acquisition* (pp. 129–145). Hillsdale, NJ: Erlbaum.

Kamil, M.J., & Lane, D. (1997, April). *A classroom study of the efficacy of using information text for first grade reading instruction.* Paper presented at the American Education Research Association., Chicago, IL.

Karolides, N.J. (1999). Theory and practice: An interview with Louise M. Rosenblatt. *Language Arts, 77,* 158–170.

Keene, E., & Zimmerman, S. (1997). *Mosaic of thought.* Portsmouth, NH: Heinemann.

Kerper, R.M. (1998). Choosing quality nonfiction literature: Features for accessing and visualizing information. In R.A. Bamford & J.V. Kristo

(Eds.), *Making facts come alive* (pp. 55–74). Norwood, MA: Christopher-Gordon.

Kintsch, W., & van Dijk, T.H. (1978). Toward a model of text comprehension and production. *Psychological Review, 85,* 363–394.

Knowledge Networks. (2002). *More kids say the Internet is the medium they can't live without.* Retrieved July 20, 2002, from http://www.knowledgenetworks.com.

Kohn, A. (1993). *Punished by rewards.* Boston: Houghton-Mifflin.

LAB at Brown. (n.d.). *Culturally responsive teaching: Nine principles.* Retrieved August 13, 2002, from http://www.lab.brown.edu/tdl/tl-strategies/crt-principles.shtml.

Labbo, L.D. (1996). A semiotic analysis of young children's symbol making in a classroom computer center. *Reading Research Quarterly, 51,* 356–385.

Labbo, L.D., Eakle, A.J., & Montero, M.K. (2002, May). *Digital language experience approach: Using digital photographs and software as a language experience approach innovation.* Reading Online, 5(8). Retrieved November 1, 2002, from http://www.readingonline.org/electronic/elec_index.asp?HREF=/electronic/labbo2/index.html.

Ladson-Billings, G. (1994). *The dreamkeepers.* San Francisco: Jossey-Bass.

Lane, N. (2002). Ethnomathematics. *Pacific Educator, 1*(3), 22.

Langer, J.A. (1995). *Envisioning literature.* New York: Teachers College Press.

Lankshear, C., Gee, J.P., Knobel, M., & Searle, C. (1997). *Changing literacies.* Buckingham, England: Open University Press.

Laturnau, J. (2002). Cultural bias in standardized tests: What do students really know? *Pacific Resources for Education and Learning,* 11–13.

Layne, S.L. (2001). *Life's literacy lessons: Poems for teachers.* Newark, DE: International Reading Association.

Leu, D.J. (2002). The new literacies: Research on reading instruction with the Internet. In A.E. Farstrup & S.J. Samuels (Eds.), *What research has to say about reading instruction* (pp. 310–336). Newark, DE: International Reading Association.

Luke, A. (2001, July 13). *How to make literacy policy differently: Generational change, professionalisation, and literate futures, keynote address at the Joint Australian Association of Teachers of English/Australian Literacy Educators' Association.* Hobart, Tasmania.

Luke, A. (2002). What happens to literacies old and new when they're turned into policy. In D.E. Alvermann (Ed.), *Adolescents and literacies in a digital world.* New York: Peter Lang.

Luke, A., & Carrington, V. (2003). Globalisation, literacy, curriculum practice. In R. Fisher, M.

Lewis, & G. Brooks (Eds.), *Language and literacy in action.* London: Routledge/Falmer.

Luke, A., & Freebody, P. (1999). A map of possible practices: Further notes on the four resources model. *Practically Primary, 4*(2), 5–8.

Luke, C. (1997). Media literacy and cultural studies. In S. Muspratt, A. Luke, & P. Freebody (Eds.), *Constructing critical literacies: Teaching and learning textual practice.* Creskill, NJ: Hampton Press.

Lynch, P. (2001). Salting the oats: Using inquiry-based science to engage learners at risk. *Primary Voices K–6, 10*(1), 16–22. [Electronic version]

Mackey, M., & McClay, J.K. (2000). Graphic routes to electronic literacy: Polysemy and picture books. *Changing English, 7,* 191–201.

Mansukhani, P. (2002). The explorers club: The sky is no limit for learning. *Language Arts, 80,* 31–39.

McDermott, R., & Varenne, H. (1995). Culture as disability. *Anthropology and Education Quarterly, 26,* 324–348.

McKeown, M.G., & Beck, I.L. (1988). Learning vocabulary: Different ways for different goals. *Remedial and Special Education, 9,* 42–46.

Miller, D. (2002). *Reading with meaning.* Portland, ME: Stenhouse.

Moline, S. (1995). *I see what you mean: Children at work with visual information.* York, ME: Stenhouse.

Moll, L.C. (1991). Literacy research in community and classrooms: A sociocultural approach. In C. Baker & A. Luke (Eds.), *Towards a critical sociology of reading pedagogy* (pp. 211–245). Philadelphia: John Benjamins.

Moll, L.C. (1992). Funds of knowledge for teaching: Using a qualitative approach to connect homes and classrooms. *Theory Into Practice, 31*(1), 132–141.

Möller, K.H. (2002). Providing support for dialogue in literature discussions about social justice. *Language Arts, 79,* 467–477.

Monson, R.J., & Monson, M.P. (1994). Literacy as inquiry: An interview with Jerome C. Harste. *Reading Teacher, 47,* 518–521.

Morgan, W. (1997). *Critical literacy in the classroom: The art of the possible.* London: Routledge.

Morrow, L.M. (1997). *Literacy development in the early years: Helping children read and write* (3rd ed.). Needham Heights, MA: Allyn & Bacon.

Moss, B. (1991). Children's nonfiction trade books: A complement to content area texts. *Reading Teacher, 45,* 26–32.

Moss, B. (1997). A qualitative assessment of first graders' retelling of expository text. *Reading Research and Instruction, 37,* 1–13.

Moss, B., & Hendershot, J. (2002). Exploring sixth

graders' selection of nonfiction trade books. *Reading Teacher, 56,* 6–17.

Muffoletto, R. (2001). *An inquiry into the nature of Uncle Joe's representation and meaning.* Reading Online, 4(8). Retrieved March 2, 2001, from http://www.readingonline.org/newliteracies/.

Murphy, S.J. (2000). Children's books about math: Trade books that teach. *New Advocate, 13,* 365–374.

Nation, I.S.P. (1990). *Teaching and learning vocabulary.* Boston: Heinle & Heinle.

National Center for Education Statistics. (n.d.). *The nation's report card: Reading.* Retrieved November 1, 2002, from http://nces.ed.gov/nationsreportcard/reading/.

National Clearinghouse for English Language Acquisition and Language Instruction Educational Programs. (n.d.). *Online library: Assessment and Accountability.* Retrieved November 1, 2002, from http://www.ncela.gwu.edu/library/assess.htm.

National Council for the Social Studies. (1994a). *Expectations for excellence: Curriculum standards for social studies.* Retrieved October 1, 2002, from www.socialstudies.org/standards.

National Council for the Social Studies. (1994b). *National standards for social studies teachers.* National Council for the Social Studies. Retrieved October 15, 2002, from http://www.socialstudies.org/standards/.

National Council for the Social Studies. (n.d.). *Notable social studies trade books: Notable social studies books for young people.* National Council for the Social Studies. Retrieved November 1, 2002, from http://www.socialstudies.org/resources/notable.

National Council of Teachers of English. (n.d.-a). *Orbis pictus award for outstanding nonfiction for children.* National Council of Teachers of English. Retrieved November 1, 2002, from http://www.ncte.org/elem/orbispictus/.

National Council of Teachers of English. (n.d.-b). *Position statement on interdisciplinary learning, pre-K to grade 4.* National Council of Teachers of English. Retrieved November 1, 2002, from www.ncte.org/positions/interdisciplinary_learning.shtml.

National Council of Teachers of English and International Reading Association. (1996). *Standards for the English language arts.* International Reading Association and National Council of Teachers of English. Retrieved October 15, 2002, from http://www.ncte.org/standards/standards.shtml.

National Council of Teachers of Mathematics Standards. (2000). *Principles and standards for school mathematics.* National Council of Teachers of Mathematics. Retrieved October 15, 2002, from http://standards.nctm.org/document/index.htm.

National Reading Panel. (2000a). *Report of the National Reading Panel.* Washington, DC: National Institute of Child Health and Human Development.

National Reading Panel. (2000b). *Teaching children to read: An evidence-based assessment of the scientific research literature on reading and its implications for reading instruction.* Washington, DC: National Institute of Child Health and Human Development.

National Research Council. (1996). *National science education standards.* National Academy of Sciences. Retrieved October 15, 2002, from http://www.nap.edu/readingroom/books/nses/html.

National Research Council. (1998). *Educating language-minority children.* Washington, DC: National Academy Press.

National Science Education Standards. (1996). Washington, DC: National Research Council.

New London Group. (1996). A pedagogy of multiliteracies: Designing social futures. *Harvard Educational Review, 66,* 60–92.

Newsweek/Kaplan Poll (2000). Plugged in at home and school. *Newsweek/Score,* (no volume), 26–27.

North Central Regional Educational Laboratory. (2002). *Policy issue scanning: The national picture.* North Central Regional Educational Laboratory. Retrieved October 25, 2002, from http://www.ncrel.org/policy/scan/national.htm.

North Central Regional Educational Laboratory. (n.d.). *Highlights of the no child left behind act of 2001.* Retrieved November 1, 2002, from http://www.ncrel.org/policy/curve/part1a.htm.

Nugent, S.M., & Nugent, H.E. (1987). Theory into practice: learning through writing: The double entry journal in literature classes. *English Quarterly, 20,* 325–330.

Ogle, D.M. (1986). K-W-L: A teaching model that develops active reading of expository text. *Reading Teacher, 39,* 564–570.

Oliver, D. (n.d.). *ESL Idiom Page.* Dave Sperling. Retrieved November 1, 2002, from http://www.eslcafe.com/idioms/id-mngs.html.

Pacific Resources for Education and Learning. (2002). *Ethnomatematics Digital Library (EDL).* Pacific Resources for Education and Learning. Retrieved October 30, 2002, from http://www.ethnomath.org.

Paisley-Jones, H., Morrison, H. & Grove, T. (2000). You be the author. Retrieved April 25, 2003, from http://americanhistory.si.edu/hohr/springer/00credit.htm.

Pajares, F. (1996). Self-efficacy beliefs in academic settings. *Review of Educational Research, 66,* 543–578.

Paley, V. (1990). *The boy who would be a helicopter: The uses of storytelling in the classroom.* Cambridge, MA: Harvard University Press.

Paley, V. (1997). *The girl with the brown crayon.* Cambridge, MA: Harvard Univeristy Press.

Palincsar, A.S., & Brown, A.L. (1984). Reciprocal teaching of comprehension-fostering and monitoring activities. *Cognition and Instruction, 1,* 117–175.

Pappas, C. (1993). Is narrative "primary"? Some insights from kindergarteners' pretend readings of stories and information books. *Journal of Reading Behavior, 25,* 97–129.

Pappas, C.D. (1991). Fostering full access to literacy by including informational books. *Language Arts, 68,* 449–462.

Pardo, L.S., & Raphael, T.E. (1991). Classroom organization for instruction in content areas. *Reading Teacher, 44,* 556–565.

Pearson, P.D., & Fielding, L. (1991). Comprehension instruction. In R. Barr, M.L. Kamil, P.B. Mosenthal, & P.D. Pearson (Eds.), *Handbook of reading research* (Vol. 2, pp. 815–860). New York: Longman.

Pearson, P.D., & Gallagher, M.C. (1983). The instruction of reading comprehension. *Contemporary Educational Psychology, 8,* 317–344.

Pearson, P.D., & Johnson, D.D. (1984). *Teaching reading comprehension.* New York: Holt, Rinehart, & Winston.

Penrose, P. (2002). *Creating a biopoem on presidential candidates.* The American President. Retrieved October 15, 2002, from http://www.americanpresident.org/lp_biopoem.htm.

Pitsco's innovative education. (1999). *Pitsco's ask an expert.* Pitsco Innovation Education. Retrieved November 1, 2002, from http://www.askanexpert.com.

Poll, N.K. (2000). Plugged in at home and school. *Newsweek/Score,* 26–27.

Pressley, M. (2001, September). *What makes sense now, what might make sense soon.* Reading Online, 5(2). Retrieved November 3, 2002, from http://www.readingonline.org/articles/handbook/Pressley/.

Pressley, M. (2002). Metacognition and self-regulated comprehension. In A.E. Farstrup & S.J. Samuels (Eds.), *What research has to say about reading instruction* (3rd ed., pp. 291–309). Newark, DE: International Reading Association.

Pressley, M., & Afflerbach, P. (1995). *Verbal protocols of reading: The nature of constructively responsive reading.* Hillsdale, NJ: Erlbaum.

Pressley, M., El-Dinary, P.B., Gaskins, I., Schuder, T., Bergman, J., Almasi, J., et al. (1992). Beyond direct explanation: Transactional instruction of reading comprehension strategies. *The Elementary School Journal, 92,* 511–555.

RAND Corporation Reading Study Group. (2002). *Reading for understanding: Toward an R&D program in reading comprehension.* Santa Monica, CA: Rand Education.

Raphael, T.E. (1986). Teaching children question-answer relationships, revisited. *Reading Teacher, 39,* 516–522.

Raphael, T.E., & Hiebert, E.H. (1996). *Creating an integrated approach to literacy instruction.* Fort Worth, TX: Harcourt Brace.

Recht, D., & Leslie, L. (1988). Effect of prior knowledge on good and poor readers' memory of text. *Journal of Educational Psychology, 80*(1), 16–20.

Rhoder, C. (2002). Mindful reading: Strategy training that facilitates transfer. *Journal of Adolescent and Adult Literacy, 45,* 498–512.

Rhodes, L.K., & Nathenson-Meija, S. (1999). Anecdotal records: A powerful tool for ongoing literacy assessment. In S.J. Barrentine (Ed.), *Reading assessment: Principles and practices for elementary teachers.* Newark, DE: International Reading Association.

Richardson, J.S., & Morgan, R.F. (2000). *Reaching to learn in the content areas* (4th ed.). Belmont, CA: Wadsworth.

Richgels, D.J. (2002). Informational texts in kindergarten. *Reading Teacher, 55,* 586–595.

Romance, N.R., & Vitale, M.R. (1992). A curriculum strategy that expands time for in-depth elementary science instruction by using science-based reading strategies: Effects of a year-long study in grade four. *Journal of Research in Science Teaching, 29,* 545–554.

Rosenblatt, L.M. (1991). Literature-S.O.S.! *Language Arts, 68,* 444–448.

Rosenblatt, L.M. (1994). *The reader, the text, and the poem.* Carbondale, IL: Southern Illinois University Press.

Rosenblatt, L.M. (1995). *Literature as exploration* (5th ed.). New York: Modern Language Association of America.

Routman, R. (1991). *Invitations: Changing as teachers and learners K–12.* Portsmouth, NH: Heinemann.

Routman, R. (2000). *Conversations.* Portsmouth, NH: Heinemann.

Routman, R. (2003). *Reading essentials.* Portsmouth, NH: Heinemann.

Salinger, T. (2001). Assessing the literacy of young children: The case for multiple forms of evidence. In S.B. Neuman & D.K. Dickinson (Eds.), *Handbook of early literacy research* (pp. 390–418). New York: Guildford.

Samuels, S.J. (2002a). The method of repeated readings. In C. M. Nichols (Ed.), *Evidence-based reading instruction: Putting the National Reading Panel report into practice* (pp. 85–90). Newark, DE: International Reading Association. [Reprinted from *The Reading Teacher* 32(4), 403–408, 1979].

Samuels, S.J. (2002b). Reading fluency: Its development and assessment. In A.E. Farstrup (Ed.), *What research has to say about reading instruction* (pp. 166–183). Newark, DE: International Reading Association.

Samuelson, R.J. (2002, May 25). Debunking the digital divide. *Newsweek*, 37.

Saramago, J. (1995). *The Stone Raft* (G. Pontiero, Trans.). Orlando, FL: Harcourt Brace.

Schillereff, M. (2001). Using inquiry-based science to help gifted students become more self-directed. *Primary Voices K–6, 10*(1), 28–32.

Schiro, M. (1997). *Integrating children's literature and mathematics in the classroom.* New York: Teachers College Press.

Schmidt, P.R., Gillen, S., Zollo, T.C., & Stone, R. (2002). Literacy learning and scientific inquiry: Children respond. *Reading Teacher, 55*, 534–548.

Schrock, K. (1995–2002). *Fry's readability graph: Directions for use.* Discovery School.com. Retrieved November 1, 2002, from http://school.discovery.com/schrockguide/fry/fry.html.

Schwartz, R.M., & Raphael, T.E. (1985). Concept of definition: A key to improving students' vocabulary. *Reading Teacher, 39*, 198–205.

Shamlin, M.L. (2001). Inquiry in kindergarten: Learning literacy through science. *Primary Voices K–6, 10*(1), 10–15.

Shanahan, T. (1997). Reading-writing relationships, thematic units, inquiry learning: In pursuit of effective integrated literacy instruction. *Reading Teacher, 51*, 12–19.

Shaywitz, B.A., Pugh, K.R., Jenner, A.R., Fulbright, R.K., Fletcher, J.M., Gore, J.C., & Shaywitz, S.E. (2000). The neurobiology of reading and reading disability (dyslexia). In M.J. Kamil, P.B. Mosenthal, P.D. Pearson, & R. Barr (Eds.), *Handbook of reading research* (Vol. 3, pp. 229–249). Mahwah, NJ: Erlbaum.

Short, K.G., & Armstrong, J. (1993). Moving toward inquiry: Integrating literature into the science curriculum. *The New Advocate, 6*, 183–199.

Short, K.G., Kauffman, G., & Kahn, L.H. (2000). "I just need to draw": Responding to literature across multiple sign systems. *Reading Teacher, 54*, 160–171.

Short, K.G., Harste, J.C., and Burke, C. (1996). *Creating classrooms for authors and inquirers.* Portsmouth, NH: Heinemann.

Short, K.G., Schroeder, J., Laird, J., Kauffman, G., Ferguson, M.J., & Crawford, K.M. (1996). *Learning together through inquiry.* York, ME: Stenhouse.

Sloyer, S. (1982). *Readers theatre: Story dramatization in the classroom.* Urbana, IL: National Council of Teachers of English.

Smith, F. (1988). *Joining the literacy club: Further essays into education.* Portsmouth, NH: Heinemann.

Smith, J. (1993). Content learning: A third reason for using literature in teaching reading. *Reading Research and Instruction, 32*, 64–71.

Smith, M.C., Mikulecky, L., Kibby, M.W., Dreher, M.J., & Dole, J.A. (2000). What will be the demands of literacy in the workplace in the next millennium? *Reading Research Quarterly, 35*, 378–383.

Smithsonian Institution. (n.d.-a). *The city of Washington at Lincoln's death: Primary source document exercise.* Smithsonian Institute. Retrieved November 1, 2002, from http://www.si.edu/archives/documents/exercise.htm.

Smithsonian Institution. (n.d.-b). *You be the historian.* Harcourt Brace. Retrieved October 30, 2002, from http://www.si/edu/harcourt/nmah/history/00intro.htm.

Spielman, J. (2001). The family photography project: "We will just read what the pictures tell us." *Reading Teacher, 54*, 762–770.

Standards for the English Language Arts. (1996). Newark, DE. International Reading Association and the National Council of Teachers of English.

Standards for Reading Professionals. (1998). Newark, DE. International Reading Association.

Statistics Canada. (1996). *1996 Census: Mother tongue, home language and knowledge of languages.* Statistics Canada. Retrieved November 1, 2002, from www.statcan.ca/Daily/English/971202/d971202.htm.

Stauffer, R.G. (1970). *The language-experience approach to the teaching of reading.* New York: Harper & Row.

Stoll, D.R. (Ed.) (1997). *Magazines for kids and teens.* Glassboro, NJ: Educational Press Association of America and Newark, DE: International Reading Association.

Storey, J. (1996). *Cultural studies and the study of popular culture.* Athens: University of Georgia Press.

Strickland, D.S. (1994). Educating African American learners at risk: Finding a better way. *Language Arts, 71*, 328–335.

Strickland, D.S., Ganske, K., & Monroe, J.K. (2002). *Supporting struggling readers and writers: Strategies for classroom intervention 3–6.* Portland, ME: Stenhouse and Newark, DE: International Reading Association.

Sutherland-Smith, W. (2002). Weaving the literacy Web: Changes in reading from page to screen. *Reading Teacher, 55*, 662–669.

Swafford, J. (2001, May). *Using viewing, the fifth language art, to facilitate comprehension across the content areas.* Paper presented at the Preconvention Institute of the annual meeting of the International Reading Association, New Orleans, LA.

Swafford, J., & Kallus, M. (2002). Content literacy: A journey into the past, present, and future. *Journal of Content Area Reading, 1*(1), 7–27.

Taba, H. (1967). *Teacher's handbook for elementary social studies.* Reading, MA: Addison-Wesley.

Tapscott, D. (1998). *Growing up digital: The rise of the net generation.* New York: McGraw-Hill.

Taylor, B.M., Pearson, P.D., Clark, K.F., & Walpole, S. (1999). *Beating the odds in teaching all children to read.* CIERA. Retrieved November 3, 2002, from http://www.ciera.org/library/reports/inquiry-2/2006/2-006.pdf.

Taylor, D. (1991). *Learning denied.* Portsmouth, NH: Heinemann.

Teachers of English to Speakers of Other Languages. (2001). *Standards, best practices, and other TESOL initiatives.* Teachers of English to Speakers of Other Languages. Retrieved October 15, 2002, from http://www.tesol.org/assoc/standards/index.html.

Unsworth, L. (2001). *Teaching multiliteracies across the curriculum: Changing contexts of text and image in classroom practice.* Buckingham, England: Open University Press.

Unsworth, L., & O'Toole, M. (1993). Beginning reading with children's literature. In L. Unsworth (Ed.), *Literacy learning and teaching: Language as social practice in the primary school.* Melbourne, Australia: Macmillan.

U.S. Census Bureau. (2000). *Language use. In United States Census 2000.* Retrieved August 2002, from www.census.gov/population/www/socdemo/lang_use.html.

U.S. Department of Education. (2002a). *Introduction: No child left behind.* Retrieved November 1, 2002, from http://www.nochildleftbehind.gov/next/overview/index.html.

U.S. Department of Education. (2002b). *U.S. Department of Education Strategic Plan 2002–2007.* Retrieved July 28, 2000, from http://www.ed.gov/pubs/stratplan2002-07/stratplan2002-07.pdf

Vygotsky, L. (1978). *Mind in society: The development of higher psychological processes.* Cambridge, MA: Harvard University Press.

Wackerly, A., & Young, B. (2002). Community, choice, and content in the urban classroom. *Primary Voices K–6, 10*(3), 17–23.

Wade, S.E., & Moje, E.B. (2000). The role of text in classroom learning. In M.J. Kamil, P.B. Mosen-

thal, P.D. Pearson, & R. Barr (Eds.), *Handbook of reading research* (Vol. 3, pp. 609–627). Mahwah, NJ: Erlbaum.

Walpole, S. (1998–1999). Changing texts, changing thinking: Comprehension demands of new science textbooks. *Reading Teacher, 52,* 358–369.

Ward, A. (1999, May). *Literacy in multicultural settings: Whose culture are we discussing?* Retrieved October 30, 2002, from http://www.readingonline.org/articles/ward.html.

Weaver, B.M. (2000). *Leveling books K–6: Matching readers to text.* Newark, DE: International Reading Association.

Weaver, C.A., & Kintsch, W. (1991). Expository text. In R. Barr, M.J. Kamil, P.B. Mosenthal, & P.D. Pearson (Eds.), *Handbook of reading research* (Vol. 2, pp. 230–245). New York: Longman.

Weir, C. (1998). Using embedded questions to jump-start metacognition in middle school remedial readers. *Journal of Adolescent and Adult Literacy, 41,* 458–467.

Wells, H.G. (1979). *Selected short stories.* Baltimore, MD: Penguin.

White, T.G., Graves, M.F., & Slater, W.H. (1990). Growth of reading vocabulary in diverse elementary schools. *Journal of Educational Psychology, 82,* 281–290.

Whitin, D.J., & Whitin, P.E. (1996). Inquiry at the window: The year of the birds. *Language Arts, 73,* 82–87.

Whitin, P.E., & Whitin, D.J. (2000). *Math is language too.* Urbana, IL: National Council of Teachers of English.

Wilder, M. (1999). Culture, race, and schooling: Toward a non-color-blind ethic of care. *The Educational Forum, 63,* 356–362.

Willey, R. (2002). Writing, reflection, and the young child. *Primary Voices K–6, 10*(4), 8–14.

Xu, S.H. (2001). *Exploring diversity issues in teacher education, 5*(1). International Reading Association. Retrieved October 28, 2002, from http://www.readingonline.org/newliteracies/lit_index.asp?HREF=/newliteracies/action/xu/index.html.

Xu, S.H. (2003). Teachers integrate diverse students' "funds of knowledge" with popular culture into literacy instruction. In J.V. Hoffman, D.L. Schallert, C.M. Fairbanks, J. Worthy, & B. Maloch (Eds.), *National reading conference yearbook* (Vol. 51). Chicago: National Reading Conference.

CHILDREN'S LITERATURE REFERENCES

Aliki. (1986). *How a book is made*. New York: Scholastic.

Aliki. (1988). *Digging up dinosaurs*. New York: Harper & Row.

Aliki. (1993). *Communication*. New York: Scholastic.

Ayer, E. H., Waterford, H., & Heck, A. (2000). *Parallel journeys*. New York: Atheneum.

Bare, C. S. (1989). *Never kiss an alligator!* New York: Puffin Books.

Barth, A. (n.d.). *In the rain forest*. Columbus, OH: McGraw Hill.

Bartholomew, A. (1998). *Electric gadgets and gizmos*. Buffalo, NY: Kids Can Press.

Beatty, P. (1992). *Who comes with cannon?* New York: Scholastic.

Beatty, P. (1984). *Turn homeward Hannallee*. New York: Troll.

Benton, M. (1998). *Dinosaurs, an A to Z guide*. New York: Derrydale.

Bridges, R. (1999). *Through my eyes*. New York: Scholastic.

Burleigh, R. (1997). *Hoops*. San Diego, CA: Silver Whistle.

Cannon, J. (1997). *Verdi*. Orlando, FL: Harcourt.

Cherry, L. (1990). *The great kapok tree: A tale of the Amazon rain forest*. San Diego, CA: Gulliver Books.

Cole, J. (2001). *Ms. Frizzle's Adventures: Ancient Egypt*. New York: Scholastic.

Connelly, L. (n.d.). *Dinosaurs dancing*. Monterey Park, CA: Creative Teaching Press.

Davidson, M. (1989). *The story of Alexander Graham Bell, inventor of the telephone*. New York: Dell.

de Paola, T. (1975). *The cloud book*. New York: Holiday House.

de Paola, T. (1988). *The popcorn book*. New York: Holiday House.

Drew, D. (1989). *The life of the butterfly*. Crystal Lake, IL: Rigby.

DuBosque, D. (1998). *Draw insects*. New York: Scholastic.

Eastman, D. (1989). *Story of dinosaurs*. Mahwah, NJ: Troll.

Epstein, S., & Epstein, B. (1964). *What's behind the word?* New York: Scholastic.

Etling, M., Folsom, M., & Kent, J. (1985). *Q is for duck*. New York: Houghton Mifflin.

Fain, K. (1995). *Handsigns: A sign language alphabet*. New York: Scholastic.

Feelings, T. (1995). *The middle passage*. New York: Dial Books for Young Readers.

Frasier, D. (2000). *Miss Alaineus: A vocabulary disaster*. San Diego, CA: Harcourt.

Gibbons, G. (1984). *Fire! Fire!* New York: Crowell.

Gibbons, G. (1993a). *Frogs*. New York: Scholastic.

Gibbons, G. (1993b). *Puff . . . Flash . . . Bang! A book about signals*. New York: Morrow Junior.

Gibbons, G. (2000). *The pumpkin book*. New York: Holiday House.

Glover, D. (1998). *Looking at insects*. Crystal Lake, IL: Rigby.

Grimes, N. (1999). *My man Blue*. New York: Dial Books for Young Readers.

Hayes, A. (1991). *Meet the orchestra*. New York: Harcourt Brace Jovanovich.

Hesse, K. (1997). *Out of the dust*. New York: Scholastic.

Hesse, K. (1999). *Come on rain!* New York: Scholastic.

Hunt, I. (1964). *Across five Aprils*. New York: Berkley Books.

James, D., & Lynn, S. (1993). *Birds*. New York: Scholastic.

Jenkins, S. (1995). *Biggest, strongest, fastest*. New York: Ticknor & Fields.

Jeunesse, G., & de Bourgoing, P. (1995). *Under the ground*. New York: Scholastic.

Johnson, J. (1995). *How big is a whale? A unique comparison of animals big and small*. Skokie, IL: Rand McNally.

Jordan, M., & Jordan, T. (1996). *Amazon alphabet*. New York: Kingfisher.

King, M. L. (1999). *I have a dream*. New York: Scholastic.

Lasky, K. (1997). *The most beautiful roof in the world*. San Diego, CA: Gulliver Green/Harcourt Brace.

Lincoln, A. (1995). *The Gettysburg address*. New York: Scholastic.

London, J. (1993). *The eyes of gray wolf*. San Francisco: Chronicle Books.

Martin, B., Jr., & Archambault, J. (1988). *Listen to the rain*. New York: Henry Holt.

Martin, J. B. (1998). *Snowflake Bentley*. Boston: Houghton Mifflin.

Marzollo, J. (1996). *I'm a seed (Hello science reader level 1)*. New York: Scholastic.

McGovern, A. (1964). *If you lived during colonial times*. New York: Scholastic.

McKissack, P. C., & McKissack, F. L. (1994). *Christmas in the big house, Christmas in the quarters*. New York: Scholastic.

Mochizuki, K. (1995). *Baseball saved us*. New York: Lee & Low Books.

Mochizuki, K. (1997). *Passage to freedom: The Sugihara story*. New York: Lee & Low Books.

Murphy, J. (1995). *The great fire*. New York: Scholastic.

National Geographic Society. (1996). *Whales*. Washington, DC: National Geographic Society.

Nayer, J. (1992). *Jungle life at your fingertips*. New York: McClanahan.

Onyefulu, I. (2000). *A triangle for Adaora: An African book of shapes*. New York: Dutton.

Parish, P. (1963). *Amelia Bedelia*. New York: Harper & Row.

Peterson, J. W. (1977). *I have a sister. My sister is deaf*. New York: Harper & Row.

Pratt, K. J. (1992). *A walk in the rainforest*. Nevada City, CA: DAWN Publications.

Reeder, C. (1989). *Shades of gray*. New York: Avon.

Reit, S. (1988). *Behind rebel lines*. Orlando, FL: Harcourt Brace Javonovich.

Rockwell, T. (1973). *How to eat fried worms*. New York: Bantam Doubleday Dell Books.

Sampson, J. (1998). *From there to here: A transportation time line*. Crystal Lake, IL: Rigby.

Sandved, K. B. (1999). *Butterfly alphabet*. New York: Scholastic.

Scieszka, J. (1996). *The true story of the three little pigs*. New York: Puffin.

Seuling, B. (1972). *Freaky facts*. Middletown, CT: Xerox.

Simon, S. (1989). *Whales*. New York: Morrow.

Simon, S. (1992). *Our solar system*. New York: William Morrow & Company.

Simon, S. (2001). *Animals nobody loves*. New York: SeaStar Books.

St. George, J. (2000). *So you want to be president?* New York: Philomel Books.

Taylor, B. (1992). *Rain forest*. New York: Dorling Kindersley.

Van Allsburg, C. (1984). *Mysteries of Harris Burdick*. Boston: Houghton Mifflin.

The Visual dictionary of everyday things. (1991). London: Dorling Kindersley.

Weisner, D. (1999). *Sector 7*. New York: Clarion.

What's inside? Insects. (1992). London: Dorling Kindersley.

Wick, W. (1997). *A drop of water*. New York: Scholastic.

Willow, D. (1991). *At home in the rain forest*. Watertown, MA: Charlesbridge.

Woods, S. G. (1999). *The amazing book of insect records*. Woodbridge, CT: Blackbirch Press.

Yolen, J. (1993). *Welcome to the green house*. New York: Putnam.

AUTHOR INDEX

SUBJECT INDEX

PHOTO CREDITS

p. 3: Tom Lindfors Photography; p. 19: Tom Lindfors Photography; p. 59: Will Hart; p. 78: Will Hart; p. 103: Brian Smith; p. 121: Richard Hutchings/PhotoEdit; p. 138: Will Hart; p. 157: Tom Lindfors Photography; p. 175: Will Hart; p. 193: Will Hart; p. 211: Will Hart.